INDIANA: A SELF-APPRAISAL

INDIANA

A Self-Appraisal

*

DONALD F. CARMONY
editor

Indiana University Press
Bloomington and London

Library of Congress catalog card number: 66-22446
Manufactured in the United States of America

PREFACE

Indiana: A Self-Appraisal was conceived by representatives of the Indiana University Press as a volume in recognition of the Indiana Sesquicentennial. From its inception this book has been developed for the general reader, though it also includes material of significance to specialists. Its chapters are historical essays which offer interesting information and thoughtful interpretation about Indiana's historical background, present status, and probable future. Each author has been asked to provide historical background for his topic, significant information about its present status, and comments about probable future developments. In addition, he has been asked to give his own appraisal concerning his topic and to suggest desirable changes.

The nineteen authors of this book come from varied backgrounds. They include professors, a business executive, a labor leader, a political writer, a secondary school principal, a politician, and a clergyman. All of them either hold or at least have held important administrative positions. Moreover, they have all had intimate acquaintance with the Hoosier scene.

There is no uniformity in the interpretations expressed by these authors. Each has been encouraged to make his own appraisal without regard to that presented by other authors. Educators have generally been more forthright in their evaluations than the other authors have been, but the discerning reader will note important exceptions to this observation. In any event, varying viewpoints are both inevitable and desirable whenever a number of authors appraise the Hoosier scene. This is especially true when they themselves are important leaders in Indiana life.

As editor I wish to take this opportunity to thank all the contributors for their fulfillment of the various tasks assigned to them. They and I are indebted, furthermore, to Miss Jane Rodman, Associate Editor of the Indiana University Press, for her tireless editorial assistance. Her own abiding interest in Hoosier history and affairs, combined with sound professional skill, has made her contribution invaluable.

Indiana's history and heritage has exhibited remarkable achievements during its initial one hundred fifty years of statehood. Hopefully this volume will add further understanding to and increase appreciation of this history and heritage. Equally important, however, it should encourage Hoosiers everywhere—including those now residing outside Indiana—to accept augmented responsibility for helping to make Indiana's history and heritage even more remarkable during its next one hundred fifty years.

DONALD F. CARMONY
Editor

Bloomington, Indiana

CONTENTS

INDIANA: A SELF-APPRAISAL

DONALD F. CARMONY

The Hoosiers and Their Heritage

Indiana has changed from a *pioneer* to an *agricultural* and then to an *industrial* commonwealth during its one hundred fifty years of statehood. During this century and a half several important influences have given the Hoosier heritage much of its particular flavor and local color. Such flavor and color are to a large extent the result of: geographical factors, the impact of the Southern element in its population, the persistent domination of rural influences, the continued existence of a diversified and generally healthy economy, an intense and abiding devotion to the Union of the States, and a strong and steadfast attachment to political moderation based on the two-party system. Other influences have indeed been important, but an understanding of these six influences is essential in explaining and interpreting the Hoosier heritage.

Indiana's abundant natural resources and its fortunate geographical location have greatly influenced its development. Only thirty-eighth among the states in size and smallest of all mainland states west of the Appalachians, it has been blessed with millions of acres

Donald F. Carmony, a native of Shelby County, Indiana, is editor of the *Indiana Magazine of History* and a professor of history at Indiana University. He has served as chairman of the Indiana Sesquicentennial Commission since it was organized in 1960.

of fertile soil, a favorable climate (especially for agriculture), varied and considerable mineral resources, a significant amount of hardwood timber, a number of rivers, and the absence of both mountains and deserts. Moreover, as James Hall, Timothy Flint, and other early nineteenth-century writers and residents of the Middle West emphasized, the region of which Indiana is a part has also been extremely rich in its natural and geographical resources. These local and regional resources made possible a diversified and expanding economy which, despite setbacks, has persisted from pioneer days.

Indiana's particular geographical location has itself been significant. An integral part of the Middle West, it has never been a natural geographical unit. Sitting astride the almost invisible continental divide between the Mississippi and St. Lawrence basins, it has of necessity been a crossroads area from the advent of the French in the seventeenth century to the present. Its location has especially fostered a diversified transportation system which today includes traffic on the Ohio and Great Lakes, state and interstate highways, truck lines, railroads, and expanding airplane routes.

Indiana's compact size, rich resources, and crossroads location have had important political and cultural as well as economic consequences. Her compactness and transportation facilities have made it possible for politicians and others to visit all sections of Hoosierdom with less difficulty than is true for most states. Its interior location and expanding trade have fostered devotion to the Union. And its generally favorable economic base and the flow of ideas into and out of the state have stimulated the development of its education, literature, and culture generally. Its borders have thus been open frontiers, inviting people, trade, and ideas from other parts of the United States and other countries of the world as well.

Indiana's natural resources and favorable location are likely to remain enormous assets to its people for an indefinite period of time. The permanency and benefits of these assets, however, increasingly depend upon wise and long-range programs for their conservation and utilization. The responsibility for such conservation and utilization rests with individuals and local units of government as well as with state and federal government.

No state of the Old Northwest, and perhaps no northern state as well, has had as large an element of Southerners in its population as Indiana. The predominance of this element during the early decades of the nineteenth century has been emphasized by John D. Barnhart in *The Valley of Democracy: The Ohio Valley, 1775-1820* (1953) as well as in other of his writings. Emma Lou Thornbrough's *Indiana in the Civil War Era, 1850-1880* (1965) affirms that Indiana had more Southern stock during the Civil War years than any other Northern state. Federal decennial census data offer convincing evidence of the continued influx of Southerners in considerable number.

The Southern stock of pioneer days consisted mainly of persons who were descendants of families which had had much experience with pioneering in the Appalachian mountain area. When they advanced through the Cumberland Gap or other passages into the Ohio Valley, they brought their cultural baggage with them. Their religious diversity and unfavorable experience with established churches fostered their commitment to religious freedom and separation of church and state. Their intimate experience with county rather than town or township government made the county much the more important unit of local government in the pioneer era. Because this stock was largely of the farmer class it provided a broad democratic base for pioneer society. This base was much strengthened by the absence of slavery and by federal legislation which made possible a wide diffusion of land ownership among pioneer farmers. In such ways the Southern element was a fundamental factor in establishing the economic, political, and cultural foundations for Hoosier life and institutions.

The influence of Indiana's Southern stock has declined since the pioneer era. The proportion of Southerners in the total population has decreased, and political power has shifted to northern Indiana where other elements have long been dominant. Economic, political, and cultural ties, disrupted by the Civil War, have developed with Eastern and other Middle Western states at the expense of former ties with the South.

Furthermore, Southern immigration since the Civil War has differed much from that of pioneer days. Numerous of its white immigrants have been displaced farmers or laborers in search of urban employment. The coming of Southern Negroes has rapidly increased, the bulk of whom have become city laborers. The generally low economic and cultural status of these immigrants, white and Negro alike, plus the bias against them, have diluted their impact on Hoosier economic, political, and cultural life. Hence, despite the fact that early Indiana was mainly an outpost of the Upper South, the influences of its Southern stock has waned for approximately a century. This influence may be expected to shrink even more in the decades ahead.

Rural influences have been dominant in Indiana from territorial days until almost the present. Prior to and including 1830, federal census returns reported Indiana's population to be 100 percent rural. Not until 1920 did the urban total slightly exceed the rural aggregate, but in 1960 the population was 62 percent urban. The census of 1840 first indicated a few towns of more than 2,500 population, but no town exceeded 10,000 before 1860. As late as 1890 only one city, Indianapolis, had 100,000 residents. Even in 1960 it had only 476,258 and was the sole urban area having more than 200,000 inhabitants.

Despite Indiana's continued high rank as an agricultural and manufacturing commonwealth, through the years it has been chiefly controlled by country dwellers and residents of numerous small towns. The diffusion of its urban element among towns and cities throughout the state has made Indiana seem less urban than it has really been. Moreover, the fact that its largest cities have likewise been widely scattered has further strengthened rural over urban forces. These cities seldom cooperate effectively with one another, often being more closely identified with the countryside and towns of their areas than with one another. Nineteenth-century Indiana was a rural Indiana. Pioneer life with its substantial degree of neighborhood self-sufficiency and isolation established basic and continuing patterns for rural life and institutions. This same pioneer life emphasized and exalted primary and intimate relationships among people within local neighborhoods. Each neighborhood usually had at least one village, general store, gristmill, sawmill, blacksmith shop, church, and the like. Some neighborhoods, particularly those which included towns, often also had schools, libraries, and newspapers. By mid-century when improved transportation facilities began to shatter this local self-sufficiency and isolation, localism had become deeply rooted among Hoosiers.

Over subsequent decades this localism has gradually melted, but not without many struggles and setbacks. The attachment to the primary and intimate relationships of small communities has likewise been modified with great difficulty. This nineteenth-century rural heritage has continued to exercise a strong influence on Indiana life in the twentieth century. It explains much of the opposition, often successful, to efforts to merge rural and small-town schools, churches, or libraries. It also explains much of the continued attachment to the civil township as a unit of government despite the fact that township government was of only limited importance in the pioneer era.

Rural ascendency, however, has waned in recent decades. The delay in legislative reapportionment from the 1920's to the 1960's braced and slowed its decline. But the legislative reapportionment act of 1965 significantly advanced urban over rural representation in the General Assembly. The influence of the rural heritage will remain for decades, but henceforth urban influences are almost certain to supersede rural ones.

Urbanization in Indiana, however, may follow significantly different patterns than in states having a single, towering metropolitan center. If numerous towns and cities of moderate size continue in the absence of such a metropolis, the political, economic, and cultural life of the state will probably reflect a strong attachment to a combination of local and regional ties and loyalties. This attachment is currently evidenced in the developing pattern of regional campuses by Purdue and Indiana universities. Whether this pattern is the best available for Hoosier students and citizens is a moot question, but it clearly reflects strong local and regional loyalties in a population already approximately two-thirds urban.

During one hundred fifty years of statehood, Indiana's economy has generally been diversified and healthy. Until about the eve of World War I, it rested mainly on agriculture and lumber. Although corn and hogs have through the years provided the principal element of Hoosier agriculture, farming has been diversified from pioneer days. During the last several decades it has become even more so with the addition of soybeans as a leading crop following World War I and the augmented commercial production of poultry, vegetables, fruit, and berries. Sawmilling, furniture, and other industries based on lumbering have likewise been of considerable significance since pioneer days.

Indiana manufacturing, like Indiana agriculture, has also been diversified. Until near the beginning of World War I, the leading manufacturing industries had long been gristmilling, meat slaughtering, liquor, and lumber. These agrarian- and lumber-based industries continue to be important; but since at least World War I industries based on metals, chemicals, and other products have been much more significant than those based on agriculture and lumber.

Though not considered a mining state, Indiana's varied mineral production has been more valuable than for some states which are so known. Coal, stone, gas, oil, gravel, clay, and other products have been very important in a number of counties. Such mineral production, coupled with variety in agricultural and manufacturing output, has given the Hoosier economy much diversification.

Despite booms and busts, Indiana's economy has generally been vigorous and healthy. Its rapid expansion has resulted in a significant and continuing increase in living standards for Hoosiers generally, while the extremes of wealth and poverty have been less than for most states. Fortunately the absence of slavery and the widespread ownership of land among pioneer farmers gave both agriculture and manufacturing a stable and solid foundation. As manufacturing has become more diversified in the twentieth century, it has for the most part added to rather than subtracted from this foundation. Thus, though only thirty-eighth among the states in size and eleventh in population, during recent decades Indiana has usually ranked approximately eighth among them for industrial output and eleventh in terms of its agricultural production. Most of its agricultural and manufacturing output now comes from the northern half of the state. A considerable amount, however, is derived from the lower half, and the contribution of this area may substantially increase in the next half century.

The Hoosier economy is likely to remain heterogeneous and at least as healthy as the national economy. Its agricultural and mineral products should remain large enough to add considerable variety and strength to supplement manufacturing, which will doubtless continue to rise. Manufacturing, however, will probably play a reduced role relative to the entire economy as transportation, banking, communication, service industries, and tourism grow in importance. The opening of the St. Lawrence Seaway several years ago, the continued improvement and rapid increase of traffic on the Ohio River, the possible development of freight traffic on the Maumee-Wabash route connecting the Great Lakes with the Mississippi, the rapid expansion of interstate highways, and expanding air travel all augur well for modernization of state and regional transportation facilities. Hence, sparing political disaster at home or military disaster in war, the economic outlook continues to be bright.

Hoosiers have exhibited persistent and staunch devotion to the Union of the States in times of peace as well as war. Late in 1832 when the tariff and nullification crisis erupted in South Carolina, Calvin Fletcher, Indianapolis lawyer and businessman, exhorted United States Senator John Tipton: "For the sake of our common country [and] for the sake of the past, the present & the future, forget Jacksonianism—Clayism & suspend all other business and strike a decisive blow against this high handed treason!" In the 1850's when agitation over slavery and related questions led to threats of disunion, Governor Joseph A. Wright emphasized: "Indiana knows no East, no West, no North, no South; nothing but the Union." Such quotations could be multiplied from Hoosiers of all periods as well as from all sections of the state regardless of party affiliation. Certainly no Civil War governor more staunchly supported the Union or more firmly insisted on its perpetuation regardless of sacrifice than did Oliver P. Morton.

This persistent loyalty to the Union has generally had two corollaries. In domestic politics Hoosier politicians have normally been strongly inclined to compromise this or that in the interests of the Union of the States. Particularly throughout the nineteenth century Indiana members of Congress often supported measures helping to harmonize sectional differences between North and South or East and West. But this staunch Unionism has helped make Hoosiers vigorous defenders of the federal government during war and often extremely nationalistic in viewing peacetime relations with other countries. Such nationalism, however, has usually been much less isolationist than many observers have claimed.

Why have Hoosiers been so strongly committed to the Union? Their attachment is grounded in important geographical considerations. As part of an interior region of unusual productivity, access to and from markets, both domestic and foreign, has always been a primary concern of Indiana residents. Sitting astride the continental divide between the Mississippi and St. Lawrence basins, the development and preservation of trade routes via the Mississippi, St. Lawrence, and between the upper Ohio Valley and states to the east of it have been of paramount importance.

But factors other than geographical circumstances have also developed strong loyalty to the Union. Of major importance was the early grant of statehood to the residents of the Middle West. Accompanying statehood were federal policies which made generous contributions to Indiana and her neighbors through purchase of land from the Indians, sale of such land, Indian removal, liberal land policy, generous gifts of land, aid for river and highway improvement, support for education, and the like. In these and other ways the federal government provided lasting and significant benefits to residents of the Middle West.

Indiana's devotion to the Union developed naturally since her sectional and national interests have been far more complementary and harmonious than otherwise. Thus, the Hoosier heritage and the American heritage have been a common heritage based on common interests. This situation is likely to continue to be characteristic for Hoosiers, encouraging them to be compromisers in domestic policies and nationalists concerning foreign relations.

Since at least the 1840's Hoosier politicians have usually traveled the middle of the political highway. Normally jostling with each other for possession of the center of the road, political leaders have seldom occupied either the right or left berm. In most elections the platform of either major party would be almost as suitable for its rival as for its own nominees! Generally lacking sharp cleavages concerning issues, Hoosier politics has frequently emphasized personalities over issues and greatly exaggerated the differences in position between the "ins" and the "outs." This situation has encouraged the "outs" to promise to do a better job of what the "ins" have been doing, but without their alleged favoritism, bungling, wastefulness, and corruption. Moreover, whenever politics has tended to move to the right or to the left, both major parties, at least in the long run, have normally moved cautiously in the same direction.

Rival political parties first developed during the period, 1824-40. Prior to these years Indiana residents had almost without exception been disciples of the Jeffersonian Republicans. By 1840, however, Hoosiers had divided into Whigs and Democrats, and Indiana has always been poor soil for third parties to sprout into major parties. In the 1850's the Whigs were succeeded by the Republicans, and for more than a century the Republicans and the Democrats have been the state's two dominant parties. Three factors do much to explain their longevity. To begin with, if third parties nourish new issues which show substantial signs of winning widespread acceptance, either or both parties are likely to endorse these issues and put them into effect. Moreover, as the "radicalism" of one generation at times becomes the "conservatism" of a succeeding era, Democrats and Republicans alike modify their platforms and then continue their jostling for the middle of the rerouted political highway. If either party gets too far ahead of its rival in such a movement, it can, if necessary, slow down its advance. At the same time, if one of the dominant parties lags too far behind in adapting to new situations, it can gradually quicken its pace. Furthermore, the attachment to the two-party system rooted in political moderation has been so great that election laws and patronage practices have long encouraged their perpetuation at the expense of third parties and independent movements.

No fully adequate explanation can be offered for Indiana's persistent attachment to political moderation. Four factors, however, explain much of the basis for this moderation. First of all, political parties were born in the pioneer era when Indiana life, as already noted, rested on a broad democratic base. Hence, during the years of party formation, leaders of both major parties naturally appealed to much the same political and economic groups. Once established on a moderate foundation, other factors tended to perpetuate its continuation. The rapid growth of a diversified, expanding, and generally healthy economy supplied an economic context which fostered and nourished continued moderation. Moreover, although political changes have mainly come piecemeal, they have principally had bipartisan support and they normally soon become widely accepted. Once these changes and adjustments are made, they are generally incorporated into a new moderate stance. Finally, as noted above, Indiana election laws and patronage practices have given prolonged and significant support for political moderation.

On the surface it would seem that the widespread moderate consensus which has characterized Hoosier politics for decades might favor merit or at least nonpartisan appointments over partisan selections. But the practice has definitely been otherwise. From the Jacksonian era to the present, Indiana politicians have fought for and then distributed governmental positions as if such a right were as inviolate and deeply imbedded in the Bill of Rights as freedom of religion! Most so-called nonpartisan appointments actually have been bipartisan selections with political plums having been divided between Democrats and Republicans according to some formula or traditional ratio. For positions which involve significant policy decisions, partisan or at least bipartisan appointments are often desirable. The victorious party should have a reasonable chance to have men sympathetic with its program in key positions. Moreover, Hoosier politicians are nearly always experienced and adept in harmonizing differing viewpoints, a process and an art of vital importance in a democracy. Nevertheless, clearing rank and file appointments of engineers, accountants, laborers on highways, park naturalists, inspectors, secretaries, and so on through political channels, though long established and well entrenched, is both costly and otherwise detrimental to the public interest.

Indiana politics will probably continue to be characterized by political moderation rooted in the two-party system for at least the next several decades. Currently Hoosier politicians are traveling the broad central highway, with some Democrats veering to the left of center as many Republicans show signs of deserting their right of center path to compete with the Democrats in the center itself. But during the 1960's, as for nearly all of Indiana's past one hundred fifty years, the right and left berms of the political highway are largely unused as moderate Republicans and moderate Democrats scramble for control of its congested central portion.

But what of the Hoosier heritage for the next one hundred fifty years? What will historians in the year 2116 have to say of the basic influences which have shaped and molded the Hoosier heritage? The rapidity of change during recent decades suggests that much larger and more far-reaching changes may come in the next century and a half than in that which has preceded us. Among the developing influences which now appear likely to have augmented impact over Indiana life and institutions during the next century and a half are public education, government itself, urbanization, and technology. The role of these and other influences may in turn largely be determined by whether freedom and justice are cherished and expanded on the home front and whether the peoples of the world are able to maintain a reasonably orderly and peaceful society in which freedom and justice can thrive.

The imprint of preceding centuries has long cast heavy, stabilizing, and significant shadows on succeeding ones. It is hoped that this process will continue, for only as each generation becomes deeply indebted to those which have preceded it can it make its full contribution to those which follow. Great and uncertain as the changes of the next one hundred fifty years may well be, many landmarks and much of the Hoosier heritage of today are likely to remain in the year 2116. Hence, this generation, as for every generation, can make decisions regarding the questions and problems facing it with needed wisdom and assurance only if it first has much understanding of and substantial appreciation for its heritage from the past. Indiana's sesquicentennial year is an especially appropriate time for Hoosiers to do the kind of self-appraisal so essential to the preservation of self-government.

PHILIP S. WILDER, JR.
KARL O'LESSKER

State Government and Its Services

The way the government of Indiana does its job makes a difference which can easily be underestimated. It is true that Indiana's location at the "crossroads of America" means that goods and people move back and forth across the state regardless of the performance of Indiana government; but job-producing plants for processing, assembling, and distributing various goods will not come to Indiana, despite its location, if governmental services are inadequate, governmental employees are unreliable, or taxation so onerous as to make location in this state risky. It is equally true that the hills, lakes, streams, and historical sites with which Indiana is favored will not move across the state's border no matter what the state government's performance may be; but unless these assets are developed, adequate access is provided to them, suitable facilities are made available for visitors, and the existence of these attractions is publicized, there will be relatively little tendency to take advan-

Philip S. Wilder, Jr., is acting chairman of the Division of Social Sciences and professor of political science at Wabash College. He has been a director of the Indiana Council for Education in Politics since 1954 and is the 1966 president-elect of the Indiana Academy of Social Sciences.

Karl O'Lessker, formerly associate professor of political science and philosophy at Wabash College, is now professor of political science at Georgia State University, Atlanta, Georgia.

tage of these assets either by native Hoosiers or by visitors from elsewhere. Across the sweep of state government activities, from law enforcement to the provision of facilities for education and from road building to help for the mentally ill, the manner in which Indiana state government performs its tasks goes a long way toward shaping the kind of life which can be lived by the citizens of the state.

The complexity of the American system is such that action by state governments can be viewed from conflicting perspectives. The significance of state activity as an alternative to federal government activity is far different from its role as a substitute for action by local governments or private institutions. In assessing a particular proposal for action by the state government, it may be helpful to think of an inclined plane slanted from private action and local government through the state government and on to Washington, with functions gravitating down this incline whenever a general feeling develops that curable needs or attainable goals are not being taken care of within the more limited arena. The nature of the effectively available alternatives varies from case to case. In some areas state government action represents a shift toward centralization and away from local or private activity while in other areas effective state action may constitute the only feasible alternative to new or broadened federal programs.

Government funds in the United States tend to be collected by larger units of government and then distributed to smaller units for expenditure. This distribution permits some transfer of funds from affluent to less prosperous areas, but the principal pressure for this process is not a desire for this redistribution but the fact that it is easier to raise funds in wider governmental units. The only major tax revenues available to most local governments come from levies on real and personal property. States can impose relatively moderate taxes on sales and incomes without inducing out-migration, particularly when each state has been compelled to levy more or less comparable taxes as a means of supporting services. National government, for a variety of reasons including its ability to control imports and monetary policy, can levy taxes at far heavier rates than the states and has done so. This development has tended to move state governments, including that in Indiana, toward the role of middleman in which grants-in-aid are received from Washington, for the support of specific programs which have been designated by federal authorities. A portion of the tax funds raised by state governments is automatically assigned to meet the matching requirements of these federally supported programs and an even larger portion of the state-collected tax funds is in turn distributed to units of local government to help finance local services. In some areas the continued significance of even this middleman role for state government is now in question, with federal funds bypassing the states and going directly to local government units, or as in the case of the Economic Opportunity Act of 1964, bypassing even units of local government and going directly to private groups at the local level.

Despite the decreased opportunity for autonomous and self-contained activity which has developed in recent decades, it is still vitally important for the welfare of a state that its government be efficiently structured and operated. This is true in part because the units of local government need effective assistance from the state level, in part because there are still many things which are in the exclusive or primary domain of the state government and will not be done satisfactorily unless the state is equipped to meet its responsibilities, in part because failure by the state to meet those demands which it could properly discharge will inevitably lead toward further movement of operating responsibility to Washington.

The basic law under which Indiana state government now operates is the Constitution of 1851. This document, like the U. S. Constitution which was drafted 64 years earlier, is now used as the framework for a governmental system far different from that which its authors had in mind. For many years there have been calls in Indiana for the holding of a constitutional convention which would replace the "outmoded" 1851 document with a new one. Most state constitutions dating from the middle of the last century have been replaced with what the supporters of the changes presumably regarded as improved models.

It is improbable that any informed observer regards the present

Indiana Constitution as perfect. This was also true, however, of the document's original authors who recognized that they had been forced to compromise among themselves on a number of points. The fact that many criticisms presently leveled at Indiana's constitution are contradictory and call for movement in divergent directions makes it clear that the meaningful question is not whether any person or group advocating a new constitutional convention in Indiana can think of a way in which this constitution could be improved, but rather, how certain is it that the document emerging from a new convention would be an improvement over the present system. The bitterly divisive experience of most states which undertake to hold constitutional conventions and the unhappy results which have stemmed from a substantial proportion of these experiences would seem to indicate that there is much to be said for working through the framework of the established constitution and attempting to develop support for individual amendments which may seem desirable.

The amendment process called for by the present constitution involves the requirement that a proposed amendment receive majority support in each house of the legislature in two succeeding biennial sessions and majority support of the voters at a subsequent election. The authors of this provision rejected the path of requiring extraordinary majorities (two-thirds or three-fourths votes, for instance) in favor of a requirement that a proposed amendment maintain majority support over a two-year period in the legislature and also be supported by a majority at the polls. From the adoption of the constitution until 1935, it was held that an amendment was defeated in the election unless it received affirmative support of more than half the total voters in that election. Since many citizens who vote in contests for elective office normally cast no vote on questions of constitutional amendment, this requirement of an absolute majority made the Indiana amendment process difficult. Since a 1935 Indiana Supreme Court decision, however, it has been held that if more people vote for a proposed amendment than against it the amendment passes. This change has substantially increased the ease of amendment of the Indiana Constitution. A further step in the same direction will be taken if the voters approve a presently pending amendment which will permit the General Assembly to give "first-session" approval to proposed amendments in sessions when amendments passed at the preceding session are up for "second-session" consideration.

One major reason the Constitution of 1851 has stayed in effect for over a century is that it is a substantially shorter and more general document than was adopted by most state constitutional conventions of the last century. The unwillingness to trust future custodians of state affairs that led authors of many state constitutions to spell out detailed governmental provisions in the constitution decreased substantially the adaptability of those constitutions to changing circumstances. Although Indiana's constitution includes a number of unnecessarily detailed provisions, they have proved less burdensome than those in most other constitutions drafted during the post-Jacksonian era.

The effective impact of constitutional restrictions depends, of course, on the availability of machinery for enforcing these limits. In Indiana as elsewhere in the American system the judiciary is empowered to invalidate any statutory provision which the judges hold to conflict with a provision of the constitution. Accepted principles of constitutional supremacy require that the Supreme Court of the state be able to invalidate unconstitutional acts, but recent experience in Indiana has raised questions whether this power of judicial oversight of the legislature might not be subject to abuse. When a county judge can suspend the enforcement of a statute passed by the legislature and signed by the Governor on the grounds, for example, that he finds the statute lacks the clarity of phrasing called for by the constitution, the machinery of judicial review may properly be subjected to critical scrutiny. The statute passed in the 1965 session which curtails the freedom of lower courts to prevent the enforcement of statutes on the basis of alleged unconstitutionality seems to have considerable merit.

One provision of the 1851 constitution which has been subjected to criticism in some quarters is the prohibition of a state debt. Current economic theory does indicate that such a provision in the constitution of a national government would create serious questions. The fact is, however, that the situation of a government like that of Indiana is such that the principles of counter-cyclical financing do not apply to it in the way they do to the governments of nation-states. In special circumstances it has proved possible to circumvent the ban on state debt through such devices as the establishment of the Toll Road Authority, and although this may ultimately involve the payment of higher interest charges, this burden has proved supportable. On balance, the prohibition of a general debt has probably served as a healthful deterrent to the periodic pressures for spending which develop in every political system where there is an opportunity to appropriate the money now and delay until some later time the decision as to how the bills will be paid.

One feature of the present structure of the Indiana government which is probably unfortunate is the relatively large number of officials who are directly elected. The people of the state are now called upon to elect not only their Senators, Representatives, and Governor, but also the Lieutenant Governor, Secretary of State, Treasurer, Auditor, Attorney General, Superintendent of Public Instruction, and the Judges and Clerk of the Supreme and Appellate Courts. The direct election of legislators and the governor is essential to the maintenance of our type of government and political system. But it would be possible to fill each of the other offices in some fashion other than direct election without doing violence to the principles of our system, and it seems probable that a shortening of the ballot would lead to improvements in the government of the state.

The ultimate responsibility for the conduct of affairs in the state government falls on the Governor. There is much to be said for giving him control over the executive branch so that he has authority equal to his responsibility comparable to the situation of a corporation's chief executive or the President of the United States. With authority dispersed as it is under the present Indiana system, no Governor can properly be held totally responsible for what goes on in his administration and we are unnecessarily providing opportunities for "passing the buck."

There seems to be no good reason why the duties currently performed by the Secretary of State and State Treasurer could not more efficiently be assigned to officials appointed by and responsible to the Governor. There should be some provision for effective audit of state accounts, but this could be handled by an office reporting to the legislature at least as well as by a directly elected Auditor. If the Attorney General is to be the chief legal officer of the state, it would be more reasonable to have him appointed by and responsible to the Chief Executive than to have him independently elected. The duties of the Superintendent of Public Instruction are such that election on a partisan ballot raises serious questions. It would seem preferable to make this an appointive office which could be responsible to a Commission of Education made up of people appointed by the Governor or through some other channel. Since all of these offices, except that of the Attorney General, are provided for in the constitution, it seems improbable that they will be abolished in the near future; but if the disadvantages of having splintered authority in the executive branch are recognized, it may be possible to devise some statutory arrangements which will lessen the handicaps under which the Governor operates. The establishment in 1961 of a Department of Administration which concentrates responsibility for various housekeeping and staff functions is an example of the kind of improvement in structure that can be made within the framework of the present constitution.

It may be desirable, though it is not essential, to have a Lieutenant Governor who serves as heir apparent to the Chief Executive. The constitution would seem to permit adoption of a plan under which the Governor and Lieutenant Governor would be voted for as a team in the fashion of present votes for President and Vice President. Even if this were done, it would seem desirable to remove the statutory responsibility for direction of the Department of Commerce from its present assignment to the Lieutenant Governor and integrate it with those agencies of the executive branch which report to the Governor.

Another handicap to more effective executive leadership is the constitutional provision which presently prohibits an Indiana Gov-

ernor from succeeding himself. It seems clear that the benefits
which would come from letting the people of the state elect a
Governor for a second consecutive term, if they chose to do so,
would counterbalance whatever disadvantages were involved in
abandoning the present arrangement. It would also seem desirable
for the state to consider moving the election for governor from
the presidential years to off-year elections in which there would
be more tendency for the choice of state officials to be shaped by
state issues rather than being affected by the pulling power of presidential coattails.

Article VII, Section I, of the Indiana Constitution provides, "the
judicial power of the State shall be vested in a Supreme Court,
Circuit Courts, and such other courts as the General Assembly
may establish." The court system established to carry out this constitutional provision includes a Supreme Court of five members,
an eight-member Appellate Court, a Circuit Court for each county,
except that in eight instances two adjoining counties constitute a
Circuit, and a number of Superior or other special courts which
have been established in those counties with populations so large
that the judicial load could not be satisfactorily handled by the
county's Circuit Court, which is restricted by the constitution to
a single judge.

The structure of the state's judiciary has been modified repeatedly in the years since the constitution was adopted and in recent
years there have been frequent calls for reorganization and realign-
ment of the various courts. These calls for changes in the state's
court system led the 1965 General Assembly to pass a bill establishing a Judicial Study Commission composed of eight legislators and
four laymen. This commission is instructed to study the state's judicial system on a continuing basis and submit biennial reports on
any changes it believes would be improvements. One reform that
the commission will certainly be urged to propose is a change in
the method of selecting judges.

The present system of filling Indiana's Supreme and Appellate
Courts through partisan nomination and election was formerly
standard in state courts but has now been replaced in many areas

with other devices. One system which seems to have worked well provides for having vacancies on state courts filled by the governor from lists of possibilities screened by the state bar association. The electoral process is used under this plan only to let the people decide whether a judge has mishandled his duties in such fashion that he should be removed and replaced. Adoption of such a system would make an Indiana judgeship far more attractive than it is under the present system in which a prospective judge is expected to wage an active campaign for the nomination, campaign for election in the fall with the other members of his party's ticket, serve out his term for a judicial salary which is lower than the income an able lawyer can expect to make in private practice, and then return to the campaign trail at the expiration of his term. Under these circumstances it is remarkable that we have as many satisfactory candidates for these judgeships as we do.

The channel through which Indiana voters communicate their views to the state government is the General Assembly, consisting of a 50-member Senate and 100-member House of Representatives. The most remarkable thing about this body is that it is in regular session for only two months every two years. The 150 legislators, approximately half of whom are new in each session, assemble in Indianapolis in early January of odd-numbered years and by early March the General Assembly adjourns, the legislators disperse, and the stage of the state's government is left to the Governor and his fellow members of the executive branch for the next 22 months.

The legislators, who represent a more widely varied sample of the state's citizenry than would be the case if legislative service came closer to demanding year-round absence from other work, receive token salaries of $1,800 per year and modest compensation for expenses but little or no provision for such assistance as secretarial help.

Several factors have combined to maintain the importance of the legislature in Indiana's governmental machinery in spite of these handicaps under which the senators and representatives labor. Most important is probably the fact that each session of the General Assembly contains enough veterans of previous sessions to serve as

a source of leadership while the new members are becoming accli-
mated. At each session, half of the senators are completing their
four-year terms and approximately half of the representatives are
people who have served in previous sessions. This continuity is
particularly helpful because it provides the basis for a system of
studying major state problems between sessions under the auspices
of a bicameral study group, the Legislative Advisory Commission.
At each General Assembly session it is likely that the legislators
will deal with the most difficult problems confronting them in two
ways: by passing a temporary or tentative statute and by referring
the general question to the Legislative Advisory Commission for
detailed study and a report at the next session. Usually some of the
legislators appointed to these interim study assignments are defeated in the subsequent election and are not available to explain
and defend the group's report, but there are always enough hold-
overs so that proposals from the LAC have strong support among
the senior members of the General Assembly.

Another factor that has tended to maintain the importance of
the General Assembly is the basic requirement that for many types
of action legislation is constitutionally necessary; and if the General Assembly does not reach a conclusion on a vital issue within
the regular session of 61 days, the Governor is empowered to call
them back to one or more special sessions of 40 days each. It is
also true that although the legislature itself has little or no staff or
research assistance available to it there are a number of interest
groups which have seen fit to support substantial programs of research on the issues with which the legislature is called upon to
deal. Even if the legislator does not have his own research facilities,
he can at least compare the arguments presented by spokesmen for
the executive branch with the material developed for the interest
groups. If these two forces view the problem from different perspectives, as is normally the case, the legislator, by playing one
against the other, may make a reasonably well-informed decision as
to where he feels truth and justice lie on the issue with which he is
dealing.

It is easy to criticize the limitation of Indiana's legislature to a

61-day regular session every biennium. However, there are significant benefits from this arrangement under which legislative service
is clearly a part-time activity. For one thing, the door to General
Assembly candidacy is kept open for people in a number of occupational groups where absences of a length called for by service
in many state legislatures would be impossible. Also, some benefit
is clearly derived from the discipline which is automatically im-
posed by knowledge that the deadline for adjournment is no more
than two months away. Budgeting in any kind of detail for a two-
year period is obviously beyond the competence of any legislature,
but the fact is that if a legislative body attempts to budget in detail
even for one year the result is inevitably unhealthy, with many of
the specific items in the appropriation schedules smelling of log-
rolling and pork barrels. For reasons which become clear only in
the light of a consideration of the inevitable characteristics of legislative activity, it seems probable that the present system of a biennial budget is more likely to advance the cause of sound and
genuinely responsible government than would a budget that was
adopted each year.

One modification of the present pattern for legislative action in
Indiana which might be desirable would involve a continuation of
the present 61-day session in the first year of the biennium with
the addition of a session, which could be of 30 days, in the off years.
This off-year session could receive and consider reports from committees which had been meeting during the 10-month period between the sessions. These committees should be adequately staffed.

The question of legislative salaries is more complicated than it
might seem. Serving in the legislature for the present 61-day session is clearly no more than a part-time job, and it seems improbable that any serious candidate for election to the legislature is primarily interested in the salary. Even if the present salary were
multiplied four or five times, there is no good reason to believe that
the caliber of legislative personnel would be improved as a result
of this financial inducement. It is true, however, that even the
present legislative service of two months plus day-by-day participation in interim study groups calls for significant financial sacri-

fice on the part of many members of the legislature. Particularly if off-year sessions are introduced or the biennial session is lengthened, it would probably be desirable to increase legislative salaries. It would also be productive even under the present 61-day session to provide funds for secretarial assistance to members of the General Assembly.

It should probably be observed that the recent furor over reapportionment of the Indiana legislature was far less important to the state's political future than were the comparable confrontations in most other states. For one thing, Indiana never did have a legislative chamber which was as grossly out of line with state population as was the case in those states where seats in the senate or house were assigned to counties or towns as such. Secondly, Indiana does not have the sharp partisan cleavage between a massive metropolitan area and "out state" which characterizes such states as Illinois and Michigan. With both parties having strong elements of strength in both the rural and the metropolitan areas, the results of reapportionment in Indiana will be relatively minor. The results of future elections in the state may well be affected less by reapportionment than by the 1965 change in election laws which provides for door-to-door registration in the more populous counties —a practice heretofore restricted to counties of under 80,000 population.

One factor that does a great deal toward setting the framework of Indiana state government is the almost unqualified and unchallenged commitment to the desirability of conducting governmental affairs through the instrumentality of cohesive political parties. This belief in the desirability of strong parties is evidenced in a number of ways.

Whereas in many states the statutory arrangements are designed to frustrate leadership of party organizations, in Indiana there is a uniquely effective provision for a pyramidal party hierarchy leading from the precinct committeemen who are elected in the biennial primaries through the county and district levels to the office of state chairman. This state chairmanship is, for both Republicans and Democrats, a salaried and normally full-time position that provides a strong focal point for party leadership.

The system of nomination for state-wide offices in Indiana which relies on the choices of approximately 2,000-elected delegates who gather in state nominating conventions and cast their votes in secret on voting machines is a political invention that has not yet been copied by any other states but may well have more to recommend it than any of the alternative nominating procedures used elsewhere. The fact that candidates for nomination to state-wide office can focus their appeals on the limited number of convention delegates rather than having to finance state-wide primary campaigns is one important advantage of the Indiana system. Since it is possible to have repeated convention ballots when there are more than two candidates for a nomination, the convention system avoids the possibility, inevitably present in primary elections, that the final choice will go to someone who has strong backing from a minority faction but is unacceptable to a majority of the party. With the introduction of voting machines to the nominating convention the unhealthy leverage which county chairmen and other leaders were able to exercise in earlier years was ended. It might be desirable to make some minor changes in the machinery for the state conventions such as the prohibition of delegates who are employees of local governments and, therefore, may be beholden to party leaders. It seems unlikely, however, that a major change in the system of nominations for state-wide offices would be an improvement.

The present system of primary elections for the nomination of congressional and local candidates seems to work well, though it might be an improvement to require a voter to signify his enrollment in a party some substantial period prior to the primary rather than permitting election-day choice of a party. Under present Indiana arrangements the selection of a party's candidates is more subject to influence by independents and even by supporters of the other party than is the case in states where primaries are more effectively "closed."

The party-column ballot, known nationally as an "Indiana ballot," which encourages support for all the candidates of a single party is entirely compatible with the Indiana assumption that the road to good government involves putting one party in power and then deciding at the next election whether it deserves to be retained or replaced. Voting machines in Indiana are equipped with party levers, the pulling of which constitutes the casting of votes for all candidates of a party in the same way that an X in the party column accomplishes this for a paper-ballot voter. The presence of the party lever on the machine is certainly a convenience and is probably conducive to responsible government. It might be desirable, however, to make the use of the party lever voluntary rather than required as is currently the case in some counties.

Indiana's presidential preference primary, which requires the delegates from the state to each national convention to support on the first ballot whichever candidate receives a plurality in the state primary, provides what seems to be a desirable opportunity for the party's members in the state to express themselves directly on their choice for the party's presidential nominee. The present law, however, is clearly imperfect and may be the least satisfactory of any presidential preference primary arrangement now in effect. It might be desirable for Indiana to consider the system used in Oregon where all actual candidates are placed on the ballot unless they act to have their names removed, the system in a number of states in which voters choose not merely between candidates but between slates of delegates to the national convention who will be likely to respond to suggestions from their first-choice candidate if he no longer has a chance for the nomination, or even the relatively innocuous advisory primary which could be much like the present Indiana system except that the delegates from the state would not be legally required to support the candidate who won in Indiana.

Personnel policy for Indiana's state government operates in a fashion that outside observers familiar with federal civil service or the system in a state like California would regard as primitive and dangerous: Many thousands of state jobs are still awarded on the basis of straightforward political patronage. Some offices, principally those which distribute federal grant-in-aid funds and are, therefore, subject to the requirements of federal personnel policy have instituted a merit system with competitive appointment. Other offices such as the State Board of Accounts and the State

Police have established their own bipartisan personnel systems distinguished by a requirement that no more than half the employees be members of either major party. For most nontechnical positions in the state government, however, clearance by the appropriate officials of the party in power is a prerequisite to appointment and the officeholder must expect to be replaced if his party loses the next election.

The maintenance of the patronage system in Indiana is a result of a desire on the part of officeholders and party leaders to be able to reward the labors of faithful party workers. This is rationalized by a belief that healthy parties are essential to healthy responsible government and that parties will not stay vigorous unless there are rewards available to the citizens called upon to do the work of those parties. The virtually compulsory contribution to the state party treasury of 2 percent of the wages of these political appointees also serves to provide the party in power with funds which can be used to support such activities as television advertising during the general election campaign.

County organizations of the governor's party receive financial support from two features of the present system. Much the more substantial is the levy of 1 percent collected from the wages of patronage employees living in the county. Less important financially but of considerable significance in motivating top leaders in the county is the practice of distributing state licenses and automobile registrations through a network of "license branches" over which the party chairman in each county has control and from which he may derive a comfortable income.

More recently the defenders of Indiana's personnel policies have gained support from critical observers of the way "merit systems" have operated in many other jurisdictions. They have pointed to charges that traditional civil service procedures have seemed to provide protection for ineffective and mediocre workers and curtail the effective authority of department heads and other administrative personnel.

In recent years various reform-oriented groups in the state have supported proposals that, instead of attempting to move toward

normal civil service, all or most of the agencies in Indiana government adopt the bipartisan personnel systems already in effect in
some offices. This bipartisan approach would involve only minimum restriction on the freedom of the agency's operating head to
administer the office as he sees fit, but by removing the chance for
direct partisan rewards through firings and replacements it would
increase substantially the possibility that an able worker could make
a career out of service in the office. This bipartisan system would
make the positions substantially more attractive than they are under
the temporary circumstances of traditional patronage.

Indiana's government is big business. During the current fiscal
biennium, 1965-67, the state will have receipts and expenditures of
just under $1.8 billion. And this does *not* include any receipts and
expenditures on the part of local units of government—cities, counties, townships—except for the monies that state government col-
lects and sends back to local units for designated purposes. Put another way, Hoosier *state* government by itself is just about a billion-
dollar-a-year enterprise.

In common with every other state in the nation, Indiana's two
principal budgetary outlays are for education and highways. Presently, 40.5 percent of the total state budget is allocated for education and 30.3 percent for highways and roads. The relative close-
ness of the two percentages is in a sense deceptive, for a far larger
portion of the highway expenditures is supported by federal grants-
in-aid and thus does not have to be raised by state taxes. The following chart, based on the official state budget for 1965-67, illustrates this point.

	Total Appropriations	Federal Grants	Percent Federal Aid
EDUCATION	$718.8 million	$ 38.5 million	5.4
HIGHWAYS	$539.3	$221.0	41.0
ALL OTHER EXPENDITURES	$519.1	$ 82.9	16.0
Totals	$1777.2	$342.3	19.3

While the federal aid-to-education program adopted by the 89th Congress will certainly increase significantly the dollar amounts received by Indiana's schools from the national government, it is safe to assume that *state* support of education will continue to remain the largest single item in the budget for as far into the future as anyone can see, as it has been since 1933.

The variety and costs of other vital state functions can be touched on only briefly in the present survey. Operation of a penal system, under the direction of the Department of Correction, involves running the state's seven prisons and its youth rehabilitation centers, probation and parole activities, and administrative functions in the department itself. Altogether they will cost Hoosiers some $27 million, or 2 percent of the 1965-67 biennial budget.

Public welfare activities, which include assistance to the aged, the blind, the disabled, dependent children, and many other types of needy citizens, will require about $31 million of state money and $54 million of federal matching grants—5.5 percent of the total state budget.

Fourteen state hospitals of various kinds, most of which are severely overcrowded, and numerous other public health activities receive appropriations of $112 million, or a bit over 7 percent of the budget.

Natural resources and recreation involve remarkably diverse responsibilities for state government, ranging from promotion of tourism to dairy control and research, from maintenance of state parks and forests to flood control and geological surveys, from operating the State Fair to keeping the War Memorial in good repair. All told, some 49 separate items appear in the operating budget under this classification, amounting to just over $20 million for the biennium. With construction costs added, including those for the new Port of Indiana, the figure becomes $56.3 million—which happens to be less than 8 percent of what the state will spend on education alone during the same two-year period.

A very minor part of the budget—1.7 percent—has been allocated to a group of functions that touch the lives of every Hoosier in direct and intimate fashion; these are called public safety and regulation and include the operations of the State Police, the Fire Marshal, the Alcoholic Beverage Commission, the Civil Rights Commission, the Labor Division, the Insurance Department, and the Public Service Commission, among many others. Given the immense importance of the work of these agencies, the current appropriation of just under $7 million for their combined activities can hardly be regarded as excessive.

To state the needs and the costs is one thing; to stipulate how they are to be financed is quite another. The gross income tax with which Indiana government financed its affairs beginning in the 1930's was an ingenious and effective device which would seem to have merited being copied by other states. In recent years, however, the pressure for expanded state spending, particularly as a result of the increased numbers of school-age children, meant that the gross income tax could no longer support more than a part of the burden without being raised to a rate at which it would have been economically disruptive. In 1963, when the state's financial situation was definitely serious but before conditions had been allowed to reach the demoralizing and chaotic state of near bankruptcy which blighted some other states' operations in recent years, the responsible officials in Indiana government devised and adopted a multi-faceted tax program which provides the revenues needed for the support of state and local services and does so in an essentially equitable fashion.

Major components of the present program include a general retail sales tax (estimated yield, 1965-67: $304.5 million), an adjusted gross income tax on individuals and nonincorporated businesses and gross income tax on corporations (estimated yield: $509.5 million), and motor fuel and motor vehicle taxes (estimated yield: $337.1 million). All other state taxes (cigarette, alcoholic beverage, etc.) are expected to produce in this same biennium $207.0 million. From the total state revenues of $1.8 billion in the 1965-67 biennium, 32.3 percent—$582.4 million—will be distributed to units of local government, most of this for schools. Although property tax rates in most Indiana communities have not been reduced in recent years, it is clear that the availability of this assistance from the state has been instrumental in avoiding the massive increases in local taxes which would otherwise have been required.

The post-1963 rash of "Indiana, Land of Taxes" automobile plates and stickers was a manifestation of emotional overaction on the part of a large number of citizens who appeared to believe that the total state tax "bite" and the sheer number of taxes in Indiana were more burdensome than those of other states. In fact, however, neither belief is warranted by comparison either with all other states or with the four states that border Indiana, which still ranks fourth out of five in this region in *per capita* state and local taxes.

The future of Indiana will depend in great measure on the way in which the state's government meets the challenges which confront it during the fourth half century of the state's history. In 1966 the governmental and political health of the state, although clearly not perfect, is by any reasonable standard in relatively good shape. That Alabama's Governor Wallace received significant support in the 1964 presidential preference primary should not be allowed to obscure the fact that Indiana has made enormous progress since the days of the 1920's when the Ku Klux Klan was a major social and political factor in the state. That in recent years there have been occasional instances of misbehavior by public officials should be taken as evidence that there is always need to be vigilant but should not obscure the fact that Indiana's record on this score has been markedly better than that of many states from Massachusetts to Illinois and beyond.

In general, the persons nominated and elected to major office in Indiana in recent years have been able and conscientious. The people of Indiana are entitled to take pride in their state and specifically in its government. The generalized denunciation of Indiana government and politics which is found in some quarters both within the state and outside is both unhealthful for the system and unjustified by the facts. When Theodore White's *The Making of the President, 1960*, for instance, refers to Indiana politics as "among the most squalid, corrupt and despicable" in the nation, the observation reveals the author's ignorance of the situation that has been in effect for at least a generation.

Indiana is presently in good shape. The best hope for its future is that a larger proportion of its citizens will inform themselves of existing institutions and programs, consider the desirability of possible modifications, and apply their energies to insure that their future government will be a credit to their state.

EDWARD H. ZIEGNER

Indiana in National Politics

Introductory Note: A few explanations are in order regarding the framework within which this chapter was written. I arbitrarily chose to limit the period covered to the years 1900-66. It seemed to me, as I got deeper into research, that these years offered the richer vein to be mined, rather than the whole period 1816-1966.

It will be seen that I have skimmed very lightly over many areas and persons and left untouched numerous others. I have done little with Indiana's governors, largely because so few won themselves a solid place on the national scene, and I have barely noted the long quarrel of Indiana's conservative Republicans with the federal government. In the latter case I made such a decision because the controversy—important as it has been to some—won only scant notice nationally.

Harold C. Feightner, politics writer for *The Indianapolis News* in the 1920's and early 1930's, and an acute and perceptive observer of the Indiana political scene for 50 years, was greatly helpful with his recollections of politics in the state. The same was true of William L. Madigan, for many years politics writer for the Indiana bureau of The Associated Press, especially in regard to Paul McNutt's activities in 1940.

Edward H. Ziegner, a native of Indiana, is state politics writer and legislative bureau chief for *The Indianapolis News*. A veteran of World War II, he has reported on state politics and Indiana government for 20 years.

The search for Indiana's image in national politics in this century may properly start with Albert Jeremiah Beveridge, just returned from the new American outpost of empire in the Philippines, making his maiden speech in the United States Senate in 1900:

> God has not been preparing the English-speaking and Teutonic peoples for a thousand years for nothing but vain and idle self-contemplation and self-admiration. No! He has made us the master organizers of the world to establish system where chaos reigns. . . . Pray God the time may never come when Mammon and the love of ease shall so debase our blood that we shall fear to shed it for the flag and our imperial destiny. . . .

The galleries roared. It was spread-eagle imperialism by a spread-eagle orator; William Randolph Hearst and Kaiser Wilhelm must have liked it. Surely young Beveridge of Indiana was on his way up.

Now come across six decades to a way station—but not a terminal point—in this state's politics and watch as the governor of Alabama, George Corley Wallace, mounts a Pickett's charge through the 1964 Indiana Democratic presidential primary, appealing to the exposed nerve-end emotions of racism, frustration, and paranoia.

The infamous Ku Klux Klan had captured Indiana's Republican party in 1924 and elected a governor; the party regurgitated the Klan after D. C. Stephenson went to prison, but many continued to look on the state as an enclave of seedy bigotry and corruption. When Wallace came in 1964, some malodorous memories were revived. He was not a pretty sight, as the Indiana and the national press trailed in his wake puzzling, guessing, how well he would do. Richard Rovere thought him "an Alabama carpetbagger bent on mischief and ready for insurrection, in which he has already had some experience. He breathes rancor, his manner is at once cold and abrasive, and his speech is an assault on the central nervous system."

Matthew Empson Welsh, a slender intellectual who had been an excellent governor, stood in for Lyndon B. Johnson and smashed the invader, 376,023 to 172,646. Rovere thought the Wallace total "a large vote for a man who stands for an ugly doctrine" and so it was, as the nation set down another footnote on Indiana politics. Wallace showed that a gifted demagogue, even with clean shirt and shined shoes, is still the spiritual heir of the white-linen-suit Southern demagogues of the early 1900's, although the angry little man did less well in Indiana than in Wisconsin or Maryland.

And in the years between Beveridge and Wallace, what men, what events, what national reactions, what attitudes, what moods have built Indiana's political heritage and image?

Kin Hubbard, throwing dead cats into privileged political sanctuaries with his immortal Abe Martin, had brought levity to the scene and helped mold the state's political image. The same was true of Elmer Davis, out of Aurora, Indiana, and working in New York as he created that quadrennial public man Godfrey G. Gloom of Amity, Indiana, the last Jeffersonian, who went to all the conventions and always knew the score.

We have held a middle ground, rarely written off completely, rarely promising enough votes, electoral or popular, to command the attention given a New York, a Michigan or a California. We have now and then been severely graded; Theodore H. White in *The Making of the President, 1960* said: ". . . those states whose politics . . . are the most squalid, corrupt and despicable . . . that Jukes family of American politics that includes Indiana, Massachusetts and Texas."

In presidential power struggles the national GOP hierarchy has normally ticked the state off as "sure Republican" since 1944, content to let the nominee pay a routine courtesy call, in the manner of the obligatory visit to the faintly boring and only modestly fixed maiden auntie. Democratic chieftains have assessed us as worthy of a quick raid, and no more. The hunting has been better elsewhere. But 1964 was an exception, for both parties; Barry Goldwater made three visits, and Lyndon Johnson two. In 1956 Dwight D. Eisenhower never came.

Who may quarrel with such pragmatism? In seventeen presidential elections 1900-64 only four times has Indiana fallen to the Democrats: Woodrow Wilson in 1912, Franklin Roosevelt in

1932 and 1936, Lyndon Johnson in 1964. Goldwater considered Indiana one of the five critical states he must have to win, but he frightened and dismayed the great bloc-voting groups, the moderates, the Negroes, and the elderly with vague and ambiguous statements which indicated his mission was to roll history back 30 years. Never had Hoosiers, or Americans, seen such a campaign, and with their votes they made it clear there would be no turning back to a gentler, simpler age. Johnson took him in the state by 259,730 votes; it was not a record, however.

For the most part our governors have never had an influence which reached much beyond the borders of Indiana, except for fleeting moments, such as the time when Henry F. Schricker, that conservative Jeffersonian Democratic link with a gentler age, nominated Adlai Stevenson at Chicago in 1952.

Those setting us down as forever birthright Republican have failed to notice that beginning in 1900 we have elected nine GOP governors and eight Democratic. One of the latter was Paul Vories McNutt, a tough-minded, ambitious man who shoved his way onto the national stage in a futile drive to sit in the White House.

We have sent substantially more Republicans than Democrats to Congress over the last quarter century. Those who took and kept their seats in House and Senate and who bore the Republican label have been almost always conservative and frequently provincial and isolationist. The nation, watching the gusty stand-pattism of James Eli Watson in the 1920's and the rigid, right-wing conservatism of William Ezra Jenner in the 40's and 50's, did not find itself especially impressed.

The only Indiana public man still on the national stage today is Charles Abraham Halleck, durable mahatma of the state's copper-riveted Second Congressional District, twice GOP majority leader in the U. S. House, after 31 years a skillful, talented, gutty professional. That biographer of Congress, William S. White, calls him "beyond doubt one of the ablest, toughest, party floor leaders of modern times. . . ." Halleck is usually conservative and occasionally moderate; he nominated Wendell Willkie in 1940, and in 1948 swung the Indiana delegation to Tom Dewey when it appeared the No. 2 spot on the ticket would be the Hoosier's. Dewey chose Earl Warren, and Halleck is still bitter. He was for Dwight Eisenhower before the 1952 convention.

In this century we have never given the nation a President. Wendell Lewis Willkie, whom many Indiana Republicans considered a Democratic wolf in the stolen fleece of the Grand Old Party, won a nomination, but not an election. And at that time he had been, for 11 years, a child of Wall Street.

Except in 1964 our presidential primaries (1916-28, 1956-64*) brought no national attention: candidates like Stuart Symington and Nelson Rockefeller have shunned the tangled briar patch of Indiana party politics. But in the spring of 1960 John F. Kennedy came against token opposition, and gave us our first hard look at the man who would be President and martyr.

He returned as presidential nominee that fall and some, remembering Catholic Al Smith losing the state by 285,000 in 1928, hoped for better things and got little—Kennedy lost Indiana by 222,000. "He never expected to carry it," recalled Theodore Sorensen in 1964, "he knew it was a tough state for a Catholic, an Easterner and a liberal."

The Republicans, in control of one or both houses of the state legislature from 1939 to 1963, shaped the clay of conservatism with a bristling anti-federal aid resolution in 1947—"We propose henceforward to tax ourselves and take care of ourselves. . . ."—and the GOP legislature of 1957 passed the first right-to-work law enacted by a Northern industrial state. It was repealed by a Democratic legislature in 1965.

While Indiana Democrats at national conventions could accept without undue strain an Adlai Stevenson or a John Kennedy, the Republicans had qualms over Wendell Willkie in 1940, went 30 for Taft and 2 for Eisenhower in 1952 and refused to change the vote after Ike's nomination. In 1960 there was an undertone of surly discontent in the Indiana Republican delegation that Richard

---

* Between 1929 and 1956 no presidential primaries were held in the state. The old presidential primary law was repealed in the 1929 General Assembly; the new one was enacted in 1953.

Nixon had knelt in the Canossa of the hated Nelson Rockefeller's duplex apartment amid Manhattan's shining towers in the wicked and liberal East, and needlessly given ground. By 1964 the dominant rightist wing of the Hoosier GOP had the man it wanted, Barry Goldwater. He proceeded to lose by more votes than Alfred M. Landon 28 years before, exploding in Indiana the durable myth that a real conservative would bring out voters aching for a choice.

But even before the John Birch Society was being formed in Indianapolis in 1958, Indiana voters had begun at least a trial separation from orthodox Republicanism. The Democrats swept the state in that year and made R. Vance Hartke the first Democrat to win a Senate race in two decades; they followed by electing Welsh governor in 1960 and capturing the state Senate for the first time in 22 years.

In 1962 on election night a *New York Times* editor, incredulous that Republican Indiana was turning its back on eighteen-year-veteran Senator Homer Capehart in favor of youthful Democrat Birch Bayh, Jr., called the *Times'* correspondent in Indianapolis and asked, "What in hell is happening out there?"

What was happening was that Indiana was slowly losing the image of a rural, conservative, always Republican state, an image with a foundation in fact that had endured for most of the twentieth century. After electing Democratic governors in 1908 and 1912, the state returned to the GOP fold in 1916 and sealed the bargain with thundering pluralities for Warren G. Harding and other Republicans in 1920. In Indiana and the nation, it was a propitious time for the triumph of an isolationist conservatism. This state had no tradition of Progressive Republicanism. Hoosiers were tired of the responsibilities World War I had brought, tired of Woodrow Wilson's New Freedom, and had years before turned their backs on Theodore Roosevelt and his demand for change.

The war over, the state had Prohibition and the Ku Klux Klan. The Republican party embraced both, with pleasing results at the polls. Indiana, after all, was still an essentially rural, white Protestant state. If a high tariff, isolationism, and business supremacy were good enough for Jim Watson and Calvin Coolidge, they were certainly good enough for a majority of Hoosier Republicans. Republican conservatism turned drab in the state with the Great Depression and the advent of the New Deal but, beginning in 1938, it reasserted itself and by 1940 Ray Willis, a rural Republican in the old mold, had been elected to the U. S. Senate, replacing New Dealer Sherman Minton.

Since conservative doctrine was again producing victories, Indiana's Republican leaders saw no reason for change, and there was none. In election after election, the party hammered the same themes—opposition to any increase in the size of the federal government, opposition to federal aid, opposition to foreign aid and foreign entanglements. In this stand there was constant encouragement from the state's Republican newspapers, and from such organizations as the Indiana State Chamber of Commerce and the Indiana Farm Bureau which, while nonpartisan, tended strongly to endorse Republican candidates and causes. Victory for the GOP seemed almost automatic. From 1940 through 1956, only in 1948, the year of the Truman upset, were the Democrats able to snip the string of Republican triumphs, and it took the remarkable Henry F. Schricker to do that. The Democrats of Indiana, burdened by aging, unimaginative, and ineffective leadership, promptly lost the 1950 election, and were all but stamped out in the Eisenhower triumphs of 1952 and 1956.

In this era, though, Indiana as a state was changing with a rapidity whose political implications were seen only dimly by the Democrats and not at all by the Republicans. The shift of population to urban counties accelerated. Increasing industrialization marched across the cornfields. The civil rights revolution began in 1954; the state's nonwhite population leaped from 175,480 in 1950 to 341,999 in 1965. Indiana Negroes had begun to drift away from the Democrats in the 1940's, and in 1952 and 1956 Dwight Eisenhower won the votes of thousands of them in the state, but after 1956 they began returning to the Democrats who were pushing the civil rights revolution. In 1960 John Kennedy commanded their hearts and their votes; in 1964 they regarded Barry Goldwater as impossible.

Members of organized labor in Indiana by the 1950's numbered more than half a million, and the bulk of them regarded the Republican party as opposed to virtually everything they wanted. They were enraged by the passage of the right-to-work law by a GOP General Assembly in 1957, just as many elderly citizens receiving Social Security benefits were upset by the incredible attack on Social Security mounted in 1959 by an ultra-conservative Republican state chairman.

The state Republican machine, so efficient and sleek in 1952, was unraveling at the seams through much of the 1950's and on into the present decade. The GOP percentage of the off-year election vote slid from 56.2 in 1946 to 53.9 in 1950 to 51.4 in 1954 and a disastrous 44.2 in 1958. The Republican primary vote declined and was surpassed by the Democrats in 1958, and the rural, conservative counties on which the GOP still relied so heavily counted for less and less in the total vote picture; by 1960 25 percent of Indiana's people lived in just two urban counties; 40 percent in only five counties, and 60 percent in just 14 out of the state's 92 counties. By 1965 less than 10 percent of Hoosiers were properly classified as farmers. The bedrock of the old GOP power base was gone.

The Democrats won Indiana's municipal elections in 1955 and again in 1959, and although they elected a minority of mayors in 1963, they still slightly topped the Republicans in total vote for the state. The people were in the cities now, and they were more and more voting Democratic. And they were more and more regarding themselves as Democrats. George Gallup, in a national poll in 1940, had found 42 percent of voters thought of themselves as Democrats and 38 percent as Republicans. In 1965, in another national sampling, his figures showed 53 percent Democrats, 25 percent Republicans. While the shift may have been less in Indiana, shift there was, and it was to the Democrats.

The state's population reflected another trend—a constantly younger population, with half of all Americans 28 or younger in 1965, and half to be 25 or younger by 1970. From 1958 on Indiana Democrats, with generally young, aggressive, and appealing candidates, found fertile ground here while the Republicans, with generally aging leadership, aging candidates, and aging ideas, found their party plows striking rock.

After Birch E. Bayh, Jr., had won in 1962, it was clear that the long pattern of voter favor for Republican conservatism had been broken at least temporarily, and perhaps for a long time. In 1958, 1960, and 1962 Hartke, Welsh, and Bayh, all Democratic liberals, had defeated doctrinaire Republican conservatives still preaching a party gospel essentially unchanged since the 1920's. But a shifting, changing, growing, younger, mobile electorate was saying, with its votes, it wanted some change.

The Supreme Court's "one man, one vote" decision on legislative apportionment and the Republican disaster with Goldwater in 1964 set the stage for the first Democratic control of the Indiana General Assembly in 28 years in the 1965 session. The Democrats reapportioned legislative seats, gave control to the cities, broke a 149-year-old domination of the Assembly by rural interests, and assured themselves of added power.

And while the Republicans were not changing much in the turbulent 20 years which followed the end of World War II, their opposition was changing a good deal. The Democrats, at last free of the influence of the generation which had come to power with Paul McNutt, had been building themselves a new party. Since 1958 their visions and aims have been both pragmatic and bold, their leadership youthful and talented, and their bone and muscle a lively professionalism tuned to the great special changes of this age and the accelerating movement off the farms and into the cities of Indiana. They are a new breed, their ranks spotted here and there with a Phi Beta Kappa, a Rhodes Scholar, a Harvard Law or Business School graduate. How long they may prevail is by no means certain, but it does seem clear that Indiana is no longer ready to hand the GOP the easy victories the party enjoyed in the 1940-56 era and that it is moving or has moved into the swing-state category in both state and national elections.

As the Indiana Democrats moved, the Indiana Republicans sat immobilized, wedded to orthodox conservatism, oriented to the business and rural viewpoints, hoping like Dickens' Micawber that something would surely turn up. The disaster of 1964 shook them as nothing had since Franklin Roosevelt's landslide of 1936. They have begun to move off dead center, they are going to win again and possibly quite soon, and they are beginning to think a rigid conservatism may not be the answer.

What of the other makers of the state's political image, between Beveridge and George Wallace? From 1900-40 the state was a forcing ground for a substantial crop; the harvest has been less bountiful in the last quarter of a century. Let us call the roll.

James Eli Watson (1863-1948), six times elected to the House, three times to the U. S. Senate, was Indiana's plumed knight of Old Guard conservatism. Floor manager for William Howard Taft in 1912, by 1919, with Teddy Roosevelt dead, Boies Penrose was telling the Indianan, "Well, Jim, we'll have enough votes to nominate you." Jim was a communicant at the smoke-filled room in Chicago which nominated Warren Harding in 1920; later in *As I Knew Them* he would blandly write that it was "simply a voluntary gathering of men, all greatly interested in the success of the party." Certainly.

He helped Henry Cabot Lodge beat the League of Nations, was a favorite-son candidate for president in 1928 in Kansas City, where he was crushed by the Hoover steamroller, then Hoover's majority leader in the Senate. Beaten for reelection in 1932, he was suggesting four years later that six million aliens "be sent back to the countries whence they came," and telling Alf Landon not to be too liberal. When he was buttonholed by Willkie in the Bellevue-Stratford lobby in Philadelphia in 1940, Watson told him he had no objection to whores in church, but could not condone their leading the choir on the first Sunday.

A Hoosier who covered him in the 1920's remembers him as a "lovable humbug." Charlie Michelson called him "wholly opportune" but one of the "experienced practitioners" of the political art. H. L. Mencken snorted that he was "a mountebank so puerile and preposterous" as to make other mountebanks seem dignified, but also called him an "adept professional." He never changed. It is trite to say that he was typical of the dominant strain of Indiana

GOP professionals in the 20's, but he was. He fitted with Harding, with Coolidge—William Allen White's Puritan in Babylon—and with Hoover. These were strange days, wrote Malcolm Moos, and then added Jim Watson's remark that "the nights were a mite peculiar, too."

Will H. Hays, Watson's contemporary, came out of Sullivan, Indiana, and up through the political chairs—county chairman, district chairman, state chairman, and national chairman when Harding won. The Hoosier knew how to organize for combat; he won elections. "Seldom has the Republican party had so effective a field general," Moos observed.

Hays called "Wilsonism" something like socialism. He told businessmen the party appreciated their "fundamental importance." In 1920 he wanted to be president. He would be, said the rumors, candidate or kingmaker; William Howard Taft believed that Hays would be the man sprung on the convention to stop Harding. In his bid Hays had a strange ally—Col. George Harvey, former editor of the *New York World*, booster of Woodrow Wilson into politics, a Democrat until 1916. Harvey gave the dinner party, in Chicago's Blackstone Hotel, which turned into the smoke-filled room. He was boosting Hays for the nomination, but got turned down at his own party. Hays didn't attend. The suite was either Hays' or shared by Hays and Harvey; accounts differ.

The new President made the man from Indiana postmaster general. The state had seen Harding first in the 1920 primary and had not liked him; he ran a bad fourth behind Leonard Wood, Hiram Johnson, and Frank Lowden. It liked him better in November; he carried the state by 185,000 votes. In the same year Indiana had its first look at Franklin D. Roosevelt, who came into the state to call Harding the tool of "Wall Street gamblers and the money trust interest."

As Normalcy unraveled, Hays got mixed reviews. Mencken called him "Elder Hays" and said he was one of the Harding "garde du corps," which presented "an appalling spectacle." To Charles and Mary Beard he was "Deacon Hays." In *America in Midpassage* (1929) they spoke of his "facile treatment of embarrassing questions" as Senate probers asked him about Teapot Dome, his relations to Harry Sinclair, and his financing of GOP campaigns. Hays went west in 1922 to become the movies' "czar"; he lived until 1954, time enough to see the Republicans win again after 20 years in the wilderness. He was our link to Warren Harding at a time when few agreed with Alice Roosevelt Longworth's judgment: "Harding's not a bad man. He's just a slob."

Albert Beveridge was a different breed of political cat from Jim Watson or Will Hays. Sonorous trumpet of the new imperialism, he married well, wore silk-lined coats, gloried in Websterian oratory, and in one campaign used the phrase "Mary of the vine-clad cottage" to point up the homely virtues of Hoosiers. Claude Bowers, hearing him on Labor Day in 1898, said, "His description of dawn was very beautiful." Many thought him arrogant, vain, and pompous.

Elected to the Senate in 1899 by the legislature and reelected in 1905, Beveridge was turned down in 1911. He went to Chicago in 1912 for T. R., and walked out with him to "stand at Armageddon and battle for the Lord." Six weeks later he keynoted the Bull Moose convention, saying: "Knowing the price we must pay, the sacrifices we must make . . . the assaults we must endure . . . we enlist for the war." He ripped off his collar for emphasis. The delegates roared. *The New York Times* called it "a Methodist camp meeting done over in political terms." In the Columbia and Marion clubs in Indianapolis they handled this deserter from orthodoxy by removing his picture from the wall. He ran as the Progressive nominee for governor and lost to Democrat Sam Ralston, but he did see T. R. top Taft in the state, 162,007 to 151,267, in Hoosierdom's long forgotten flirtation with Progressive Republicanism.

He ran unsuccessfully as a Progressive for U. S. Senator in 1914, began to write his four-volume life of John Marshall, returned to the party fold in 1916, beat Harry New in the 1922 senatorial primary, and lost another election to Ralston in November. He was through.

Across the spectrum from Beveridge was Eugene Victor Debs of

Terre Haute, an all but forgotten Indiana political image maker. Secretary of his lodge of the Brotherhood of Locomotive Firemen at 20, he was an organizer of the American Railway Union in 1893 and a leader of the Pullman strike in Chicago a year later. Indicted for his part in the strike, Clarence Darrow defended him, but he went to jail. Debs called his bride, Kate Metzel, "Duckie." His politics failed to bother poet James Whitcomb Riley; they were good friends.

By 1895 he was a Socialist. Votes, he told the workers, could "make and unmake presidents and congresses and courts. . . ." He went out to get them; the Socialists nominated him for president four straight times beginning in 1900. In 1908 he campaigned on "The Red Special," the crowds would scream "Debs, Debs, Debs!"; at Evansville he drew more people than Taft. He got almost a million votes in 1912, 36,931 in Indiana, in the year in which Jim Watson had helped stop T. R., Beveridge had keynoted the convention which nominated the Rough Rider, and Tom Marshall of Columbia City was on his way to Washington as Woodrow Wilson's running mate. It was a vintage political year for the state.

Debs opposed American involvement in World War I and was nominated for president for the fifth time by the Socialists in 1920, hearing the news of his selection in the warden's office at Atlanta. He had been arrested for violation of the Espionage Act during the war and sentenced to ten years in prison. He got almost a million votes again in 1920, 24,703 in Indiana. Wilson had said, "I will never consent to the pardon of this man." Harding, though, commuted his sentence December 23, 1921. Debs made a strange visit to the White House, saw the President, came out and said, "We understand each other perfectly." It was hard to explain. It made sense to Arthur M. Schlesinger, Jr., however, who wrote, "Terre Haute and Marion, after all, were much the same."

When Debs got off the train, home at last, the band played the "Internationale" and "Hail, Hail, The Gang's All Here." Now he was sick, old, tired; one of the last things he did was to tell the faithful to vote for Bob LaFollette in 1924; perhaps he was pleased that LaFollette got 5.64 percent of the vote in Indiana, the same percentage Debs had received in 1912. When he died, at 70, in 1926, history had overtaken him. He was a remarkable man.

In 1888, less than 32 years after he was born in County Monaghan, Ireland, Tom Taggart, Democratic chairman of Marion County, Indiana, carried the county for Grover Cleveland over Benjamin Harrison, a local boy who should have done better in his own backyard. Harrison made it to the White House, anyhow. People began to talk about Taggart. Three times mayor of Indianapolis, state chairman, national chairman, national committeeman, U. S. Senator by appointment but twice loser at the polls, the boy from County Monaghan was getting on.

He owned the big, flossy hotel at French Lick, furnished luxury suites and Pluto Water to the millionaires who rode their private railway cars in for some relaxation, and became a millionaire himself. A national power in the party, the "Boss of Indiana," he was one of the most charming and skillful politicians ever produced by any state. He had the right friends, and made some of the right enemies; Hearst called him "a plague spot in the community spreading vileness." D. W. Brogan wrote in *Politics in America* that "men went out to French Lick to talk to Tom Taggart and, if they were wise, usually listened to what he had to say. . . ."

Tom went to Baltimore in 1912 pushing Marshall for president. It looked a weak hand—just 30 delegates from Indiana—but Taggart knew the deck. He dealt with Wilson's manager, who was looking for help, moved Indiana behind the Princeton scholar on the twenty-eighth ballot, and saw him nominated on the forty-sixth. The nomination of Tom Marshall for vice president followed.

His last great show was in New York in 1924 as the Democrats, in the course of 103 ballots, proceeded to tear themselves to pieces over the Klan and Prohibition. Taggart had Sam Ralston in the race as a favorite son; the squire of French Lick set up shop at the old Waldorf-Astoria and began to talk to the party's power brokers. He could; he belonged to the club. Taggart ran Ralston up to 94 delegates on the fifty-third ballot, but Ralston wanted out. It was whispered that he was tied to the Klan; he denied it, but wired Taggart July 1, and again two days later, to stop. Taggart stuck the first wire in his pocket and showed the second to politics writer Harold Feightner of *The Indianapolis News*, who got a national news beat and a $5 raise. Taggart took Ralston out and started dividing Indiana's 30 votes, with 20 for William Gibbs McAdoo and 10 for Al Smith. What would Taggart do? the convention asked. He was a man to watch. Suddenly Ralston was back in again, and climbing; by the ninety-second ballot he had 196¾ votes, trailing only Smith, with 355½, and McAdoo, with 314. John W. Davis, who would be the nominee, had 69½. Now Taggart took Ralston out for keeps. It was all over.

Had Taggart really wanted to nominate Ralston, and did Ralston want it? Feightner thinks not. Taggart knew it was hopeless to elect anyone in 1924, Ralston was ill (he died two years later), and Taggart looked ahead to what a man might get done in 1928. The chance never came. Ill himself, he couldn't go to Houston in 1928 and died in March 1929, two days after Herbert Hoover took the oath of office. Taggart kept Indiana on the national political stage for a generation. We have never had another quite like him.

There were others in this era—Tom Marshall, Harry New, Charles Warren Fairbanks—who played supporting roles and moved on.

Thomas Riley Marshall was a country lawyer from Columbia City who drawled slowly, had a good mind, and thought quickly. The twenty-sixth governor of Indiana (1909-13), Tom Taggart got him the 1912 nomination for vice president; he won with Wilson and was reelected in 1916, the first No. 2 man able to claim that honor since John C. Calhoun.

He was witty and sometimes irreverent. No one had to tell him the post of second consul carried little prestige, influence, or importance. A man of more than passing ability, he is remembered most for his cracks about the vice presidency. The Senate found him charming and liked him, even though he called the chamber "the cave of the winds." Working one day in his Capitol office, he looked up to see a group of tourists gawking through the door. The Vice President of the United States invited them in and they declined; they had more important things to do. "Well, if you can't come in, throw me a peanut," Marshall shot back. They went on.

He and Wilson had some differences, but Wilson quashed attempts to drop him in 1916. With Wilson ill, Marshall waved away suggestions that he assume some presidential duties. He died in Washington, D. C., in 1925.

Harry Stewart New, Republican national chairman in 1908, a Taft backer and convention arrangements chairman in 1912, always seemed to be getting tangled up with fellow Indiana Republicans. In 1916 he beat Jim Watson in the state's first senatorial primary; Watson made it to the Senate, anyway, when he won a short-term vacancy which opened up. New showed up at the smoke-filled room in Chicago in 1920. Two years later Albert Beveridge beat New in the senatorial primary. He found himself able to laugh about it. A few weeks after his defeat, hurrying down a Senate corridor, he was stopped by a befuddled woman tourist, demanding to know how you get out of the Senate. "Madam," said New graciously, "I suggest you try an Indiana primary."

Charles Warren Fairbanks, United States Senator, got to be Roosevelt's running mate in 1904 but wasn't renominated in 1908. He was back in harness in 1916, as running mate with Charles Evans Hughes; they carried Indiana, but lost nationally to Wilson and Tom Marshall. Whichever way it went that year, Indiana was bound to have a vice president.

As in 1912, 1940 was another vintage year for the state; it raised up Paul McNutt and Wendell Willkie.

Handsome, silver-haired, tough-minded, ambitious, McNutt served in World War I, became law school professor and dean, and national commander of the American Legion. By January 1933 he was governor of an Indiana with an empty treasury, and a desire for change. He was the first Democrat to sit in the governor's chair since Sam Ralston. He picked up the state, shook it like a terrier, and set out to make a national reputation for himself. He wanted to be president. Indiana's Republican newspapers began calling him a dictator; he told a reporter, privately, "They [the newspapers] think they're running the state. They're not. I am."

At the White House the latchstring was not always out for him. Indiana had guessed wrong at Chicago in 1932 and climbed aboard the Roosevelt express much too late. In 1935 a dying Louis McHenry Howe, FDR's man Friday, would fret over the "absurd impertinence of a premature drive for . . . McNutt for vice president in 1936" and "the grinding friction of the antique Indiana machine."

Out of office as governor, McNutt went to the Philippines as high commissioner, came back as Federal Security Administrator. The President, thought Bronx Boss Ed Flynn, "encouraged McNutt's aspirations to such a degree that the . . . Indianan seemed to conclude there had been a 'laying on of hands.'"

He was wrong; Franklin Roosevelt wanted a third term. The hopes of being a presidential nominee were abandoned; the hopes of the second spot on the ticket were kept alive. Indiana took over a gate at the convention hall in Chicago in 1940, and hundreds of Hoosiers flowed in, with or without tickets, to yell for Paul McNutt. The convention, unhappy with the third term, was rebellious. Did McNutt have a chance for the second spot? No. Wayne Coy, keeping in touch with Harry Hopkins, got the word that FDR wanted Henry Wallace. McNutt went to Hopkins' suite; from there he phoned the President to pledge his support. It was a bitter pill, but he was playing the good soldier.

Back in session, the convention readied itself to choke down a Henry Wallace it did not want. McNutt started to the rostrum to withdraw. The delegates and galleries began to roar and boil and surge. A majority of them wanted the man from Indiana, not Iowa.

McNutt, at the podium, started, saying "I want . . ."

"NO!" came the screams. Seven times he started, and had to stop.

Finally he got it out: "He [Roosevelt] is my commander-in-chief. I follow his wishes, and I am here to support his choice for Vice President of the United States. . . ."

He lingered on the national stage as War Manpower Commissioner, went back to the Philippines as first ambassador, and then built a lucrative law practice before his death in 1955. Had Franklin Roosevelt not sought a third term, he might have been president.

Wendell Lewis Willkie, wrote Washington correspondent Roscoe Drummond, was "no more humble than he was simple. He was neither modest or immodest; it just never occurred to him to be anything other than successful." This he was. Small-town, middle-class boy from Elwood, maverick at Indiana University, Army veteran of World War I, Democrat, he went on to New York to become the $75,000 per year president of Commonwealth & Southern. He bitterly fought the New Deal, but stayed within the party fold, voting for Herbert Lehman in New York in 1938. The 1940 edition of *Who's Who* still listed him as a Democrat.

Like Paul McNutt, he wanted to be president. Almost no one in the party knew who he was as 1940 opened; he began an outwardly amateurish but actually brilliantly organized drive for the Republican nomination. Some of the GOP professionals refused to take him seriously. By the time the convention met in Philadelphia, he was getting stronger. Old Jim Watson was outraged. He tried to get Dewey and Taft together to stop the interloper who, while he owned farms near Jim's own home town of Rushville, was a newcomer, a renegade Democrat, and a child of Wall Street. It was almost too much for Jim to bear.

Charlie Halleck nominated his fellow Hoosier and, slashing at the rumblings that Willkie was too new a Republican, asked, "Is the Republican party a closed corporation?" Even with Halleck pushing, Indiana was reluctant on the first ballot, giving its native son only 9 of 28 delegates. Paul McNutt, hearing the results back in Indianapolis, smiled and said, "Well, Wendell's learning about politics." He was learning. His own state still moved slowly, 15 for him on the fourth ballot, 20 on the fifth; on the sixth and last, before the shift, 23 for Willkie and 5 for Taft. Jim Watson stalked off the floor; he had had enough.

Nominated, Willkie relaxed on the yacht of Roy Howard, came back to bucolic Rushville, borrowed a big, red brick house, leaned on the fence and looked at his cattle, and made like a candidate. The whole business, said the Democrats, was of ersatz quality. He accepted the nomination August 17, 1940, in Callaway Park in Elwood. Old Socialist Norman Thomas said it appeared to him that Willkie agreed with Roosevelt's whole program "and said it was leading to disaster." Harold Ickes called him "a simple, barefoot Wall Street lawyer." He had swallowed so much of the New Deal, said Mencken, that he now appeared to be "a man choking on his own false teeth." Later John L. Lewis endorsed him. Reporters called the Willkie campaign train "The Squirrel Cage"; he traveled 19,000 miles in 51 days, lost to FDR, but carried Indiana by 25,000 votes. "How could we lose?" cried Edith Willkie. "We tried so hard."

When he died in New York in October 1944, *The New York Times* called him "as American as the countryside of his native Indiana." He was ahead of his time, ahead of his party, and almost out of sight from the conservative Republicans of Indiana. They never liked him much; they were waiting for Bob Taft and Barry Goldwater, and they have forgotten him and what he stood for. He was an able man.

After McNutt and Willkie faded from national view, there were few to keep Indiana on stage. Halleck did, and still does. Frank McKinney of Indianapolis became Democratic national chairman in 1951 and Harry Truman called him "the best national chairman the party ever had." Paul Butler of South Bend won the job in 1955 and stayed almost five years, better than par for the course.

William Ezra Jenner, who served two terms in the U. S. Senate (1947-59) and who ran the GOP in Indiana for most of the years between 1945 and 1960, bolstered the national image of the state as a citadel of right-wing Republican conservatism. He called General George Marshall a "living lie," lustily defended Joe McCarthy, and became increasingly critical of Dwight Eisenhower. In the national press Jenner got poor marks. Comparing Jenner to Pat McCarran of Nevada, Elmer Davis said the Hoosier had "nothing like the intellect and force of Old Silvertop." Rovere reported Bob Taft had "nothing but scorn" for Jenner. Sam Lubell said one should call senators like Jenner "disillusionists," not isolationists. But Jenner never gave a damn about what the press said. He retired voluntarily from office at the close of his second term, has never again run for an elective job, and his influence on the party in Indiana has considerably waned.

Our last show which drew a national audience was the 1964 presidential primary, both a grim and gaudy affair. George Wallace provided the grim side. The other came from such candidates as Faye T. Carpenter-Swain, a woman of indeterminate age who wore a wristwatch on an ankle and who threw jelly beans at reporters and voters. In the Democratic primary she got 7,140 votes, perhaps a testimonial to the appeal of comic opera.

If one tired of the jelly beans, there was tireless Harold Stassen, running against Barry Goldwater in the Republican primary. To the surprise of everyone, Stassen got 107,157 votes to Goldwater's 267,935. A few perverse readers of election statistics noted that when Stassen's vote was added to that of two other Goldwater foes, it showed one GOP voter in three in Indiana didn't want the man from Arizona. It was an omen for November that almost no one noticed.

In voting for presidents, Indiana has been a reliable weathervane. In the 38 contests since we became a state in 1816, we have been with the winner 29 times, and with the loser only 9. Four of our nine wrong guesses have come in the last 25 years; we went down with Willkie in 1940; Dewey in 1944 and 1948, and Nixon in 1960. In short, the mood of the nation has usually been ours, but less so in recent years.

Today Indiana is rather far down on the national totem pole of influence in both great parties; only Halleck can fairly be rated as a national figure, and even he—his post of minority leader taken from him in 1965—speaks with a muted voice.

The new generation of men, Republicans and Democrats, who will carry the banner in future years are only a few steps along the road, or not even yet started. Some of the young Democrats who have come to power in the last few years in the state show promise —but we cannot be certain they will keep on winning nor how far they may go if they do. The Republicans have not been winning, and they have even further to travel than the Democrats.

EARL L. BUTZ

Agriculture—
An Industry in Evolution

A scientific explosion is occurring in our midst. American agriculture is an industry in the middle of a far-reaching scientific and technological revolution which is shaking the very foundations of its traditional institutional patterns. It is changing from a way of living to a way of making a living. It is changing from a business of arts and crafts to a business undergirded with large amounts of science and technology. The advances in the next decade will be unparalleled in American agriculture. It will be the decade of the most far-reaching change in our entire history.

Although it is the smallest state west of the Allegheny Mountains (except Hawaii), Indiana is one of the richest agricultural areas in the world. Agriculture is one of the truly great growth industries for Hoosierland, and the future never looked brighter. "Big and basic" characterizes the agricultural industry in the Hoosier economic picture. Farmers not only produce an annual

Earl L. Butz, a native of Noble County, Indiana, has been Dean of Agriculture at Purdue University since 1957. A Purdue graduate, he was head of the department of agricultural economics at that university for eight years before serving as Assistant Secretary of Agriculture in Washington from 1954 to 1957. On 8 trips abroad, he has visited 30 countries, studying food and agricultural conditions.

flow of new wealth but also generate the wide variety of processing, manufacturing, and distribution activities that grow out of farm production. It is estimated that with the generation of every one dollar of new wealth produced on our farms, from three to five dollars of related economic activity keep men working and industry humming "along Main Street" of literally scores of Indiana towns.

Because farming is done with considerably less manpower today than a generation ago, too many people think that agriculture is a declining industry. Instead, Hoosier agriculture is an expanding industry in every important respect except one—the number of people required to run the farms. Its agricultural plant each year uses more capital, more science and technology, more purchased production inputs, more managerial capacity, more specialized marketing facilities, and more research than the year before.

Although the declining trend in farm population is viewed with alarm by some politicians and rural fundamentalists, it is a sign that American agriculture has entered the age of science and technology. Brainpower has replaced horsepower as the central ingredient of success on our farms. The total U. S. agricultural output has increased some two thirds in the last two decades, while workers on farms have decreased almost three million. The result has been that production per worker on farms has doubled in the last 20 years. This remarkable increase in production efficiency is unmatched by any other major sector of the American economy.

Along with the decline in farm population there has been a decline in the number of farms. The 1964 farm census reported 108,082 individual farms in Indiana, a decline of 20,000 farms in five years and twice that number for the entire preceding decade. Although the number of farms has been decreasing two to three percent annually, acres per farm have been increasing about three percent per year. The 1964 census put the average size per farm at 166 acres compared with 145 acres only five years earlier. It is predicted that changes of this approximate magnitude will continue in the next decade. The total amount of land in farms has been relatively stable, however, decreasing approximately 100,000 acres per year. Total land in farms in Indiana on January 1, 1966, was estimated at 18,800,000 acres. This is about 73 percent of the total land area of the state, about 23,158,400 acres.

Indiana's farm production is now at an all-time high. Compared with 20 years ago, Hoosier farmers are now producing more than twice as much corn, nearly three times as many soybeans, five million more bushels of wheat (on 400,000 fewer acres), one billion more pounds of milk, 300 million more pounds of beef, and nearly 1.4 million more hogs marketed.

In 1965 Hoosier farmers achieved a record-smashing 94 bushels of corn per acre for an all-state average yield. This was the highest among the fifty states. In the same year these farmers equaled their own previous record soybean yield of 28 bushels per acre, and were second in the nation. Although Indiana is only thirty-eighth in size among the states, she ranks eleventh in total farm production, third in the production of corn, third in hogs, third in soybeans, third in the production of tomatoes for processing, third in the production of mint, twelfth in poultry, fourteenth in dairy cattle, and eighteenth in beef cattle.

The advance in Hoosier agriculture during the last century has been even more spectacular than for the entire nation. For example, average corn yields have moved from 39 bushels per acre in 1915 to the remarkable 94 bushels per acre in 1965—an increase of 140 percent. Wheat yields moved from 18 to 34 bushels per acre. Soybeans, scarcely known in 1915, moved from 14 bushels per acre in 1930 to 28 bushels per acre in 1965—a 100 percent increase. Hay yields increased by more than 50 percent in the interval from 1935 to 1965.

In the 30 years since 1935 Indiana's livestock programs moved ahead vigorously. Hog production has more than doubled, beef production was up substantially, broiler production went from nothing to over 25 million birds annually, turkeys went from a very small number to 3.4 million birds, milk production per cow more than doubled, egg production per hen more than doubled, and so on and on.

Indiana farmers have gross cash receipts of about $1.4 billion annually. In 1965 total cash receipts were $1,396,000,000. Of this amount, $766 million came from sale of livestock products, $530 million from sale of crops, and nearly $100 million came from government payments. If we assume that from three to five dollars of related economic activity arises from every dollar of primary farm income, it is at once apparent that Indiana's total agricultural industry is well in excess of $5 billion annually.

Much of this $5 billion industry is found in the "off-the-farm" phase of agriculture. In the quarter century since 1940 total inputs going into American agriculture have remained approximately the same. While farm labor input has been nearly cut in half, the use of capital has practically doubled. We have doubled our inputs of power, machinery, fertilizer, lime, insecticides, seed, breeding stock, commercial feeds, and the like. These items are produced off the farm and funneled to the farmer through commercial channels. In 1910 American farmers spent—counting the value of their own capital, land, and labor—$5.8 billion to produce crops and livestock. In 1954 many fewer farmers spent about $30 billion, or nearly six times as much. In 1965 the nation's farmers had a total gross income of $44 billion, or four times as much as twenty-five years ago. Most of this was spent in one way or another—for living if not for production expenses.

The total personal income of the U. S. farm population in 1965, after taxes, was better than $18 billion. This is two and a half times as much as it was 25 years earlier, although the farm population is less than half what it was then. Farm people are an important market for family cars, television sets, home furnishings, appliances, clothing, cosmetics, pharmaceuticals, and the whole range of consumer goods. At the same time there is the tremendous farm market for production items. Farmers now buy annually more new trucks than new tractors. New automobile purchases top them all. Each year farmers purchase about 150,000 new tractors, 200,000 new trucks, and 500,000 new automobiles. About 12 percent of our farmers will purchase new automobiles annually, as compared to 11 percent of the entire population.

More personal income originates in agriculture than in any

other industry except wholesale and retail trade and contract construction. As farm mechanization and automation become even more widespread, farm people will have added time for leisure and recreation. The rural market for consumer goods and services will continue to expand very rapidly.

Agriculture is one of the biggest users of capital in modern America. The total assets of American agriculture on January 1, 1965, was $238 billion—a record high. This is over four times the investment in American agriculture in 1940. The investment per farm and per worker is also at an all-time high—and growing. To the total investment in agriculture may be added another $80 to $100 billion invested in agri-business, which is an essential component of modern agricultural production and marketing. This makes a total investment in agriculture and agri-business of around one third of a trillion dollars.

The total debt in agriculture on January 1, 1965, both real estate and non-real estate was $37.5 billion. This is a record high figure, even though it does represent only 16 percent of the total assets of agriculture. In recent years the total debt has been going up about $2.5 to $4 billion per year, even though the percentage of proprietors' equity in the entire agricultural plant remains relatively constant at about 84 to 86 percent.

The expansive character of agriculture is indicated by the large capital requirements on commercial farms. Farm account records from a group of some 500 farms throughout Indiana, kept in cooperation with Purdue University, show that the capital investment per farm has more than doubled from 1950-54 to 1963 (see Table 1), while the labor force per farm has remained constant at 1.7 men equivalent. This means that the investment per worker has more than doubled. At the same time the size per farm has increased from 233 to an average 339 acres, or 46 percent. It is projected that by 1970 a further increase of forty acres will have occurred.

Investment per worker on these farms was $74,000, while a comparable figure for investment per worker in American industry is approximately $20,000. Thus it takes between three and four times as much capital investment to create one agricultural job on Hoosier family commercial farms than it does in American industry.

In the last quarter century the physical volume of output from farms increased more than 50 percent, with a third to a half fewer farm workers. The result has been that the output per worker in American agriculture has more than doubled in these years and has roughly quadrupled in the past 50 years. Indeed, the productivity of the American farm worker is so high that our problem in America is how to live with plenty, in sharp contrast to the rest of the world, where there is a constant struggle to produce enough food to prevent widespread famine and human misery. American agriculture now feeds our growing population, with a great abundance beyond domestic needs to feed tens of millions of hungry people around the world. About $100 billion of the American consumers' annual expenditures go for food and clothing provided by or made from the products of agriculture. Nearly three fourths of all our basic raw materials are of agricultural origin. A day's factory labor buys 50 percent more food than it did in 1940, and this is some four times as much as it does in Russia.

Tens of millions of Americans never give a thought about tomorrow's food. They are so used to a well-laden supermarket just down the street, with its wide variety of tempting, palatable, healthy, and nutritious foodstuffs, that they assume without a second thought that, even as abundant food has been their fortune so far in life, they need have no apprehension on the food front for tomorrow.

Why has this opulence occurred in the United States rather than in Argentina, for example, where there is similar land and climate? Or why not in Western Europe, which has a larger population, ample resources, and intelligent minds? Or why not in Russia, with more than 200 million people, almost self-sufficient resources, and capable scientists as illustrated by their progress in space? Why is America's problem one of "too much food," while in Russia they repeatedly have trouble getting their agriculture off the launching pad?

The application of scientific research and technology to agri-

TABLE I

State-wide Averages of Characteristics and Earnings
of Indiana Farm Account Farms*

	1950-54	1955-58	1959-62	1963	1970 Projected
Acres per farm	233	268	314	339	380
Acres in corn	63	82	109	116	140
Bushels of corn per acre	63	72	92	105	110
Number of feeder cattle bought	9	17	25	30	40
Number of hogs raised	168	235	322	366	500
Capital invested per farm	$61,221	$79,871	$109,725	$125,702	$164,000
Labor force per farm	1.7	1.7	1.7	1.7	1.7
Investment per worker	$36,000	$47,000	$65,000	$74,000	$97,000
Net farm income	$7,303	$7,414	$11,730	$12,885	$15,000– $17,000
Income to labor & management	$4,243	$3,421	$6,244	$6,599	$7,000– $9,000
Rate earned on investment	8.5%	5.6%	6.0%	5.9%	5%–7%

* Sample of commercial family farms: average of 586 for 1950-54; average of 513 for 1955-58; average of 509 for 1959-62; average of 494 in 1963. These farms are judged to be in the upper third in Indiana in efficiency and earnings.

culture forms the very cornerstone of the high standard of living that Americans enjoy. Modern scientific agriculture is so efficient that America now feeds and clothes its entire population with something less than six percent of its workers on farms. Over nine tenths of its population is available to produce the wide variety of goods and services that make up the fabulous American living standard.

By way of contrast, Russian agriculture is so inefficient that some 45 percent of their workers are required to produce enough food to keep the population going at a subsistence level. As a consequence, there just isn't enough manpower (or womanpower) left to produce things to make life more pleasant. So long as our output per agricultural worker remains five times above theirs, there can be little doubt concerning the ultimate outcome of the struggle between our two systems.

The American food industry has advanced more in the last fifty years than in all the preceding years of its history. Research and the application of trained brainpower is the big reason for this advance. Human energy is much less important than formerly in today's farm operation. Energy can be purchased so much more cheaply than it can be provided by man. Today's farm operator is a combination manager-applicator of the life sciences, the physical sciences, and the social sciences. The research undergirding modern agriculture ranges all the way from physics to physiology, from biology to business. It is just as complex and just as far on the periphery of knowledge as is the research done in the laboratories of the nuclear scientist or the electronics engineer.

Scientists and educators seek to apply their knowledge in an effort to increase the total productivity of the economy. There is no "cult of science," and knowledge is not pursued for knowledge's sake. The end of science is the advancement of human welfare and human happiness. This philosophy guides our agricultural colleges and experiment stations.

Agriculture in 1975 will be further ahead of 1965 than it is now ahead of 1955. One worker on farms today feeds and clothes himself and 32 others. This ratio has trebled in the last generation. By 1975 fewer workers on farms than now will be feeding 225 million Americans. One farm worker will feed and clothe about 50 other persons, and better than ever before in history. Only about 4 percent of our total population will be members of farm families in 1975, in contrast to 6 percent now, and over 25 percent a generation ago. By 1975 there will be a fifth fewer farms than now, just as there are now about one fifth fewer than ten years ago.

During each year of this decade our agricultural plant will use more capital, more science and technology, more managerial capacity, more purchased production inputs, more specialized marketing facilities, and more research than the year before. Those writers and analysts who refer to agriculture as a "declining" industry are looking only at a single aspect of this growing and important American industry.

By 1975 the unduly long hours of farm toil and drudgery will be only a conversation topic among the old-timers. We'll use a fourth fewer man hours of labor for farm work to produce a fourth more output. Chore-time labor in 1975 will be reduced by a third as building rearrangement and automation bring us closer to "push-button" meat production. The livestock feeder won't necessarily be tied to his "twice a day" chore-time stint at the barn. He can take the weekend off, if he chooses, for a pleasure trip with his family, just as his city cousin does now.

Family farms will be larger with much more capital—*but still family farms.* It will not be uncommon for a good family farmer to operate a unit of 600 to 1,000 acres, with over a quarter million dollars invested in his business. In such cases, $100,000 or more will represent working capital, such as machinery, livestock, feed inventory, and current supplies. An increasing share of this capital will come from off-the-farm sources, either from specialized credit agencies or from farm suppliers through some contractual arrangement. This does not mean that the individual farmer will lose his independence through integration. Instead, it means that he will enlarge his earning potential by increasing his volume through the use of outside capital and planned coordination of his farm production with the processing and selling phases of the total food and fiber industry.

Farmers will produce to a predetermined market with respect to quality, time of marketing, and type of product. No longer will they produce anything and then seek a market at whatever price it will bring. They will use their knowledge of genetics, physiology, and environmental factors to produce "to specification" for a particular kind of market demand, just as industry now does. This will enhance selling price and income.

One-fifth fewer farmers in 1975 than now by no means portends decay of the rural community. It will be stronger than now, although substantially different. Large numbers of urban workers, many of them former farm families, will live in the country. There are very few rural families in Indiana who do not live within commuting distance of urban employment. As these urban-oriented families intermingle with farm families in church, school, 4-H Clubs, and social occasions, a new culture will emerge which will combine the best of our present rural and urban cultures. This may be called the new *Rurban* culture.

In this environment the commercial family farm, using large amounts of capital, science, and technology, will increasingly assume the characteristics of a business establishment. The farm manager will assemble "packages of technology" which have been produced by others on a custom basis. The share of total farm receipts spent for production items will increase still further; the gross margin per dollar of receipts will become narrower, and profits will depend increasingly on growing volume.

The rural "businessman" running the farm of 1975 will think and act much like any other businessman, whether he happens to live in city or country. A new community culture will emerge in which the farmer will be less conscious of his vocational identity, just as the lawyer, the doctor, or the machinist now loses much of his vocational identity in his own community life. The differences between rural and urban living will have narrowed markedly. The farmer will be a businessman in much the same sense as is his city cousin. He will demand and will receive comparable levels of income and satisfactions from life.

Organized and imaginative research is the vehicle which will push the scientific frontier beyond limits we scarcely dare dream of today. If we can keep our economy free and preserve an environment in which individual scientists are free to dream a little about new techniques and new ideas, and to enjoy the fruits of their dreams, we shall experience phenomenal progress in the next generation.

JOHN F. MEE

Dominance of Manufacturing

Indiana's sesquicentennial of statehood provides the ideal occasion to recognize the dominance of Hoosier manufacturing and to consider how it developed, its present status, and its probable future.

Although Indiana ranks only thirty-eighth in size among the fifty states, it stands eighth among them in the total value-added by its manufacturers and ninth in the number of employees engaged in manufacturing industries. On a per capita basis, the ranking is fourth in industrial output. Among the Hoosiers working in nonagricultural employment, 41.2 percent were engaged in manufacturing occupations in 1965 compared to 29.9 percent in the nation.

Some of the Indiana firsts in industrial activities include:

The invention of the machine gun by Richard Gatling in Indianapolis in 1862. It fired 250 shots a minute.

The first gasoline pump was installed in Fort Wayne in 1885.

One of the first automobiles was designed by Elwood Haynes in Kokomo in 1893-94. Some other automobiles manufactured in

John F. Mee is the Mead Johnson Professor of Management in the Graduate School of Business and Dean of the Division of General and Technical Studies at Indiana University.

Indiana were the Apperson Jack Rabbit, Cole, Marmon, Auburn, Cord, Duesenberg, Stutz, and Studebaker.

One of the first automatic telephone systems in the world was put in service at La Porte in 1892.

The first household gas refrigerator was made in Evansville in 1926.

On the basis of census study and the values of products involved, Indiana ranks as follows in the nation:

First in biological products, musical instruments, morticians' goods, and prefabricated building.

Second in book printing, wood office furniture, storage batteries, and veneer mills.

Third in steel production, aircraft equipment, motors and generators, refrigeration machinery, and pharmaceutical preparations.

From the time that Indiana entered the Union on December 11, 1816, as the nineteenth state, there has been a continuous growth in manufacturing activities. Dominance in manufacturing was not achieved easily or quickly, however. Hoosier perseverance and leadership were essential through several stages of growth and development.

Manufacturing began in Indiana in the period between 1800 and 1860. The economy was characterized by isolation with poor transportation facilities and a spirit of self-sufficiency. Production in excess of home or local consumption was not the general practice. Indiana Territory in 1810 contained the following types and numbers of manufacturing resources among a total population of 24,520: 33 gristmills, 14 sawmills, 3 horsemills, 18 tanneries, 28 distilleries, 3 powder mills, 1,256 looms, and 1,350 spinning wheels. The total value of manufacturing was estimated at around $300,000 for the year. When Indiana became a state in 1816, records show the following production facilities at Vincennes, the former territorial capital: 4 blacksmiths, 2 gunsmiths, 3 shoemakers, 3 saddlers, 4 tailors, 2 cabinetmakers, 3 hat factories, 1 silversmith, 1 tin factory, 1 chairmaker, 1 tobacconist, and 1 tannery.

Early manufacturing facilities played a role in a treaty with the Miami Indians in 1818. The Miami ceded the federal government 7,036,000 acres of land, most of which is within the boundaries of Indiana. In return they received $15,000 in silver, one gristmill, one sawmill, and 160 bushels of salt annually. They also received the promise of the government to provide and support one blacksmith and one gunsmith for their requirements.

The initial foundation for Indiana's development into a manufacturing state primarily involved pork packing, flour and grist mills, sawmills, tanneries, distilleries, and brickmaking. In 1820 the single manufactory in Indiana was at Cannelton (where cotton was cultivated for local use). It made cloth by the use of 108 spindles driven by power from oxen on an inclined plane. Ironworks at Mishawaka and Rochester became important around 1838. Terre Haute and Madison led the state in pork packing. In 1850 Indiana, with Ohio, packed one half of all meat products and "provisionary supplies" in the United States. Steamboat building became an important industry in New Albany and Jeffersonville; one company is still making boats in the latter city. Most of the early manufacturing took place in the southern region and especially in the river towns of Madison, Lawrenceburg, New Albany, Evansville, and Terre Haute. Leather and tannery products were important along with wagonmaking and carriage making.

Before 1860 only the seeds of future manufacturing prominence were to be found in Indiana. Early manufacturing activities were rooted in the household processes of the earliest settlers. Crafts and trades developed, followed by shops, mills, and small factories. The domestic industries evolved from products made from materials that were wrested or raised from nature. The emergence of trades, mills, shops, and factories encouraged a division of labor as special skills were developed by the pioneers. As urban communities evolved, they attracted a greater diversity of workmen who preferred production and trade to a rural life with agricultural hardships. About 5,200 business establishments operated in Indiana in 1860. The average annual output per factory was about $8,000. They produced approximately $27 million in primary goods and an equal amount in processed goods. The leading industry was timber.

The evolution of manufacturing has been the principal factor in changing the economic base of the state since the Civil War and especially since the advent of the twentieth century. The increasing production of goods at lower costs has favored Indiana with the benefits of economic growth and social progress. By 1910 the total value-added by manufacturers amounted to about $245 million compared to an estimated $300,000 in the Indiana Territory in 1810.

During the evolutionary period agriculture continued to be the dominant economic pursuit, and manufacturing depended upon the resources of agriculture and lumber. Among the industries of the state immediately after the Civil War, the "big four" continued to be meat products, flour and meal, lumber, and liquor. By the turn of the century the important Hoosier industries were iron and steel, railroad cars, foundry and machine-shop products, glass, carriages and wagons, furniture, and clothing. Furthermore, the most important manufacturing localities were now located in the northern half of the state.

One of the earliest industries was the glass industry that centered around Muncie during the 1880's. Ball Brothers began operations in 1888, and the weekly payroll at that time for 125 employees amounted to $1,200. The natural gas boom was the major reason for the growth of the glass industry in central Indiana. When the supply of gas was exhausted, most of the industry declined.

The Studebaker Brothers began making wagons in their blacksmith shop in South Bend in 1852. An interesting sidelight of their success are the contracts drawn by the two brothers in 1863:

I, Henry Studebaker, agree to sell all the wagons my brother Clem can make.

(Signed) Henry Studebaker

I agree to make all he can sell.

(Signed) Clem Studebaker

By 1875 the sales of the Studebaker Brothers exceeded $1,000,000. In 1902 Studebaker made its first electric vehicle. Its first gasoline-powered automobile was made two years later. When it celebrated its centennial in 1952, the Studebaker Company became the only Indiana-based automobile company to achieve this distinction. Studebaker Larks and Hawks were the last of the line to be manufactured at South Bend; they continued until 1962. Six companies in Indiana, however, are still making horse-drawn wagons.

Historical research into the pioneer automobile industry discloses the known number of Hoosier-made cars to be 208. The first automobile made in Indiana is still a subject for argument. A car made by C. H. Black around 1890 is in the Children's Museum in Indianapolis. Black did not begin commercial manufacturing until 1899, however. Elwood Haynes began making plans as early as 1890, but it was not until July 4, 1894, that his first car made a successful run and demonstration on Pumpkinvine Pike near Kokomo. It was built in the machine shop of Elmer and Edgar Apperson and is now in the Smithsonian Institution. Haynes and the Appersons made cars together for seven years and then separately until the 1920's. The automobile-making boom spread to 30 cities in the state. In Indianapolis 44 different cars were made at one time or another. Studebaker in South Bend was the last one to survive. The production of component parts for the automobile industry remains a major factor in Indiana manufacturing, however.

The Lake Michigan area was especially attractive for the manufacture of steel, which requires water both for production and transportation. The Inland Steel Corporation chose East Chicago for its site in 1901. Five years later the U. S. Steel Corporation established and built Gary and its mills. The Universal Atlas Cement plant there was completed almost simultaneously with Gary Steel Works. On July 23, 1908, the first cargo of iron ore was discharged at Gary. The first heat of steel was tapped from an open-hearth shop on February 3, 1909; the new rail mills turned out their first finished product that same month. Judge Elbert H. Gary, chairman of the board of U. S. Steel Corporation, was the first to envision a great steel-producing complex in the then barren dunes along the southern tip of Lake Michigan. From this wilderness there emerged in Indiana one of the foremost steel-manufacturing complexes in the world.

In 1907 the largest manufacturing plant in the state was the Haskell and Barker plant at Michigan City; it was the forerunner of the present Pullman-Standard Car Manufacturing Company.

The period from 1901 to 1917 has usually been called the "Progressive era" in American history. During these years government regulation of the economic life of the manufacturing industries increased. As in many states, the need became apparent for Indiana manufacturers to form an association to solve mutual problems. In 1901 the Manufacturers and Merchants Association was organized. Some of the early objectives of the association were legislative activities and the study of state and local taxes and their impact on the development of manufacturing firms. Several name changes ensued. In 1906 it became the Indiana Association of Manufacturers and Commerce and in 1913 the Indiana Manufacturers and Shippers Association. Since 1915 the name has remained the Indiana Manufacturers Association. A major portion of its program continues to be devoted to the protection of state manufacturers from unfavorable legislation and taxation. Emphasis on industrial relations problems has become another important aspect of its program. In addition, consideration is given to compensation rates, insurance, better working conditions, a favorable business climate, and the serving of new and established industries in the state.

Between 1890 and 1910 Madison and New Albany were displaced as leading manufacturing areas by new manufacturing towns, most of them in the northern part of the state. Census data in 1910 show $508,717,000 invested in manufacturing in Indiana. There were 7,187 establishments classified under 55 separate industries and an additional 772 without classification. Of the total capital involved, about one third was invested in five leading cities: Indianapolis, South Bend, Fort Wayne, Evansville, and Terre Haute. The next ten manufacturing cities were Hammond, Mishawaka, Richmond, Anderson, Michigan City, Muncie, La Porte,

Elkhart, East Chicago, and Elwood. The leading industries represented investments ranging from $47,781,000 for the iron industries to $15,857,000 for the output of flour and grist mills.

Employment in manufacturing firms increased along with the capital investments. Of the state's total population of 2,700,873 in 1910 manufacturing provided employment for 208,263. The number directly employed in manufacturing amounted to 186,-984 or 6.9 percent of the population at that time. Immigration had become an important factor in the development of Indiana industry. Germans, Irish, Italians, Greeks, Poles, and Belgians provided competent labor for the mills and factories. Foreign immigration slackened after 1920, however, and virtually ceased during the depression years of the 1930's.

During the evolutionary period of manufacturing, the output per worker increased with the growing use of machinery and mechanization. The State Federation of Labor was organized in 1897. Transportation facilities improved. Electric interurbans crisscrossed the state in competition with steam railroads. Real highway construction increased and improved. Urban areas developed as the population drawn from agricultural pursuits and immigration clustered around the new and developing manufacturing establishments. Fortunately, the manufacturing firms were scattered throughout the state and had avoided a single high concentration area as had happened in some of the neighboring states. Shortly after the turn of the century it had become apparent that Indiana was destined for greatness as a manufacturing state with a decreasing emphasis on agriculture.

The third stage of progress in Indiana manufacturing began about 1910 and continues to the present. Manufacturing has become independent of agriculture and now far exceeds it in importance to the economy. Although agricultural output has continued to increase, the farm population in Indiana accounted for only 10 percent of the total population in 1965. Nationally the farm population amounted to less than 7 percent with a rapidly shrinking trend.

Employment of Hoosiers in manufacturing increased from 520,-000 in 1955 to 636,300 in 1965. During the same decade employment in services for manufacturing increased from 106,000 to 161,000. Manufacturing and services now provide employment for over half of Indiana's nonagricultural workers. In 1965 the average hours worked per week were 41.7 at an average earnings of $2.91 per hour. The aggregate value-added by manufacturers exceeded $8 billion.

The Indiana State Chamber of Commerce was founded in 1914 and admitted to the U. S. Chamber of Commerce in 1915. It was reorganized and revitalized in 1939 with a view toward the development of the best possible economic and governmental climate for business operations and development. Over 5,400 members cooperate in programs for the improvement of legislation, taxation, personnel relations, transportation, and education. The state chamber serves as the spokesman for Indiana business through the "working together" of the following affiliated local and state organizations: 179 local Chambers of Commerce and 98 trade and professional associations.

In this dominance of manufacturing era the leading industries are now iron and steel, transportation equipment, electrical machinery, other machinery, food and related products, chemicals and related products, stone and glass products, printing and publishing, plus rubber and plastic products. Although the increase in manufacturing activities has fortunately been widely diffused throughout the state, the northern half has developed into the main area of manufacturing with heavy concentrations in Lake and Porter counties. Manufacturing of heavy industry now depends more upon the advancing technologies of mechanical engineering and chemistry and less upon an agricultural base.

Indiana is the headquarters for several of the 500 largest industrial corporations in the nation. According to sales volume in 1963-64, they rank as follows: Eli Lilly, Indianapolis; Studebaker, South Bend; Essex Wire, Fort Wayne; Cummins Engine, Columbus; Stokely-Van Camp, Indianapolis; Inland Container, Indianapolis; Miles Laboratories, Elkhart; Arvin Industries, Columbus;

and Mead Johnson, Evansville. Many of the other largest industrial companies are represented by important decentralized plants in the state, especially in the automobile, steel, petroleum, electrical, and rubber industries.

Size alone has not resulted in the state's dominant position in manufacturing. Over 1,600 member companies of the Indiana Manufacturers Association employ less than 200 workers in widely diversified operations. Throughout Indiana manufacturing produces a large assortment of items, such as cigars, snaths, chicken-picking equipment, pig warmers, calendars, pianos, bird cages and dog beds, corsets, gloves, toothpaste, shoehorns, ink, peat moss, smoking pipes, archery products, map globes, caskets, cheer-leader costumes, lightning rods, frog-gigging guns, sponge rubber, church furniture, mining machinery, and muzzle-loading rifles. The largest manufacturer of metal shoehorns in the world is Steel Industries, Inc., of Crawfordsville. With the C. G. Conn Company, Elkhart is the band music instrument center of the nation.

> If you want your pigs warmed or your chickens plucked or your snath replaced or your peat mossed or your muzzle loaded or any of a couple of dozen other things, you get it done with an article that was "Made in Indiana."

Although Indiana has so many diversified small-business firms, it is the large-business establishments which provide the greatest employment opportunities. In March 1964 38,491 establishments employed 1,161,000 persons covered by the Indiana Employment Security Act. This act includes about 95 percent of the total employment in all manufacturing firms. The 275 establishments with 500 or more employees accounted for almost 37 percent of all covered employment and 45 percent of the covered payroll. Yet they represented only 0.7 percent of the covered establishments. Despite the net gain of 4,135 business establishments between 1959 and 1964, there was little change in their proportionate sizes. Exhibit I portrays the classes of establishments by size in the state.

The dominance of manufacturing in the economy of the state and its impact on the Hoosier way of life can be illustrated by the

EXHIBIT I
Number of Establishments by Size
March 1959 and March 1964

	NUMBER OF ESTABLISHMENTS			
	MARCH 1959		MARCH 1964	
Number of Employees	Number	Percent of total	Number	Percent of total
Total, all classes	34,356	100.0	38,491	100.0
0 – 3	6,193	18.0	7,683	20.0
4 – 19	21,077	61.4	22,618	58.8
20 – 49	4,188	12.2	4,936	12.8
50 – 99	1,489	4.3	1,653	4.3
100 – 499	1,177	3.4	1,326	3.4
500 – 999	141	0.4	168	0.4
1,000 and over	91	0.3	107	0.3

Source: Indiana Employment Security Division

types of occupations in which the citizens earn their livelihood. At the time of Indiana's sesquicentennial 41.2 percent of the citizens who were not engaged in agriculture were employed in manufacturing. Furthermore, there is a much larger percentage of people engaged in manufacturing in the state than in the entire United States. Exhibit II illustrates the trend in the relationships of occupations for Indiana workers with those in the nation.

The evolution of manufacturing in the state to its position of dominance today has provided a typical example of economic growth. Indiana has progressed through the three stages of economic development. The first stage finds an economy devoted mainly to agricultural production. In the second stage there develops a manufacturing sector of the economy with a declining emphasis on agricultural activities. Manufacturing becomes dominant in the third stage. Agriculture continues to decline in its relationship to the total economy, and there is an increase in the service occupations, such as personal services, transportation, finance, communications, governmental services, and education.

EXHIBIT II

Occupations in Indiana and the United States

Type of Occupation	1960		1965	
	Indiana	U.S.	Indiana	U.S.
Mining	.6	1.3	.5	1.1
Contract Construction	4.8	5.3	4.2	4.9
Manufacturing	41.4	30.9	41.2	29.9
Transportation and Public Utilities	6.6	7.4	5.7	6.6
Wholesale and Retailing	19.8	20.9	19.3	21.1
Finance, Insurance, Real Estate	3.9	4.9	4.1	5.1
Service and Miscellaneous	9.8	13.6	10.4	14.6
Government	13.1	15.7	14.6	16.7
	100.0	100.0	100.0	100.0

Source: Indiana Manufacturers Association

Changes in three variables—productivity, advancing technologies, and the desires of man—exert pressures on this sequence of economic development. The increasing income from productivity and technology also increases per capita personal income. This in turn provides people with incomes in excess of that required for basic needs. The excess income is used in the services market which accelerates the demand for services.

By 1965 Indiana had progressed far into the third stage of development. Manufacturing was dominant but not increasing, and the service occupations were. Any continued expansion of manufacturing will result from the expansion of the services, such as transportation, education, public health, recreation, and communication. In this third stage attention must be given to a proper balance of manufacturing and services by the managers of private enterprise and the public administrators.

The figures for personal income derived from manufacturing demonstrate its importance to the economy of Indiana. They indicate the degree of employment in an occupation and reflect the amount of wealth produced from a source, such as manufacturing. Within a population of over 4,700,000 in 1963 approximately 32.6 percent of all personal income in the state came from the manufacturing area and amounted to nearly three times that from the second most important area, wholesale and retail trade, which was 11.1 percent. Other sources of personal income were services with 4.9 percent, transportation with 3.2 percent, contract construction with 3.3 percent, utilities and communication with 1.8 percent, and agriculture with 4.2 percent.

In 1965 the major source of personal income centered around the following leading industries: iron and steel, electrical machinery, transportation equipment, chemicals, and other machinery (except electrical). These industries employed 75 percent of all workers in manufacturing and accounted for 70 percent of the total value-added by manufacturers in the state. They have a high capital investment per worker and a tremendous production capacity. Individual workers with the help of machines can turn out large quantities of products that have considerable value.

Two of the most promising growth industries have been identified as electrical machinery and primary metals. The new Bethlehem Steel Works at Burns Harbor can add to the growth of the latter industry. Since 1960 the furniture industry in the southern region of the state has shown growth potential. It employs double the number of employees compared to the national average, with a rising trend in 1964. The stone industry located in the Bloomington-Bedford area has operated at a constant level of employment; it provides employment for about 2 percent of the nonagricultural workers in the state. Industries declining in importance for their contribution to personal income are food, apparel, petroleum, and coal.

Indiana's economy has become strong through the contributions of manufacturing to employment and personal income. During its 150 years of statehood Indiana has developed into a major industrialized state. There are indications, however, that point toward a leveling off of growth in manufacturing with some services gaining in importance. Nevertheless, employment in manufacturing has been maintained and increased in the state to a greater degree than in the neighboring states in the Middle West. Exhibit III portrays the percentage change in recent manufacturing employment.

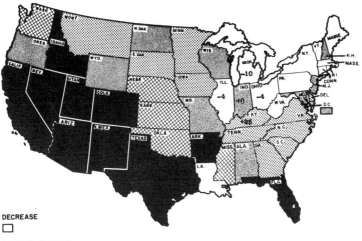

Exhibit III

Percent Change in Manufacturing Employment,
by State, 1947-62

DECREASE
☐

PERCENT INCREASE
▨ 0 – 14.9   ▨ 30.0 – 44.9
▨ 15.0 – 29.9   ■ 45 and over

National Average: 8 percent increase
INDIANA: 8 percent increase

Source: State agencies cooperating with U.S. Department of Labor
Data for Alaska and Hawaii not available for 1947

The change in the state from an agricultural to an industrial society dominated by manufacturing industries has disturbed existing institutions and patterns of living. As industrial communities have developed, the population has migrated to large urban centers, leaving only 10 percent of the people on farms in 1965. Many people have resorted to automobile-commuting practices in transportation to places of work. More and more highway systems have been developed for the needs of employees who live 50 or 60 miles from their places of employment. Adjusting school systems to accommodate the population shifts has caused changes in the policies and methods of taxation to support an increasing number of school-age children.

Population clusters in the urban communities that have developed around huge industrial complexes have disturbed the long-standing voting districts of the state. Reapportionment of the state legislature became necessary. Furthermore, it became necessary to adjust the tax structure and tax rates to provide for changing conditions in recreation, transportation, conservation, and urban affairs, as well as in education.

Long-range planning for the highest and best use of land has created political implications in the struggle to allocate land intelligently to industrial, residential, farming, mining and quarrying, recreational, and business uses. Adjustments to life in an industrial society have demanded greater cooperation for a better way of living among the political, industrial, business, educational, and religious interests of the state. Present indications point toward a continuing disturbance of the social and cultural patterns of life as the impact of manufacturing penetrates further into the economy of the state and the nation.

Indiana manufacturing in its dominant stage has been moving toward consolidation, mergers, and more diversified operations. Numerically the small firms have continued to maintain a stable ratio to the very large ones. However, the fewer large organizations have increased in the numbers of workers employed, the amount of payrolls, and the total value of output. New products have influenced the manufacturing activities, such as plastics, electronics, computers, and synthetics. The trend in new products has depended less on agricultural raw materials.

Increasing mechanization and automation have reduced the requirements for physical labor in manufacturing processes. Consequently the labor market has changed, and there is a greater demand for technicians, engineers, scientists, and idea men. Certain types of employment opportunities have increased, especially those types that require higher levels of education and training. There has been an increasing need for the continuous training and retraining of workers. Although mechanization and automation have created the demands for higher skills and greater knowledge among the workers, the advantages of increasing productivity have provided a higher standard of living, more leisure time, and decreasing costs for consumer goods. In addition, the service industries have been developing in importance for additional employment opportunities and a better way of life. Service industries have been providing a greater percentage of growth for employment than manufacturing.

Various factors have contributed to Indiana's achievements and dominant position in manufacturing:

1. The industriousness and ingenuity of the people who settled in the state and developed its potential must be given primary credit. Indiana has always been blessed with good political, religious, business, and educational leadership.

2. An important advantage resulted from its agriculture and timber as a foundation in the development of manufacturing for an industrial economy.

3. Railroad, water, and highway transportation systems have been a boon to Indiana manufacturing. Recent developments concerning air travel and interstate highways have further improved the total system of transportation. The state's favorable geographic location, combined with its transportation facilities, has put substance into its motto—"The Crossroads of America."

4. Conservative tax policies and an intelligent tax structure have been adequate and conducive to economic growth.

5. The labor force has been capable, effective, varied, and sufficient to provide the manpower requirements for the competitive advantages and growth of manufacturing establishments.

6. Available power from sources of gas, coal, and electricity has contributed to the development of manufacturing industries. Furthermore, the water supply has been adequate for manufacturing needs.

7. Economic diversification with decentralized factory locations also has been a contributing factor to stability and the best uses of land.

8. A well-planned public education policy and educational op-

portunities have provided an intelligent work force for manufacturing.

The future of Indiana manufacturing will depend upon the capacities and abilities of the Hoosiers to make the transition from an industrial to a technological and scientific-based economy. Both the technological revolution and the explosions of knowledge from all areas of research will have a significant impact on the future development of manufacturing.

Indiana is fortunate in having a solid base of industry that manufactures both consumer and industrial products. Severe economic fluctuations have been avoided because of the location of the basic industries in the state. The expanding population in the world should continue the market demand for Indiana's consumer and industrial goods.

During the decades immediately ahead the prevailing factors that made Indiana a leading manufacturing state should continue their influences. The state's urban population is widely diffused among cities and towns of moderate size so that there is room for expansion without excessive costs. Southern Indiana has the potential for manufacturing sites suitable for the new science-based industries. A number of rivers and artificial lakes are capable of providing needed water for cities, factories, and recreation. The importance of water will be realized to a greater extent in the future of manufacturing and the people who support it. Service industries to manufacturing are developing. The population of the state is growing but not as fast as that of the nation. The projection for Indiana's population growth between 1965 and 1975 is about 605,000 or 12 percent compared to a national growth of 18 percent.

In 1965 a publication entitled *Why Industry Prospers in Indiana* was released by Lieutenant Governor Robert L. Rock (Director of the Indiana Department of Commerce) with a special message from Governor Roger D. Branigin. These state officials attributed Indiana's industrial growth to geographic location, natural resources, a skilled work force, a favorable tax climate, and broad diversification. They reported that industry's optimism concerning Indiana's future is exemplified by the growth of capital expenditure for manufacturing from $301,247,000 to $568,000,000 during the 1954-63 decade. The report also mentioned that educational attainments of Indiana's population challenge the best in the nation. In 1960 99.1 percent of the population over 25 years of age had attended school.

Personal capacities, capabilities, traits, and values or attitudes of Hoosiers will be the greatest determining factor for economic growth and social progress. In the future the new "knowledge industry" explosions and the force of technological advances will have more influence as society moves from an industrial to a scientific-based economy. Knowledge from education and research may be more important than land or capital in determining Indiana's future position in manufacturing.

Science-based industries became the "growth industries" following World War II. These industries are dependent upon educated people who possess high managerial, scientific, and technical qualifications. Such industries differ from the previous basic industries that depended upon locations with available physical raw materials and low-cost transportation facilities. Preferred locations for science-based industries are characterized by a congenial climate in which to live with abundant cultural and intellectual attractions.

Indiana has achieved a position of dominance in manufacturing with industries that developed because of a generous endowment of natural resources. These industries, with locations near iron and coal deposits with low-cost transportation, have engaged in the mass production of standard items with standardized production techniques. The contribution from mechanical engineering, scientific management, and a large investment of capital have transformed raw materials into valuable products. In the latter portion of the twentieth century the science-based industries, in contrast, will work with relatively small quantities of expensive raw materials in very complex fabrication processes. The emphasis will be on elaborate systems of process control for a huge total system of processing. Computer technology and electronic data-processing systems will resolve the problem of materials and parts handling, production flow, and quality standards.

The future for Indiana manufacturing appears promising if progress is made in developing a share of the new science-based industries in addition to maintaining and developing the health of the present basic industries. Growth in the state's manufacturing industries will be heavily dependent upon educated people. The human asset, composed of people with managerial, scientific, and technical skills, will become as important as capital assets.

Inasmuch as education provides the principal nourishment for an industrial economy with scientific overtones, a change becomes necessary in the educational philosophy and institutions of the state. The number of eighteen-year-olds in Indiana increased from 72,000 in 1960 to 86,000 in 1964 and to 93,000 in 1965. Another sharp increase to almost 100,000 by 1970 is on the way. These boys and girls will be seeking employment or continuing their education for stable employment careers. Since opportunities in agriculture are decreasing, they must depend upon employment in manufacturing, retailing, wholesaling, and service industries or in governmental occupations. By 1970 the number of workers in the labor force under 25 years of age is expected to be 60 percent greater than in 1961.

During the next stage of Indiana manufacturing there must be a greater contribution from the educational resources of the state if growth is to continue. In addition to the public school system, there will be greater dependence on the state-supported and private universities and colleges to provide industry with vital personnel requirements. Technological assistance can come from Indiana University's Aerospace Research Applications Center and Graduate School of Business in cooperation with Purdue University's McClure Park and Schools of Engineering. Furthermore, Purdue's School of Technology, Indiana University's Division of General and Technical Studies, and the Indiana Vocational Technical College can provide the leadership in developing qualified personnel with the essential technical skills to advance the manufacturing industries both in the traditional and the scientific-based manufacturing operations.

Hoosier leadership has so far faltered in planning and providing for the vocational, technical, scientific, and engineering education of the state's youth for life and work in a growing manufacturing economy with the promise of a developing scientific society, but changes are underway. Public school officials have started to plan for area vocational high schools. The Indiana Vocational Technical College has been established but has not moved into operation. Purdue's School of Technology offered its first programs in 1965. Indiana University's Division of General and Technical Studies was established in 1965; its first programs were initiated in 1966. Both Indiana and Purdue are now offering technical education in several regions of the state in response to community needs for technically trained personnel in manufacturing.

Indiana University's Graduate School of Business and Purdue's Schools of Engineering have been educating highly qualified personnel for leadership in management and engineering. Large numbers of these graduates, however, have been exported to other states with the new science-based and technologically advanced industries. Unless the leadership in Hoosier manufacturing can develop new industries characteristic of the new scientific society in the space age, this so-called "brain drain" of college graduates from Indiana will continue.

A self-appraisal of Indiana manufacturing during the past 150 years leads to the conclusion that Hoosiers have made a magnificent transition from an agricultural to an industrial economy. For the future the principal uncertainty lies in whether or not Hoosier leadership in private enterprise (both worker and management), public administration, education, and religion can cope with the gradual transition to a scientific and technological economy. If an attitude of achievement continues to prevail among Indiana's citizens, the state will not only be able to maintain and strengthen its position in manufacturing but will attain even greater economic growth and social progress.

L. LESLIE WATERS

Transportation

The section of North America known today as Indiana has always had problems in transportation. The Indians struggled to conquer space but were unacquainted with superior forms for movement of goods and people. The white men who came knew of better means but were frustrated by the lack of roads and navigable waterways. Little or nothing was done during territorial days because the sparseness of the population restricted economic demand. Travel conditions as late as 1816 were abominable; railroads, canals, and roads were yet to come, and travel on foot was virtually as fast as on horseback or by wagon. Only the Ohio River served the state. Steamboats came to the Ohio very early, but the falls at Louisville limited "through" navigation to periods of high water.

Many stories have been told to illustrate travel conditions of the past. One anecdote concerns two students from Madison, Wisconsin, who journeyed to college in Bloomington in a manner that suggested they might already have read Chaucer. The boys owned

---

L. Leslie Waters is an export of Kansas who was subjected to intellectual processing in Missouri and Illinois. He has had a long career in transportation as a teacher, researcher, writer, consultant, and director of companies in the United States and abroad. Currently, he holds the special rank of University Professor of Transportation and Business History in the Graduate School of Business at Indiana University.

one horse. One rode for two hours, tethered the horse, and began walking. The other had started walking and, when he reached the horse, mounted and rode until he caught up with his friend. In 1965 another student also faced a difficult transportation problem at the opening of the school year. He could have flown his father's airplane, although this really was not a choice. The dilemma arose from ownership of three automobiles—a sports car, a station wagon, and a sedan. Each seemed essential to life at school, and he could not drive all three. The solution was to drive one to the university and send two underclassmen via bus to fetch the remaining cars.

The following pages bridge the gap between the stories and sketch the development within the state of Indiana of a complex transport network which is connected with all parts of the continent by land and air and the entire world by water and air. Where once the state had problems connected with little or no transportation, it now has problems connected with an intricate system, an immense investment, and extreme problems of fiscal equity—but enhanced opportunities for serving the well-being of the citizenry.

The white man followed the Indian trails during territorial days and in many cases these developed into roads and highways. The trails had all sorts of shortcomings. In general, they took a fairly direct route, but they also took the path of least resistance, going around hills rather than over. They were subject to washing from above and were impassable in bad weather. In the southwestern part of the state between Louisville and Vincennes, the best-known of the trails originated not with Indians but with buffalo. The Buffalo Trace was heavily relied upon from before the days of George Rogers Clark to about 1816. The surface of the route, approximately 114 miles long in Indiana, was extremely hard from long use by the herds. Wide in places, it was so narrow in others that it could be traveled only on foot.

A treaty between the Potawatomi Indians and the United States in 1826 ceded to the state of Indiana enough land to build a road from Lake Michigan to the Ohio River. The route ultimately settled upon was from Madison to Indianapolis to Logansport and then to the mouth of Trail Creek, the present site of Michigan City, and construction got under way in 1832. Regrettably, the road turned out to be of very poor quality. Bridges washed out, potholes developed, and at best the road was usable less than two thirds of the year; nevertheless, with all its shortcomings, the road was immeasurably better than nothing.

The National Road, which had reached the Indiana-Ohio border in 1827, promised to become the first good highway in the state. The line did prove to be the best of the early roads but, unfortunately, dwindling finances required the state to choose specifications substantially below those used elsewhere. Contractors were permitted to leave stumps 15 inches high in the middle of the road, but were at least required to round them to minimize damage to carriages. Roads of many types were built by private and local public interests, some of planks and others of logs (corduroy). Most of them were poorly constructed and soon proved to be financial fiascoes. Nevertheless, numerous stagecoach companies and freight lines were organized. The stage lines had colorful names such as "The June Bug Line, "The Oyster Line," "The Good Intent Line," and "The Shake Gut Line." (The latter got its name from the jelly-like appearance of one of its fat drivers as his equipage bounced over the road.)

Pressure for internal improvements in the new state of Indiana, exerted by all sectors of the economy, culminated in a mammoth internal improvements act in 1836. The state, which was to be served by networks of roads, canals, and railroads, promptly began borrowing and spending money—but could not possibly have chosen a less propitious time. The panic of 1837 gripped the country. Canal costs were underestimated, and the state fell heavily into debt. Interest could not be paid and, finally, some settlements were forced upon creditors.

One of the projects undertaken is especially noteworthy because of recently renewed interest in it. The Wabash and Erie Canal, which was constructed over a period of many years, began at Toledo, Ohio, and utilized the Miami and Erie Canal to Defiance. It entered Indiana in Allen County and ran southwesterly to the Wabash River at Lafayette, then down the Wabash to Terre Haute and Evansville. This canal, like some of the other projects of its time, generated more enthusiasm than traffic. The early promise of railroads dampened interest in both road and canal building, but the Ohio River continued to serve the state of Indiana by means of steamboats, rafts, scows, and flatboats until 1850.

Railroad construction by 1850 was fairly well developed. Some 19 railroads had built 212 miles and had 993 more under construction out of a projected total of 4,205. Most of these were local railroads with local titles, such as the New Albany & Salem. This was in contrast with railroads incorporated elsewhere in the country, which were more likely to have a title like the Canadian, New Albany, Salem and Gulf. As these little lines became established, they were merged into the trunk-line systems that came to serve the territory for the area north of the Ohio and east of the Mississippi. The New Albany & Salem, which was built from New Albany to Michigan City (including the branch to Indianapolis via Mooresville), was estimated to have cost $5 million and was officially completed in 1854. Although the outlay for the early railroads was low in terms of today's costs, great difficulty was encountered by the promoters in floating stocks and bonds. Local companies sold what they could in the territory either for money or for kind. Most of the funds were raised in New York and, ultimately, through connections in Europe.

In the last half of the nineteenth century in Indiana, one depended on horses and buggies and wagons for local transportation and on the railroad for traveling longer distances. History tends to make these methods of transportation seem very romantic, though like so many features of the "good old days" they are most highly regarded in nostalgic memories. Balky mules and horses, heaterless buggies, and slow trains are better to contemplate in the comfort of mid-twentieth-century living than to experience.

Interurbans appeared near the end of the century and provided intermediate passenger travel. Most of the principal communities of Indiana were connected as part of a speculative venture that was said to permit travelers to go from Boston to Dallas, Texas, by electric lines.

Sweeping changes in transport began with the new horseless carriage. Manufacture of automobiles was concentrated initially in Michigan and Indiana; in fact, at one time the Hoosier state had an excellent chance to become the "motor state." Dozens of automobiles were manufactured in Indiana, including the Haynes, Elcar, Stutz, Cole, Duesenberg, and Studebaker. The era of automobile consolidation and the success of mass producers squeezed smaller firms, and one by one they fell by the wayside until only Studebaker remained in the 1930's. This firm was to drop out in the 1960's.

Automobile manufacturing, however, did not end in Indiana. Indeed, this branch of industry expanded, but in a different form. Indiana became a component maker and, to a lesser extent, an assemblers of cars. In addition, truck manufacture prospered in the state, and Cummins in Columbus led in the output of engines. In the early days of auto manufacturing, some buses were turned out, especially by Studebaker. These were essentially touring cars with extra seats on a long base. They were so highly regarded that the president of the company that came to be Southeastern Greyhound specified in his will that the executors of his estate should always buy Studebaker buses. In due time, the manufacture of regular intercity buses shifted outside the state, but the manufacture of bodies for school buses soared. Plants in Indianapolis and Mitchell, as well as elsewhere, outfitted a disproportionate number of the school buses of the nation.

The development of the automobile was followed by the manufacture of trailers, an industry that expanded during the Great Depression of the 1930's. It was helped rather than hindered by World War II because trailers provided quick and mobile housing. After the war, the trailers evolved into progressively larger and more luxurious units. They softened much of the postwar housing demand and continued to sell even after conventional houses became available. The manufacture of mobile homes, as they came to be known, is concentrated in northern Indiana, especially in Elkhart.

By the 1920's the days of the interurban were numbered; the depression of the 1930's completed the liquidation of the industry. Interurbans were, to a certain extent, superseded by bus companies, which dominated the short for-hire business. Initially, bus companies were small enterprises, but, through amalgamation, large companies came to dominate the industry. Since trucking became an established business, Indiana has been provided extensive service; in fact, states contiguous to the Great Lakes have the most intensive truck routes anywhere in the country. Hundreds of trucking companies serve Indiana locally, and many of them reach to one coast or another, and a few to both coasts, in addition to the Gulf of Mexico. Fully 75 percent of all products shipped by Indianapolis industry move on rubber. In-bound materials, when in limited bulk, are likely to arrive the same way. Items of freight move 100 percent by the road. Trucks also move almost all livestock from the farm to the cattle pen in the stockyard. Partly because of the strategic location of the state of Indiana, many trucking companies are organized and headquartered here. For some reason, the state has attracted household goods movers; Fort Wayne, Indianapolis, and Evansville are hosts to three of the largest.

The burgeoning automobile, truck, and bus population put great strain on the road-building capacity of the various governmental units. The state lies athwart the main east-west routes of commerce, and the highways must bear cross-country as well as local traffic. Through state licenses, gasoline taxes, and federal aid, as well as local revenues, an enormous investment has gone into the road network. When the interstate and defense highway system of the United States was authorized in 1956, 1,115 miles were designated to be built in Indiana. The city of Indianapolis with six legs has more than any other city in the United States. Of the interstate mileage in Indiana, 157 were made up by the Indiana toll road, which had been built in the 1950's across the northern part of the state. The state, like many others, has had a difficult time keeping road building ahead of sales of vehicles, even though at times the rewards incidental to construction have been higher than they should have been (or, at least, the criminal courts thought so). An enormous amount has been accomplished in the face of persistent low compensation for officials and lack of a merit system throughout most of the history of road building.

By the early 1970's, Indiana's interstate system will have been completed; the state will have limited-access roads of high quality over the main routes. This system will be expanded with federal encouragement, and the state will go ahead to raise the standards of the great mileage outside the interstate and defense network. Difficult financing problems loom. The interstate and defense highway system is financed on a 90-10 basis. The federal government puts up the larger amount, but all of the maintenance expenses are borne by the state. This accounts for mounting pressure from the states (including Indiana) to get the federal government to assume a percentage distribution of maintenance costs in order to avert a situation in which the states would use their highway funds for maintenance and have nothing left for new construction.

Because vehicle sales run ahead of provision for driving and parking facilities, the state, along with its sister governmental units, faces the dismal prospect of increasing congestion. Even the smaller towns and cities of Indiana must contend with their own predicaments—too many vehicles for too little space.

The impact of the automobile has affected Indiana and other states in diverse ways which are generally familiar. Three are singled out for mention. First, the domiciles of people have been altered drastically. Cities have sprawled out over the countryside like confused amoebae. Large numbers of people have abandoned the swollen metropolitan areas and become part of the "rural nonfarm" populace. Ribbons of settlement have developed along our highways so that miles of roads are lined with one-hundred-foot lots and ranch-style homes. This has in turn led to an increase in accidents along our numerous unlimited-access routes. The second observation is that the automobile and its driver have evolved into a lethal combination on the roads. Only cornpickers and unloaded guns seem as dangerous. Deaths and injuries per mile driven dropped precipitously from the 1930's to the 1960's, but the increased number of cars and their use have led to higher absolute losses.

A final phenomenon of the motor age has been the emergence of regional factories. Components may be made in several cities and the parts rushed to another city for assembly. Highways have become a part of the assembly line itself—but outside the plant rather than within. Speed, dependability, and good communications enable assembly plants to operate on parts inventories of a few hours. A factory, in a broad sense, might well be scattered over northeast Indiana, southeast Michigan, and northwest Ohio.

Aviation in Indiana has kept pace with that of the nation or perhaps lagged a little. By the 1960's, over 100 public and private facilities were in service. Major trunk lines early established routes that crisscrossed the state; feeder lines dominated by Lake Central took care of short hops; and fixed-base operators provided taxi and charter service. Some military bases were established, and the skies of Indiana were home to thousands of aircraft of every type. The state not only acquired a great many airports but, by some standards, has too many. Communities have tended to build their own small airports rather than unite in building a medium-sized port that might generate enough traffic to have regular air service. Moreover, airport development went ahead with little or no cognizance of the improvements in the road system that might have made fewer airports logical.

A paradox in the development of air transport in the state can be observed with the introduction of jet aircraft: for a period of years, the quality of air service into and out of Indiana deteriorated. The large jets with their insatiable need for passengers could not afford to come down in Indiana cities. Service finally came to Indianapolis, but on a limited basis for several years, and in due time smaller commercial jet aircraft enabled a few additional cities to enjoy improved service. On the occasion of the sesquicentennial of Indiana, the possibility exists that once again the airlines may bypass Indiana. The superjets, which will carry 400 or more passengers, and the supersonic jets can stop only in large cities for economical operation. The ports in Chicago, Cincinnati, and Louisville have played major roles in serving Indiana; in the years ahead, Chicago may well prove to be the tie-in point for residents of Indiana who contemplate long trips. Much of what has been said about air passenger service applies to air freight. Trucklines generally serve as the feeders to air cargo carriers.

The twentieth century has witnessed a comeback in transportation by water. Virtually all of this development, though, as it relates to Indiana, is quite different from that of the previous century. Rivers within Indiana have not been used. Modern water transportation has been on the Ohio River—where commerce in the 1960's dwarfs that of the century before—and at that part of Lake Michigan which borders the state. River transportation has come back on the Ohio River for several reasons. The Corps of Engineers has improved the river substantially with new locks and dams, such as the project at Markland. The pusher towboat with barges has superseded the old steamer. Diesel engines, kort nozzles, and multiple screws, as well as radar, have drastically reduced operating costs.

Shipbuilding has retained importance in Indiana through the activities of the Jeffboat Company, successor to the Howard Shipbuilding Company. Evansville has served as one of the major southern ports with its extensive activities in conjunction with the Mead Johnson Terminal. For the most part, port sites on the north side of the Ohio River in Indiana have been limited; however, development has occurred recently, and the growth is expected to continue.

In the late 1950's the St. Lawrence Seaway was completed, although the 27-foot channel into Lake Michigan under the Blatnik Act was not opened unttil 1962. The immediate effect was to stimulate export and import business as well as domestic tonnage at the ports in northwestern Indiana. The seaway also stimulated a substantial expansion in steel manufacturing in the area and induced the state to provide a public port at Burns Harbor. The facility promptly became the target of various groups with vested dollar interests or genuine concern about the paucity of recreation facilities in northwestern Indiana. The battle of port versus park became one of the most spirited political issues in recent Indiana history. Completion of the St. Lawrence Seaway has revived interest in river improvement and canal building in Indiana to connect the Ohio River with either Lake Michigan or Lake Erie. Interests along the Wabash River authorized studies that have yielded promising results. Not too much attention has been devoted in these studies to the financial troubles of 125 years ago, but times have changed.

One of the least-known modes of transportation is the pipeline. About one sixth of all the ton-miles of traffic in the nation are accounted for by pipelines carrying crude oil and refined products. The state of Indiana naturally has its share of mileage. As was mentioned earlier, it's hard to get around Indiana. Pipelines from the mid-continent fields and those to the south go through the state with the citizenry oblivious to this vast underground movement. Some oil comes up the Ohio River by barge and is then piped to refineries in central and northern Indiana. To date, the state's pipelines have not carried such unusual products as gilsonite, wood pulp, coal, or tea, nor is such in prospect.

The railroads of Indiana were reasonably profitable up to 1929, though overbuilding in the previous century had made rates of return low as compared with other industries. The railroads were operated by the government during part of World War I, then returned to private ownership. The lines suffered acute distress during the depression and, with the exception of a few major lines, either entered trusteeship in bankruptcy, receivership in equity, or flirted with these distressing possibilities. By 1930, almost 90 percent of all intercity travel had shifted to the automobile. Bus companies cut into rail revenues. Moreover, trucklines organized in great numbers during the 1930's and solicited the high-class freight that meant so much to the railways.

Gasoline and tire rationing during World War II restored volume to the railroads. Profits rose, but not to great heights, and, after the war, the prewar trend away from the railroads returned with increased intensity. The percentage of intercity ton-miles of the railroads of the nation and of Indiana dropped well below 50 percent. Furthermore, other modes had skimmed the cream, so that the quality of traffic tended to be lower.

Many factors accelerated the distress of the railroads. New generating stations were located near the source of their coal supply; in effect, the coal was wired on high-transmission lines. (Future generating stations will probably substitute atomic energy for coal and relocate power production again.) Decentralization of industry and assembly plants, and local purchases of components cut cross-country movements. Moreover, the acceptance of the concept of physical distribution and logistics put new emphasis on services other than mere hauling, so that executives considered inventory, warehousing, packaging, and other costs in addition to the rates. The result was a shift of traffic to trucks, air cargo, and private fleets, and away from the common-carrier railroads.

The decrease in traffic and loss of mail contracts caused the railroads operating in Indiana to discontinue passenger trains and even abandon lines, thus ending both passenger and freight business. Employment in the industry from the early 1920's to the middle 1960's dropped approximately 70 percent; employment in the manufacture of railroad equipment also declined. By the middle 1950's, passengers could no longer buy tickets after 5:00 P.M. in the Indianapolis Union Station, and famous trains made their final runs.

Beginning in the late 1950's, management sought to stabilize and rationalize the industry, and began to see that hope lay in reduced rates and improved and imaginative services. Trunk lines carrying large quantities were developed; less-than-carload business disappeared and was replaced in part by piggyback. Another cure was sought in railroad mergers in the hope that two sick friends could get well together. This led the ICC in 1966 to approve the merger of the Pennsylvania and the New York Central, a decision of vital concern to the state of Indiana. The third fifty-year period in Indiana is certain to witness additional railroad consolidation. A hard core of trunk lines will have high survival and service values.

Those who read this essay within a decade of its publication will be intimately acquainted with the death of another industry. The streetcar has long passed from the scene, to be followed by the trackless trolley and, in due time, the local bus. Increasing car ownership, rising wage costs, and a variety of other factors have caused all of the transit companies in Indiana to encounter difficulty. City after city has lost its transit service or averted the loss by converting from private to public ownership. By the 1960's the rate of return on private transit companies in Indiana was essentially on a break-even basis with no reward for investment. The systems in the major cities were a little better off than those in the smaller cities, yet these larger companies were so weak that they sought and received state relief of inadequate proportions. Only subsidies seemingly offered hope of keeping the industry alive.

The possibility exists that Indiana might go back to the jitneys of days gone by and have station wagons or small buses cruise along established routes. If this is not done, private transportation will be supplemented only by taxi service. The rise in the number of private automobiles has brought distress to another industry. The automobile insurance companies are plagued by increased numbers of accidents and rising costs of repair, as well as judgments obtained under the jury system. The rate of return of transit companies in Indiana was exceeded on the downside only by the return of automobile insurance companies.

The people of Indiana are blessed with an abundance of commercial transportation service at extremely attractive rates. Competition is lively within and between the various modes. Furthermore, neither the Interstate Commerce Commission nor the Public Service Commission of Indiana deters the transportation companies from extending favorable prices to shippers and travelers. The thesis can be plausibly argued that the state of Indiana has a gross oversupply of for-hire companies. Furthermore, we have an incredible supply of private automobiles, trucks, and airplanes. This vehicular abundance gives our goods access to markets near and far, opens up sources of supply for industry everywhere, and enables extensive travel to and from the state. It is likely that Indiana will continue to enjoy improved transport. The state's location is so strategic that it is likely to be benefited by most innovations—with the probable exception of larger and faster aircraft. If hovercraft, hydrofoils, and beltlines become feasible, this state will doubtless see these, too.

In retrospect, the state of Indiana has come a long way from the Buffalo Trace, the old and improved Ohio River, and Clear Creek. Hoosiers have come so far in the area of transportation that they now look back on the old days and old technology with genuine affection. Now they buy aluminum canoes to paddle on man-made lakes. They pay $2 to $4 an hour for the discomfort of horseback riding. They drink skimmed milk rushed to them in fast trucks from distant dairies. This is even more paradoxical. (In days gone by, skimmed milk was judged unfit for human consumption and best for hogs.)

Finally, a few enterprising Hoosiers preserve steam locomotives, keep them in running order, and charge hobbyists for excursion rides. We have come to have a superb transportation system in an absolute sense and could have a poor system only in a relative sense. With innovation in other areas of commerce and industry, the state can use its transportation to achieve new levels of well-being for its citizens.

ROY C. ECHOLS

Public Utilities

Water, heat, light, power, communication—all are essential to the way we live and work here in Indiana in 1966. We need all these in our homes and in our offices. We need all these to operate our factories and our farms. We depend upon an ample and uninterrupted supply, ready when wanted regardless of the hour of the day or the day of the year. We do without any one with difficulty, even for brief intervals. All are made available to most of the five million people in our state as services sold to the general public by Indiana's public utility organizations.

The term *public utilities* includes also organizations that provide certain forms of transportation services. Since transportation is the subject of another chapter, the comments here will be confined to the water, gas, electric, telephone, and telegraph utilities. I shall note, briefly, their first appearance on our Hoosier scene, discuss their problems and progress, their impact on our society, and then suggest some implications for the future. In the short space of a

Roy C. Echols, a native of Texas, has spent more than 47 years in the Bell Telephone System, becoming president of Indiana Bell Telephone Company in 1960. He has become an enthusiastic Hoosier, a director and officer in numerous business, civic, and charitable organizations devoted to the progress and welfare of Indianapolis and of Indiana. Mr. Echols has just completed his second year as president of the Indianapolis Chamber of Commerce.

single chapter it is impossible to do justice to any one of these dynamic industries, much less to the individual companies that comprise them. Each has its own pioneers, its own leaders, its own record of accomplishment. It seemed better in this chapter to discuss the growth and the improvement of these utility services in terms of ideas rather than to cite a multiplicity of statistics.

As in many other fields of endeavor, Indiana has been among the leaders in the development of public utility services. From their beginnings—less than a hundred years ago, for the most part—the desire and the incentive of utility organizations to serve the people of the state, and serve them well, have contributed a great deal to the progress of the state as a whole. By making essential services more widely available and improving their quality and reliability, public utilities have not only grown with Indiana, but they have also helped the state to grow. And public utility people, carrying their ideals of service into other aspects of community life, have done much to make the cities and towns of the state better places in which to live.

Public utilities are business organizations that are "clothed," as the law says, with an unusual public interest. The services they provide are fundamental to an increasingly urbanized, industrialized, interdependent society. They are services that can best be furnished by limiting the number of suppliers, rather than by encouraging the "open" competition that is characteristic of most other fields of American business enterprise. Public policy, developed through the trial and error of experience and enacted into law, requires that public utilities offer specified services of good quality in specific places and that the prices of these services be subject to regulation by public authority. In a very real sense, regulation by public authority in the utility field is the practical substitute for regulation by the forces of "open" competition.

Most utility service in Indiana is provided by private enterprise, but both municipal and cooperative ownership are well represented here. Water is the one utility service to be furnished in more places by publicly owned than by privately owned facilities. In fact, water service is provided by the municipality in more than two thirds of the cities and towns in Indiana. A number of electric systems also are municipally owned and operated. They provide distribution facilities only, purchasing power at wholesale rates from the state's large investor-owned power companies that generate it. These same generating plants also supply power to 43 member-owned electric systems organized under the Rural Electrification Membership Corporation statutes that now serve some 185,000 farms and rural establishments in 90 of the state's 92 counties. One of the principal gas suppliers, the Citizens Gas and Coke Utility in Indianapolis, is a public charitable trust. Communications services, in all but a few places, are provided by private enterprise.

For the most part, Indiana's utility companies specialize in providing a single form of service, be it gas, water, electric, telephone or telegraph. There are some notable exceptions. For example, Northern Indiana Public Service Company supplies a large area with both electricity and gas, as does Southern Indiana Gas and Electric Company. Indiana Gas and Water Company supplies the two services included in its name.

The first water system was under development at Madison even before Indiana became a state. Pioneer accounts of water being "piped" into Madison from springs in the surrounding hills between 1814 and 1817 have since been featured in the Madison *Courier*. The water is said to have been "cold and pure." First used were wooden conduits, but they soon deteriorated. Iron pipes followed, and a reservoir and pumps were added to the system. By 1849 Madison had a waterworks, one of relatively few in the country at that time. The early entrepreneurs of water service sold their company to the municipality in 1852.

Connersville is credited with the second Hoosier water system, established in 1869. Construction of the first system for Indianapolis was begun in that same year. By 1900 there were at least a hundred others. Terre Haute installed the first water purification plant in the state in 1889. Indianapolis is one of the few large cities in the nation to be supplied with water by an investor-owned corporation. The Indianapolis Water Company, now in its eighty-sixth year, has two large reservoirs, and others in the planning stage that will help supply the city's needs for the foreseeable future.

Indiana, in contrast to many other populous areas in the country, is blessed with sufficient rainfall, reasonably well distributed by areas and reasonably dependable from year to year. As population continues to grow and industry to expand, the principal problems of adequate water supply are likely to be in the development of the additional reservoirs that will surely be needed and in the building of additional distribution facilities. As the small communities in the state grow, they will require new water plants. And as the present cities and towns expand, their distribution systems will have to be extended.

Initially, the development of the gas industry in Indiana was based upon manufactured gas rather than the product of nature. The early discoveries of natural gas in the state were of poor quality, and the wells were uneconomical to develop. Gas was first used principally for street lighting, first appearing in Madison in 1851—in the same year that the voters of Indianapolis refused to pay a tax for street lighting. New Albany installed gas lights on its streets in 1852, and the following year the property owners in two blocks in the capital city did agree to pay for street illumination. Gas manufacturing and distribution companies were organized soon after at Fort Wayne, and others followed during the next few years.

Discovery of the Trenton natural gas field in the vicinity of Muncie in September 1886 ushered in central Indiana's famed "gas boom." More than 5,000 wells were drilled within the 7,000-square-mile Gas Belt. Natural gas became so plentiful that it brought unprecedented industrial development. Factories moved into the area at the rate of one or more per month to take advantage of the so-called "free" fuel. Gas City took its name from the boom. The seemingly limitless resource was wasted shamefully. Visiting dignitaries were entertained with roaring wells that shot flames skyward a hundred feet or more.

By 1901 the supply of gas began to falter. Conservation efforts were too late and output dwindled sharply. But in those years the need for gas had grown tremendously, and manufactured gas undertook to shoulder the demand through consolidation of companies. Not until the 1930's, with the arrival of pipelines from the huge natural gas fields of the Southwest, did the natural resource again become the leading factor in Indiana's gas supply.

The larger units of Indiana's gas industry include Northern Indiana Public Service Company, which supplies gas to customers in the northern third of the state; Indiana Gas and Water Company, with customers in 31 counties; Central Indiana Gas Company at Muncie; Citizens Gas and Coke Utility in Indianapolis, and Southern Indiana Gas and Electric Company headquartered at Evansville. In all, there are sixteen gas utilities serving the state. Underground storage of gas has become commonplace in Indiana, utilizing geological formations, often in locations where there were formerly producing wells.

The basic problem inherent in the natural gas industry is in exploration rather than in distribution. There is presently no shortage of reserves, nor does it seem likely that there will be, but as the use of gas increases in industry and in the home, new sources must be continuously discovered to maintain the nation's reserves.

Electricity can be said to have arrived in Indiana about 1880, for in that year four big electric arc lights were mounted on the courthouse tower at Wabash. When turned on with considerable fanfare, Wabash laid its claim to being the first community in the United States to be *wholly* lighted by electricity.

Rapid growth in the capacity to generate electricity and in its use for light and power has been characteristic of the industry. This has been particularly true since 1900, when Indiana began to become an industrial state. It is said that the output of electricity increased about forty times from 1900 to 1940, and has since been doubling every ten years. The use of electric power in homes and industries continues to proliferate. Increasingly efficient generating plants tend to lower unit cost, and per capita consumption trends upward. With further advances in the population and prosperity of Indiana, the use of electricity seems certain to continue to increase.

Most of the state's electric power is produced by five large electric utility companies: Northern Indiana Public Service Company, Indiana and Michigan Electric Company, Public Service Company of Indiana, Indianapolis Power and Light Company, and Southern Indiana Gas and Electric Company. The Indiana and Michigan Company's Tanners Creek Plant at Lawrenceburg and the new generating station being developed near Petersburg by the Indianapolis Power and Light Company are outstanding examples of new additions to generating capacity to keep ahead of Indiana's growing needs for electricity.

High-voltage transmission lines are the backbone of power distribution systems, carrying electricity to all parts of the state for the use of consumers the electric companies serve directly and also to supply the needs of the municipal and the cooperative organizations. The first electric cooperative in the United States began business in Boone County in 1936.

The telegraph was the first of Indiana's public communications services by some thirty years, arriving in 1847 and 1848. The first line was built by the Ohio, Indiana and Illinois Company from Dayton to Chicago by way of Richmond, Indianapolis, and Lafayette, with a branch extending from Lafayette to Terre Haute and on to Evansville. It was known as the O'Reilly line, named for the principal owner, Henry O'Reilly, who had acquired building rights from Samuel F. B. Morse, the telegraph's inventor. The first message from Indianapolis to Dayton was sent May 12, 1848. Other lines were built around Lake Michigan's tip, in southern Indiana, and as parts of interstate systems. The Western Union Telegraph Company built a line along the Indianapolis and Cincinnati Railroad in 1854 and in time acquired the facilities of the other companies.

The major impact of the telegraph in its early days in Indiana was on the newspapers in the state. News of national and international importance began to be available more quickly for publication, though speed in publishing did not always seem to be a matter of first importance. In 1864 there was a seventeen-year-old telegrapher working at the Indianapolis Union Station. His associates long remembered him for his persistence in plying them with annoying questions about electricity. His name was Thomas A. Edison.

With the passing years and the coming of the telephone and other means of communication, the public wants for telegraph service have changed. The Western Union Company became the dominant supplier for the nation, and it has developed new services for the use of business as well as by individuals. Its facilities today are far more sophisticated than the open wire lines that were first built paralleling most of the nation's railroad tracks a century ago.

In the fall of 1877 a pair of Alexander Graham Bell's telephones was exhibited at the Indiana State Fair. The novelty of speaking over a wire appealed to some of the Indianapolis business people, and shortly thereafter telephones were installed by several firms to connect separated offices. In 1879 the first telephone exchange in Indiana was opened in downtown Indianapolis, and a new service to the public had begun. Other Hoosier cities opened exchanges in rapid succession. To La Porte goes the distinction of having the world's first automatic telephone exchange in commercial use, established in 1892.

In the 1890's, after the original Bell patents expired, telephone companies were organized locally in all parts of the state, often more than one in the same community. Direct competition between telephone companies proved impractical, financially disastrous to the supplier, and seriously restrictive to the quality and the convenience of service to customers. Through a long series of consolidations, duplicating service was eliminated. The number of companies providing telephone service in the state has declined to about one hundred now. Only a few serve more than a small area.

The bulk of Indiana's telephone service is presently provided by Indiana Bell Telephone Company, General Telephone Company of Indiana, United Telephone Company of Indiana, Illinois Bell

Telephone Company (in the northwest corner), and Indiana Telephone Corporation (in several southern counties). All but the latter are units of multi-state organizations. The trend toward fewer, stronger companies has been characteristic of the industry as a whole, as technological progress has made the task of providing good telephone service infinitely more complex. Regardless of size, all the telephone companies work together to furnish a well-coordinated service throughout the state, so that the customer who makes a long distance call anywhere within the state is not aware that two or more companies may be involved in its completion.

These brief flashbacks to the early beginnings of our major utilities serve to dramatize the fact that, in general, these differing services have been developing simultaneously. Most of the development has taken place, and has been accelerating, during the latter half of Indiana's 150 years of statehood. In communications particularly, as in gas and electricity and to a lesser extent in water, there has been an evolution from small local suppliers to large-scale enterprises that serve many communities in large areas of the state. The responsibility for public service that utilities must accept has increased as the numbers of customers have grown. It has increased even more as the services themselves have become basic to the state's economy and fundamental to the health and welfare of its people.

In developing from babyhood to maturity each industry has faced its own trials, and each of the surviving organizations has overcome its own obstacles. There are some problems that all utilities share, however, problems that are inherent in the rapid expansion and development of public service.

For the private enterprise segment of the public utility industries, which provides the bulk of the services, certainly the acquisition of adequate capital is a problem in common. Utilities, characteristically, require an investment in facilities that is much larger than in most other business in relation to the annual sales dollars that physical assets will produce. If rapidly growing public needs for service are to be met, met well and on time, utility companies must have a continuing in-flow of capital obtained on reasonable terms. This can be difficult even for the most capable management if the economic climate is temporarily unfavorable, or the regulatory climate restricts utility earnings unduly. The need for capital and financial strength has been one of the factors in the trend toward fewer and larger companies. The major companies that provide utility services in Indiana today are owned, directly or indirectly, by investors, large and small, in all parts of the nation.

One of the reasons often advanced to justify federal financing of cooperatively owned electric companies and federal loans at very low rates of interest to some of the smaller telephone companies is to speed development of service in areas where potential revenues are insufficiently attractive for large outlays of private capital obtainable through normal channels at much higher cost.

Technological progress, too, has tended to add to a utility's need for capital. As the capabilities of equipment have been increased, as new and versatile devices have been developed, and as much of the heavy and repetitive work in utility operations has been mechanized, the investment needed to provide the most economical up-to-date service has climbed.

During the years in which the utility companies have been growing toward maturity, the long-term trend of prices has been upward. Improvements in technology tend toward greater efficiency, lower costs, and lower rates. But the impact of rising wage rates, tax rates, and higher costs of materials and supplies is toward higher costs and higher rates. No two utilities are affected in the same way or to the same degree by these opposing trends in their costs of operation. However, it has been a common problem to keep the rates for service in tune with such changes. The regulatory process, by its nature, requires considerable time, and regulatory "lag," as it is sometimes called, has been a frequent experience when upward rate adjustment is needed. The loss occasioned to the utility, though temporary, is irretrievable and if long continued can adversely affect a utility's ability to expand and improve its services.

Attracting and retaining qualified, capable people to provide utility services is a continuing problem of all, a problem that is heightened by rapid organizational growth and service expansion. Specialized skills and training are necessary for most utility jobs, and there is no substitute for experienced, dedicated employees. Employment with a utility company must therefore be recognized as good, dependable employment in relation to other job opportunities available in other fields. Wages, benefits, working conditions, possibilities for advancement, and all other aspects of employment, considered together, must have an appeal to many young men and women who are looking for a worthwhile career in business. In the larger companies, professional abilities in a number of fields are required, and as operations become more complex, administrative talent of a high order is necessary to the successful conduct of public utility enterprises. Generally speaking, the quality of service is no better than the quality of the people who provide it.

A third problem that public utilities have in common is the need for maintaining public understanding and public support. By nature, these public services affect the entire population, personally and directly, many times every day. In some instances, the proper use of the service by the customer has much to do with the satisfaction the customer receives from that service. Misunderstanding, or lack of understanding, of service capabilities or objectives on the part of any segment of the public leads to higher operating cost and in extreme cases can lead to restrictive legislation that handicaps a ultility company in furnishing service.

And certainly among the problems that utility companies share are those that arise out of change. For change—dynamic, far-reaching change—seems to be the outstanding characteristic of the era in which we live. Research and development in science and engineering are changing the ways in which utility services are furnished, and adding to their usefulness. Economic change is altering customer needs for these services, and the places and times they are needed. To serve the public interest it is essential that new knowledge and new techniques be incorporated promptly in public utility services and that changes in the public's wants and needs not only be met, but be anticipated.

From the standpoint of those who are responsible for the success of investor-owned utilities, the concept of service in the public interest is very broad indeed, and is becoming broader with the passing years. Good service—to customer, to communities, and in some instances to the state as a whole—is the basic reason why a public utility exists. Wherever a public utility serves, it has the obligation to serve without discrimination all who apply and conform to reasonable rules. Implicit in this obligation is a responsibility to extend service to additional customers as communities grow and the needs for service increase.

Commitments of capital for major expansion of facilities can involve no small financial risk. It is important to have forecasts of service growth that are realistic, long-range planning that is imaginative, and highly competent engineering. To be in the long-range public interest utility growth must be prudent growth. On the one hand, all essential public needs must be met promptly; on the other hand, the rise in operating costs, operating revenues, and plant investment must be kept in good relationship. Well-balanced development is often difficult to achieve, but it is one of the keys to an expanding service at reasonable rates over the long term.

Utilities have a responsibility also for utilizing the advances in science and engineering in developing new methods and techniques. Improvement of this kind usually requires additional investment, and here again there is the need for maintaining good financial balance.

Water, gas, and electricity may be viewed as commodities delivered by the supplier to the consumer to be used in such quantities and for such purpose as the consumer elects. The development of machinery and devices in business and industry and of new types of appliances for the household has added new uses and values to these three services. Communications services are of a more personal nature, carrying the customer's voice or his messages in a number of forms anywhere he wishes. The communications companies, themselves, have had the leading role in developing the usefulness of their services. The telephone industry, with which I am most familiar, has introduced many new forms of service for general use, provided a wide choice of styles and colors in the equipment the customer uses, and has designed many highly specialized local and long distance services to meet highly specialized communications needs of various types of business. Western Union Telegraph Company has developed many new and improved services in the telegraph field.

Service in the public interest carries with it the obligation to be a good employer. As a result of prudent growth and improvement, employment in the state's public utility industries has reached 36,000, according to recent estimates of the Indiana Employment Security Division. In addition, there are many other thousands who earn their living in jobs with local firms that furnish the utility companies with goods and services, materials and supplies. For example, the largest of the electric companies, Public Service Indiana, uses one of every ten tons of coal mined in Indiana. Western Electric Company manufactures at Indianapolis nearly all the Bell telephones used throughout the nation. Associated with Western Electric's Indianapolis Works is a branch of the Bell Telephone Laboratories. If all of the Hoosiers who directly and indirectly gain their livelihood from utility services were to live with their dependents in one place, "Utility City" would be one of the largest metropolitan centers in the state.

Employment in the utility field is unusually stable, not as subject as most other industries to wide swings of customer demand that have occurred from time to time throughout Indiana's economic history. And in providing equal employment opportunity for minority groups I believe that our utility companies are deeply concerned with the importance of merit as the standard in employment and advancement, regardless of race, creed, color, or national origin. In view of the satisfactions, the opportunities, and the monetary rewards of utility employment, it seems fair to say that Indiana's utility companies are among the state's progressive firms and, as such, have contributed to making Indiana a desirable place to work.

Most of the men, and many of the women, who are attracted to utility work soon come to regard it as a career, remaining with th same company or in the same industry during their working years. They become service-minded by training and by tradition. So it is natural that their interest in serving others should carry over into other activities not directly related to their daily jobs. Throughout Indiana, the men and women of the public utilities are engaged in all manner of useful work on behalf of their communities, helping to make their neighborhoods and their home towns better places in which to live. They help in their churches, the schools, young people's groups, local hospitals, and other charitable organizations. They lend support and leadership to the service clubs and to civic projects of all kinds. Some take part-time assignments on school boards and in other aspects of local government. There is no measure of the result of all their individual efforts. And when disaster strikes, in the form of a blizzard, tornado, fire, flood, explosion or other emergency, these same people work round the clock to maintain and to restore essential utility services for the public. Wearing a uniform in time of war, Indiana's utility people have served their country with great distinction all around the globe.

Just as utility people are a part of the community life of their home towns, so the facilities of utilities are an integral part of the physical structure of the communities they serve. Utility plant is there to stay. Unlike some businesses, utilities do not move away, and the future of their service area is inseparable from their own future. It follows therefore that the broad concept of service in the public interest includes good citizenship on the part of the public service companies. Many projects for civic betterment and area improvement win strong support from the utilities—with publicity, with leadership from utility managers, and with financial contributions. And in recent years the trend has been to extend and increase this corporate support, including within its range such important state-wide concerns as aid to the privately supported educational and cultural institutions of the state.

As public utility properties increase, so does their value for purposes of state and local taxation. According to the Indiana Tax Foundation, the assessed valuation of public utility property in

Indiana now exceeds $2.5 billion. This means massive tax support for public schools, roadways, and all other governmental services. Since federal funds also contribute substantially to employment in this state and to its economic activity, it is worthy of mention that public utilities, characteristically, are large federal taxpayers.

Utilities have a strong interest in good, responsible government that transcends partisan politics. Some companies actively encourage their employees to take part in the political life around them, working on behalf of the political party and candidates for public office of their own choosing. In general, utility people feel that, with government as with utility services, the people of Indiana are entitled to the best.

Because of the services they provide, some of the state's utilities become engaged in projects and programs that relate directly to the defense of the nation. Whether it is serving a strategic air base, furnishing links in a nation-wide or world-wide communications network for the military, or cooperating with the government in training programs, Indiana's utilities fully recognize that the needs of the nation come first.

To summarize: Through prudent financial management of service expansion and improvement, by introducing better methods and utilizing new technology, and by the development and orderly marketing of service in new forms, Indiana's public utility companies, in my opinion, continue to meet their increasing obligations for service and to meet them well. In so doing, they contribute to the growth and progress of the areas they serve. They are living up to their greater responsibilities as employers, creating, as they grow, more and better jobs with greater opportunities. Utility companies generally are meeting their increasing responsibilities of good corporate citizenship and utility people, as individuals, are among the state's most responsible and useful citizens.

Meaningful generalizations on the trends of the rates in public utility services are most difficult. The factors involved in the cost of furnishing service vary widely from industry to industry. For example, the cost of the services of employees can be relatively major, or relatively minor, depending upon the industry. The cost of coal, a major item in the production of electricity, is inconsequential in furnishing communications. And, as has been mentioned, some companies provide more than one of these basic utility services. Let me simply state that it is my feeling that most utility customers in Indiana through the years have received increasingly better values from their utility dollars than from dollars spent for most other products and services.

Most utility rates have undergone changes—sometimes upward, sometimes downward—in keeping with the changes in the economic factors affecting the services. In some cases the trend has been decidedly downward. The most dramatic example of steadily declining rates for service that I know of is the reduction of the charges for long distance telephone calls to faraway places. For instance, in 1915, when the purchasing power of $1.00 was a little more than three times as much as it is today, the cost of a three-minute, station-to-station call from Indianapolis to San Francisco was $15.95. Today, the rate is only $1.00 after eight o'clock in the evening and all day Sunday. The call goes through in seconds instead of minutes, and it isn't necessary to shout to be heard. Through cycles of economic expansion and contraction, through years of peace and of war, the underlying long-term trend of costs and prices has been upward. In my opinion, the accomplishments of public utility management in making essential public services available at a greater bargain, considering both value and price, has been one of the most outstanding aspects of serving the public interest. And for the most part, Indiana's investor-owned utilities have retained their vigor and gained the additional financial strength they have needed as a result of reasonable earnings and dependable dividends to their share owners.

It should be pointed out that public utilities are not immune from the competitive business world. They compete with all other businesses in many ways: for capital, for qualified employees and managers, for materials and supplies, and for a share of the growing market for goods and services that add to the convenience of living. Some services of regulated public utilities are in direct competition with alternative services offered by nonregulated industries. Some utility services compete directly with each other, such as gas and electricity for cooking and heating.

Sharing the interest of utility companies in serving the public well and formally charged by the state legislature with the responsibility to assure good service at fair rates is the Public Service Commission of Indiana. This body was created in 1913, replacing a Railroad Commission established in 1905, and given jurisdiction over the public utilities in addition to railroads. Prior to 1913, regulation of utilities had been in the hands of the legislature and the individual municipalities. Though there have since been changes in the regulatory laws, the duties, powers, and responsibilities of the Public Service Commission have remained much the same. The present commission chairman is Judge Merton Stanley. Other commissioners are Philip Bayt and C. Patrick Clancy. The commission's staff now numbers about sixty people.

Chairman Stanley expressed his view of regulation in a dynamic economy in a recent address at a conference at the University of Iowa attended by regulators, the regulated, and academic authorities in this field:

> Commissions must encourage utilities to incorporate new types of equipment into their plant and to adopt new operating methods that will result in savings and better service to their customers. . . .
>
> A utility must have an adequate rate of return and depreciation rates that are realistic in this period of change and obsolescence. . . . A utility that is hard-pressed financially cannot make the improvements in its services that a strong, healthy company does as normal operating procedure. . . .
>
> Many studies have indicated that adequate rates of return and realistic depreciation rates, more often than not, result in lower rates to the customer as well as better service. For good service is not always cheap, but poor service is always expensive.

Commenting on the rate-making process, a former chairman of the Indiana Commission has said: "We appreciate the fact that rate-making is not an exact science, since there are many variables which fluctuate with the business cycles, seasons of the year and demands of the public. In attempting to allow a fair return, we do not guarantee a profit, but provide an opportunity to earn it. . . ."

The chairman of the Illinois Commission recently expressed a similar philosophy in these words: "The interests of the public can best be served by utilities which, like unregulated businesses, have profit motives to do a constantly better job for the consumer. I believe in utilizing the hope and promise of economic reward as a means of goading the management of all companies to exert exceptional efforts to meet customers' needs, to innovate, to introduce new and improved services and to step up their operational efficiency."

A public service commission sets the regulatory climate within its jurisdiction, and if the climate is such as to encourage good management to be forward-looking and progressive, the commission deserves a good share of the credit for the progress that is made. And I think this is true in Indiana.

It seems reasonable to believe that the progress of utility services in the future will be more rapid, perhaps more dramatic, than all their previous accomplishment. Indiana, located as it is in the heartland of America, seems certain to develop at an accelerated pace, particularly as a center of industry, education, and culture. Its population seems sure to continue to grow.

Growing out of steady advances of science and technology are several major developments that are making an appearance in utility operations. The computer revolution, for example, is in progress and is requiring most companies to re-think their objectives and goals and to reorganize their operations. Until recently computer use has been concentrated on turning out the paper work—payrolls, customers' bills, and other clerical tasks—at a speed and with an accuracy that has never before been possible. With the advent of the large-capacity, "on-line, real-time" computers, frequently referred to as the "third generation" of these amazing machines, computers will be more a part of the day-to-day process of serving customers.

In the telephone industry we believe that the full impact of computer science will affect us more than most other businesses. Coming advances in communications also include electronic switching systems that are expected to replace, by the end of this century, most of the electro-mechanical central offices in use today. Electronic components will make possible new Custom Calling Services that are not available now. These will include automatic transfer of calls to another telephone, dialing of three-way conference calls, a tone that tells the customer using the telephone that someone else is trying to reach him. A customer will be able to select eight telephone numbers anywhere in the country and reach any one of them by dialing a single digit.

The new Touch-Tone calling makes it possible to reach a telephone and then transmit additional signals that can operate all sorts of equipment used in business or at home. Household bills, for example, could be paid through Touch-Tone instructions to a bank's computer. Picturephone service that enables people to see each other while they talk is becoming more feasible as a commercial service.

Just as remarkable will be the evolution of other utility services through their research and development. The possible use of nuclear energy to generate electric power in Indiana is under consideration. The state's leading power companies are in close touch with the progress of the industry in this venture. Some are associated with power companies in neighboring states in the East Central Nuclear Group, a research organization studying the possible development of sources of nuclear energy to serve the Middle West. Storage of gas in liquefied form is being considered, telemetering is being applied to distribution systems. Water and telegraph companies are also looking ahead to provide the facilities and the services that the people of a growing, prospering state will want and need in the remaining third of this century and on into the next.

As the explosion of scientific and technical knowledge proceeds, and the population keeps on growing, who can foresee the dimensions of Indiana's future? I am confident that the men and the women who will supply these indispensable services around the clock to the people of our state will find their work more interesting and more challenging as the years go by. And I am just as confident that the people of our state who are furnished these services will find them increasingly useful, offering more value in relation to their cost, and more and more satisfactory to use in Indiana's next 150 years.

Organized Labor

A self-appraisal of organized labor and its history in Indiana is somewhat "bittersweet." While many of the goals of organized labor have been achieved, the struggle continues for a society in which mankind can find peace, abundance, and equal opportunity for all.

The history of organized labor in Indiana had its beginning in the earliest days of the American labor movement. Like that of the rest of the nation, it received its greatest impetus during the industrial organization, because of the many basic industries, such as automotive and steel, located in the state. Many of the early giants of organized labor were well-known residents of the state, and Indiana provided many of the national leaders who were responsible for the creation of the American Federation of Labor (AFL) and the Congress of Industrial Organizations (CIO).

Eugene V. Debs, who lived in Terre Haute, organized the first industry-wide union (The American Railway Union) in 1893. He was also the Socialist Party's candidate for president of the United States from 1900 through 1912 and again in 1920.

Dallas Sells, a native of Anderson, Indiana, is president of the Indiana State AFL-CIO. A veteran of World War II, he is an industrial electrician by trade. He is a member of many civic, state, and national committees.

Only thirty years ago John L. Lewis sat in a big chair in front of the English Hotel in Indianapolis, smoking his after-dinner cigar. From an eleventh-floor office in the Merchants Bank Building he ran the United Mine Workers of America. The union's secretary-treasurer was William Green, who later would be president of the AFL. In offices on East Michigan Street "Big Bill" Hutcheson was the dynamic boss of the Carpenters Union. Dan Tobin, also an Indianapolis resident, headed the Teamsters Union. Other unions with international headquarters in the Hoosier capital were the Barbers (William Brightright), Bookbinders, Bricklayers, Masons and Plasterers, Laundry Workers, Stone Cutters, and Typographers (Woodruff Randolph). The Painters and Decorators were located in Lafayette. Of these, only the headquarters of the Stone Cutters, the Barbers, and the Painters and Decorators are still in the state.

In 1880 the Indianapolis Central Labor Council was organized and five years later the Indiana Federation of Trade and Labor Unions. Some of the unions represented at the Federation's meeting in 1896 no longer exist: Cigar Makers (none in Indiana), Citizens Street Railways Employees, and the Working Girls Union. Most of the delegates represented the Barbers, Typographers, Retail Clerks, Carpenters, and county labor councils.

The Indiana Federation of Labor was founded on October 8, 1903. And twenty years after the Indiana State CIO was organized on November 16, 1938, the two organizations merged to form the Indiana State AFL-CIO on May 24, 1958.

Statistics provided by the Indiana Employment Security Division show that in terms of employment and wages Hoosier workers have made reasonable gains over the past few years. In 1935 there were 350,100 and in 1964 625,600 workers in manufacturing in the state. The unemployment rate, as a percentage of the labor force, is presently at 3.8 percent. In the past fifteen years the highest rate of unemployment—8.2 percent—occurred in 1958. The hourly wage rate of Hoosier workers (industrial) has risen from 55¢ in 1936 to $2.81 in 1964; weekly earnings have shown a corresponding increase from $22.15 to $115.80. Hoosier workers have kept progress with and even exceeded the national average. Much remains to be done, however, particularly in raising wages of unorganized workers in the state.

Today there are approximately 400,000 organized workers in Indiana (both AFL-CIO and independent). The Indiana AFL-CIO has a membership of about 60 percent from the former Congress of Industrial Organizations and 40 percent from the former American Federation of Labor groups. The largest groups are the United Autoworkers and the United Steelworkers from the industrial unions and the Carpenters and Electrical Workers from the craft unions. The two largest local unions in Indiana are U.A.W. 662 and U.S.A. Local 1010; each has a membership of over 15,000. There are local unions with as few as 7 members, however. Indiana compares favorably with its neighboring states in ratio of union membership to the number of workers in manufacturing:

	Number of Organized Workers	Number of Workers
Indiana	400,000	625,600
Illinois	1,030,000	1,300,700
Ohio	1,100,000	1,317,100
Michigan	800,000	1,094,300
Kentucky	175,000	206,200

In the early formative days of labor organizations in America, Indiana played a central role. This was due, in part, to the many industries in the state which were the first organized, such as mining, printing, and construction. In those early days the struggles were more turbulent with frequent clashes on the picket line; today while the issues—wages, hours, and working conditions— remain the same, the fighting is now done chiefly at the bargaining and legislative tables. When the emphasis of the national unions shifted from organization to organization *and* political action, the center of the labor movement moved to Washington, D.C. Hoosier labor then became more directly concerned with state problems, as was true of most other state labor organizations.

Even during the first half of the nineteenth century many union leaders in the American labor movement recognized the necessity of political education, since it was obvious that the power of the state and federal governments was being used to prevent the organization of workers. At that time labor was fighting for a shorter work day, restriction of child labor, and free public schools. Not until 1906, however, did the AFL, which had been organized in 1886, begin a formal program of political action, taking an active part in every national campaign from that year through 1924. Under the leadership of John L. Lewis, the CIO, organized in 1935, created PAC (Political Action Committee) on July 7, 1943. The AFL formed LLPE (Labor's League for Political Education) in 1947, marking its return to the political field at the time of the enactment of the Taft-Hartley Act and the new drive for passage of right-to-work laws in the several states. The joint activities of PAC and LLPE resulted in the passage of more liberal legislation.

COPE (Committee on Political Education), a merger of PAC and LLPE, was created by the first constitutional convention of the AFL-CIO in 1955 in New York City. COPE's objectives are to advance the cause of organized labor and to work for the general welfare of all the people through political education and action. The position on action is determined in state and national conventions and candidates are endorsed by the organized workers living in the geographical area in which the candidate is elected. In 1956, the first year of COPE's operation, President Eisenhower became the first president in history to win by a landslide vote who did not carry his party into control of Congress. In 1962, Birch E. Bayh, Jr., who had been endorsed by Indiana labor, scored the biggest upset in senatorial races in the country by defeating incumbent Senator Homer Capehart.

Labor became active in the field of social legislation to protect itself from the political activity of employer groups who had found that, while they were losing at the bargaining table, they could gain at the legislative table. From the beginning, labor's legislative goals had been aimed at legislation to benefit all citizens and not just organized union members only. While some goals have been achieved, labor in Indiana has still not been as successful as the employers. A review of some of the major legislative goals follow

For years the labor movement in Indiana has attempted to g
some form of a wage and hour bill through the General Assembl
Since the merger of the state AFL and CIO in 1958, every sessio
of the legislature has had a bill introduced for this purpose. In 195
the bill would have established a state minimum wage of $1.00 a
hour and require time and one half for all work over eight hours
day. It passed the House by a vote of 62 to 22 and was then assigne
to the Senate Labor Committee, where it died without a hearing
Two years later S. B. 347 was introduced to establish a minimur
wage of $1.25 an hour; it was then assigned to the Senate Labo
Committee and was never considered. Another attempt was mad
in 1963 with S. B. 211, which provided for a state minimum wage o
$1.25 an hour and time and one half for work over eight hours
day or 40 hours a week; it also was assigned to the Senate Labo
Committee and was never considered. Finally in 1965, although i
was not the bill of the AFL-CIO, H. B. 1012 was introduced as
result of the state Democratic party platform pledge. It passed bot
houses and was signed by Governor Roger D. Branigin. The ac
exempts a wide area of workers and many who need it the mos
are all but excluded. In fact, Indiana has a wage and hour law *in
name only*.

The Indiana workmen's compensation laws passed in 1915 ar
elective, that is, the employer has the option of either accepting
or rejecting them, except in the coal mining industry, where ap
plication is compulsory. The intent of these laws was that worker
injured in the course of their employment would be assured promp
payment of benefits regardless of fault, and a minimum of lega
formality would be needed. Today an injured worker still ex
periences delays, however, and the services of an attorney ar
generally needed to win a contested compensation case.

Although the laws have been amended many times by the legis
lature, the benefit pattern has not kept up with the average wage
Weekly benefits have declined over the years from 63.5 percen
of wages in 1939 to only 37.2 percent of wages in 1965. The averag
wage is now above $130 a week, and the maximum weekly benefi

for an injured worker is $45 a week. The trend has now reached the point where some international unions have negotiated into the contracts with their employers what is called supplemental workmen's compensation.

On March 3, 1936, the Indiana General Assembly, in a special session, passed the State Unemployment Compensation Act, creating the Indiana Unemployment Compensation Division in the state Treasury Department. The following year the first amendments were made, mostly of a technical nature to make the law easier to administer. They eliminated contributions by employees so that, after April 1937, only employers contributed. In 1941 the legislature approved substantial changes in the act: The name was changed to the Indiana Employment Security Division, the waiting period was changed to one week, and benefits were increased to a maximum of $16 per week for 16 weeks. The wage credits of Hoosiers in the armed forces were "frozen," to be available as the basis for claims upon their return. Since that time there have been gradual increases until today the maximum weekly benefit is $40, with an additional $3 for a nonworking spouse, for a maximum of 26 weeks of benefits. Even with these increases Indiana still has one of the lowest benefits for an industrial state.

"Right-to-work" laws have reached the ballot or legislative stage of development in at least 39 states. They have been rejected by 21 and adopted by 18 states; most of the latter are located in the South, the Great Plains, and the Rocky Mountains. Florida and Arkansas were the first two states to enact these laws; they did so by constitutional amendment in 1944. In 1947, when Congress passed the Taft-Hartley Act and invited states to pass "right-to-work" laws, 11 states accepted this invitation. The so-called "right-to-work" law is designed to eliminate union security provisions. In effect, it restricts the freedom of both the employer and the employee to make a contract which would include some form of union security. It does not restrict the worker's freedom of choice, as proponents claim, inasmuch as the employee makes his decision when he applies for a job knowing the conditions under which he will work. Labor opposes this law because it restricts the right of contract between employer and employee and hinders due process in our industrial economy.

A "right-to-work" law, introduced in the Indiana Senate in 1953, received no consideration and did not come to a vote. It did not come to a vote again in 1955. Before the next session of the legislature an organization, which became known as the "Right-to-Work" Committee, Inc., had been established and dedicated to the enactment of this particular law. In addition, both Crawford Parker, who was elected lieutenant governor in 1956, and George Diener, who was selected House speaker, had campaigned on platforms advocating its passage. In February 1957 the House passed the bill by a vote of 54 to 42, and on March 1, after limited debate, the Senate passed it by a vote of 27 to 23. Attempts to repeal it were made in the 1959, 1961, and 1963 sessions. After the Democrats had won control of the General Assembly in the 1964 election, the first bill introduced in the Senate was a repeal of this law. S. B. 1 was passed by the upper house by a vote of 38 to 12 on January 14, 1965, the House approved it by a vote of 74 to 21 on January 25, and Governor Branigin signed it into law three days later.

In 1935 the Indiana General Assembly passed the Prevailing Wage Law:

> Any firm, individual, partnership, or corporation which is hereafter awarded a contract by this state, or by any political subdivision thereof, or by a municipal corporation, for the construction of any public work, and any subcontractor thereon, shall be required to pay for each class of work on such project a scale of wages being paid in the immediate locality for such class of work as hereafter determined. For the purpose of ascertaining what the prevailing wage scales are in such immediate locality, the awarding governmental agency, prior to advertising for such contract, shall set up a committee of three (3) persons: One (1) representing labor, to be named by the State Federation of Labor; one (1) representing industry, to be named by the awarding agency; and a third (1) member to be named by the Governor. . . .

Several attempts have been made to amend this law. In 1959 a bill was introduced to change the method now employed by the state to establish wage rates on projects where public funds will be used. In 1961 the bill would have weakened the law so that construction workers would have received wage reductions of as much as $1 an hour in more than 60 percent of the counties. It passed the House by a vote of 59 to 29 and died in the Senate Labor Committee. In 1963 two attempts were made: S. B. 212, which provided that the prevailing wage schedule on public projects should be that of the county where the project is located, and S.B. 339, which eliminated prevailing wage where the contract was paid from local tax levies. Neither bill passed the Senate. In the 1965 session the first attempt was made to make improvements in the law; the bill provided for replacing the existing three-man committee with a commissioner and giving him greater authority to enforce the provisions of the act. The bill passed the House by a vote of 71 to 19, but it failed to receive a constitutional majority in the Senate, where the vote was 23 to 20.

For many years the Indiana AFL-CIO has been interested in social legislation at both the state and national level, such as social security, health insurance for the aged, the war on poverty, the plight of the farm workers, civil rights, employment of handicapped workers, and education. It supported the long overdue "medicare" program, based on social insurance principles.

Among the national AFL-CIO legislative proposals to implement President Lyndon B. Johnson's "war on poverty" are (1) enactment of a vast new federal job retraining program; (2) expanded coverage under the Fair Labor Standards Act, with an increase in the minimum wage to $2 per hour; (3) reduction of the basic work week to 35 hours with an increase in the overtime penalty; (4) improvement of unemployment compensation through the application of federal standards; (5) to end all provisions of existing federal labor law that conflicts with the established policy of the United States to further collective bargaining.

The national AFL-CIO advocates better wages and working conditions for farm workers; they should have all the protection of social welfare legislation enjoyed by other workers. Farm workers are the most poverty-stricken, most depressed, and most underprivileged working people in America. They earn an average of less than $1,000 a year and work an average of less than 140 days a year. They often must travel hundreds of miles to find jobs of short duration or no jobs at all. Their housing is often miserable; health conditions are sometimes scandalous. Education for their children is generally inadequate, if available at all.

The national AFL-CIO is for the Negro's civil rights without reservation and without delay. Unfortunately, to the shame of the nation, discrimination still exists. It must be wiped out if the United States is to be truly the champion of freedom in a world where non-whites are an overwhelming majority. The national constitution invites "all workers" without regard to race, creed, color, or national origin to share in the full benefits of union organization. We are pledged in equal measure to see that all workers share fully in every aspect of American life; for our cause is the brotherhood of workers and the brotherhood of man. Handicapped workers are a group that often suffers from prejudice, discrimination, and inadequate opportunity. The national AFL-CIO wishes to help them win their full status as productive citizens.

There must be available to every qualified young person an opportunity to continue his education through undergraduate and graduate work. The cost of higher education must be low enough to be within reach of all young people. Low-cost higher education requires much greater public support, including federal aid, than has been available so far. In addition to direct aid to the colleges, there is need for a federal scholarship program.

The role of the union as a full partner in community life received added emphasis during World War II. Without lessening their interest in the economic well-being of union members, both the AFL and CIO had begun to organize specific programs centered around the health and welfare needs and problems of union members' places of employment. A maturing labor movement was moving into the mainstream of community and national life, not only in terms of economic issues but also in all matters affecting the welfare of its members, their families, and the communities in which they lived. This interest was not new. Labor's concern for such things as decent housing, health, and education is as old as the labor movement itself. All too often, however, this concern had to be subordinated to the cold facts of union organization and the basic issues of shorter hours and better pay.

The extent and nature of personal and family problems facing many union members during World War II brought about a new field of union service, that of community services and community relations. Housing was at a premium; transportation was difficult; women without prior employment experience were entering the work force by the hundreds of thousands; many families were on the move. It was a period of excitement, strain, and restlessness. These conditions, just as much as working conditions, can affect employees adversely. It was recognized by the labor movement that, if war production was to be maintained at peak levels, the unions must do all within their power to help members resolve those off-the-job difficulties that might interfere with work attendance and job efficiency.

Obviously neither the AFL nor the CIO was equipped to establish, staff, and maintain specialized social services and facilities to handle such problems as the day care of children of working mothers, transportation, emergency housing, health services, etc. Instead, organized labor looked to the community's network of government and voluntary social agencies and services to provide these basic kinds of assistance. Here was a vital point of contact between organized labor and social agencies. Both recognized the importance of working together for common goals.

Early in the war literally hundreds of new welfare agencies and relief committees were established that resulted in the duplication of needless and annoying fund appeals. It was an unusual week that passed without the local unions receiving several appeals for funds for this or that war-related cause. To bring about some order in this multiplicity of fund appeals, both the AFL and CIO became members of the newly created National War Fund, a nation-wide, once-a-year campaign to raise sufficient money for local and national voluntary social services.

From these beginnings, labor's community relations and community services grew. By the war's end this new dimension of service—of union activity—was an integral and vital part of the American trade union movement. One fact, however, needs to be emphasized. From the very outset the relationship between organized labor and community social services, especially voluntary agencies, was one of working partners. Neither the AFL nor the CIO wanted to establish labor-sponsored social agencies. Rather than duplicate what already existed in the community, labor merged its interests, efforts, and manpower with the traditional agencies, asking only in return that such organizations and their services be administered democratically in behalf of the total community.

The goals and objectives of organized labor in Indiana remain the same. The emphasis is different because of the nature of the changing society in which we live. Samuel Gompers, the first AFL president, stated that one word could summarize all the goals. That word was MORE. He went on to add more and better schools, hospitals, roads, etc. Philip Murray, president of the CIO, put it a little differently when he said, "What we seek is pictures on the walls, carpets on the floor, and music in all homes." George Meany, president of the AFL-CIO, has stated that what organized labor really seeks is the right of every citizen to equality of opportunity. A man should be judged on his own merit and not by his religion, color, or ethnic background.

In Indiana we still have a long way to go to achieve these goals. We need to upgrade our welfare legislation to make it more meaningful in a nuclear age. We need to more fully implement unemployment compensation to a more realistic level compared to the individual's "take-home" pay. Education needs to be expanded and the cost borne by something other than the property tax, preferably a tax based on the ability to pay. We need educational opportunities not restricted by the present economic barriers, and we need more educational emphasis on the non-degree skills. We need to look honestly at the civil rights problems in our state and to overcome the Ku Klux Klan attitude that all too often lurks beneath the surface.

Our goal is to make our members useful, productive, and participating members of the community in which they live—a community in which all citizens have a sense of dignity with economic as well as political freedom. We ought to do those things needed to bring about such a community through the private sector of our society where possible and the public sector where necessary. We do not fear our government. We respect it. We must participate in it as organized labor and as individuals, for "politics is the practical housekeeping job of a democracy."

At times we have failed to recognize our own weaknesses. At times we have misused our responsibility and authority. This is true of all organizations and individuals of all ages. Yet the American trade union movement has a glorious history of fighting for the rights of individuals. But success in an affluent society, which it has helped to create, has led to the danger of labor's becoming institutionalized rather than remaining a crusading, pioneering force for good. I am sure "we shall overcome." We shall continue to be in the forefront of the battle for freedom, politically and economically. And we shall achieve peace, abundance, and equal opportunity for all mankind.

JOHN E. MITCHELL

Natural Resources

Never before has there been so much popular concern about the natural resources in Indiana. This growing interest involves their conservation, preservation, utilization, development, and management. But before we take up these activities, we must consider the human resources of the state, the people—the people of today and tomorrow. What natural resources will they require for their benefit and enjoyment in the years to come? What will be the needs of their children's children when they become responsible citizens 50 to 100 years from now?

It has become increasingly difficult to make correct decisions about such questions. We have learned many lessons from the history of our country and state about conserving the resources that once were so abundant, and we have access to scientific know-how today that gives us much needed information about their development. But we still need much more knowledge. There is also a basic and growing need for trained persons to guide and

---

John E. Mitchell, a graduate of Purdue University, lives on the family farm near Flat Rock in Shelby County. After serving four years in the General Assembly, he was appointed secretary of the Indiana Flood Control and Water Resources Commission and then director of the Department of Natural Resources, 1965-66.

direct resource development, utilization, and conservation. And we need a public that says: "Give us the thoughts of the trained minds and we'll give you the support to move ahead in the conservation of our natural resources."

It is relatively simple to develop a particular resource if consideration does not have to be given to the possible effects of its development upon other resources. As we construct a dam across a river basin to provide water for communities, flood control for areas downstream, fish and wildlife enhancement, water quality control, and recreational facilities, we may have destroyed those benefits derived from a naturally free-flowing stream. And we may have obliterated some great natural scenic beauty that was being enjoyed by many people. Free-flowing streams offer a tremendous value, but so do reservoirs. The choice is always difficult and government becomes the judge of the balance that must be maintained. Similar decisions must be made in other areas of natural resource development.

The basic question is: How do we settle the conflicts, how do we make wise decisions when we have more than one use of a resource to consider? The public is aware that we need to develop our natural resources, although it may have different ideas from those of the administrators or the trained, professional people about how to do the job. But all agree that we must move ahead and we must accomplish worthwhile results. The task of government is to plan a program of action after considering all the needs of the people and all the alternatives, *make* a decision, and then complete the projects.

In 1899 the Indiana Forestry Association was organized to promote a forest management program for Indiana. In 1901 the state appointed a five-man forest board to make recommendations, and two years later the legislature appropriated money for a state forest reservation in Clark County. During these years other resource agencies had been formed and all were brought together in a state Department of Conservation in 1919. At the same time similar groups were being organized on the national level.

Although we have about four million acres of forest land in Indiana, less than a million acres is government owned and under the management of the U. S. Forest Service or the Indiana Department of Natural Resources. One continuing need is the program of fire prevention in the forests. Another is the preservation of our forests and stopping their depletion. We have finally reached the point where we are producing as many board feet of timber each year as we are harvesting. In fact, we produced more board feet of lumber on the stump than was harvested by our lumber industries in 1965. The major problem now is the acute shortage of certain species of timber, such as walnut, where production is much lower than the amount harvested each year.

Proper management of the three million acres of forest land under private ownership must be encouraged. As part of Indiana's forestry program, eleven forest districts are located throughout the state and in each of these areas professional foresters work with the local landowners, giving them the needed technical assistance. There are fringe benefits in developing the forest resources, and one is the opportunity for outdoor recreation, which can often accompany this program.

As we harvest coal or other minerals by surface mining, we must take advantage of the opportunities to reclaim the land by reforestation. We must have a continuous program of reclamation and be prepared to provide adequate planting stock from our nursery program to cover the areas denuded by the surface mining industries.

Oil and gas are the resources most difficult to manage from the administrator's viewpoint. No longer do we assume that oil and gas will always exist and that we do not need to be concerned with their conservation. These underground resources are there to be used not by just one generation but by many generations. How long they will last depends upon how wisely we utilize them. In the area around Gas City, Marion, and Muncie, known as the Trenton Field of the late 1800's, ill-advised judgment was used in the harvest of natural gas. Gas lights lit up the sky for miles to invite people and industry to an area where gas was cheap and where it was assumed that the supply was inexhaustible. This illusion is now a pathetic footnote to Indiana history. A tremendous resource was wasted because the knowledge, know-how, and desire were not available to guide and direct its proper development. Today Indiana has some of the best oil and gas regulatory laws in the nation. As we discover new sources of oil and gas, we have the laws, the knowledge, the know-how, and the desire to make the decisions that will conserve these resources for the future. Recent explorations and discoveries in Indiana have shown that we can meet the new opportunities in an orderly and conserving manner.

Stone, gravel, sand, coal, and gypsum are other resources that will continue to serve the state in the long-term future. As we take these resources from the ground, we still need to ask what are the proper methods of harvest? We need to know more about their proper utilization, and we need more know-how in the field of management. The laws and statutes governing these resources should be periodically reexamined in the light of new technology. Recovery of underground minerals is important to our Indiana economy, but we must insist that the harvest and reclamation methods employed conserve them for the best long-term use by the people.

In 1837 the governor appointed David Dale Owen of New Harmony the state geologist. He was instructed to survey the whole state, account for all discoveries, analyze mineral substance and soils, and make geological examinations. And in 1869 the General Assembly created the Department of Geology and Natural Sciences. These were some of the first steps in the movement to conserve the state's natural resources.

One of the agencies which assists us today in the search for knowledge is the Department of Natural Resources' Geological Survey Division, headed by the state geologist and located at Indiana University. Its personnel is charged with the research relating to the geology and mineral resources of Indiana. The Geological Survey has a very important role in the study of underground resources. As a result of its research the discovery of new gypsum deposits in southern Indiana is bringing new wealth to the state. More yet may come from other recent discoveries in the northern part of Indiana. The duties of the Oil and Gas Division are to conserve these resources by regulation of the recovery of oil and gas and to prevent waste.

One major natural resource often not recognized as such is our wildlife, since many people tend to regard it as of interest only to fishermen and hunters. But it is a resource that we harvest and utilize and we need to conserve. Indiana has a Fish and Game Division to supervise the harvest of wildlife resources and to manage them for the greatest good of the people, both now and in the future.

The management of game, which is related to the hunting opportunities of the public, is a most difficult problem. For instance, we are losing hunting areas at the rate of almost one-half county per year in Indiana. As land is converted to man-made purposes, such as housing developments, shopping centers, suburbia, and interstate highways and as the methods of agriculture are drastically changed, the countryside habitat that once produced many different forms of wildlife is rapidly disappearing. It has already disappeared in some of the Eastern states. The challenge to conserve, manage, and develop wildlife resources, especially game, is extremely urgent. Our programs must be geared to the changing times and based on scientific knowledge. The modern trend to larger and cleaner farms and changing practices of land management will bring about a reduction in the amount of wildlife as well as new patterns of wildlife growth and development.

In southern Indiana we are moving from a pasture and cover-crop agriculture to a predominantly forested area. Because of the decrease in their preferred habitat, we shall have fewer rabbits and quail, but at the same time we shall have more deer, grouse, and squirrels. In northern Indiana, where we have fields of continuous corn and row cropping, less land remains in pasture or cover crops and less wildlife will be produced. We must develop habitat in any area that we can find available. If we do not, we shall not keep up with the demands of a growing population along with a diminishing supply of land suited for wildlife habitat.

We are adding new hunting opportunities. We have transplanted ruffed grouse to the state and opened six counties—Bartholomew, Brown, Morgan, Monroe, Jackson, Lawrence—to grouse hunting for the first time in 28 years. We have also imported wild turkeys into the southern part of the state, and we are experimenting with several foreign species of pheasant. For almost 30 years there were no deer-hunting opportunities in Indiana; in fact, deer disappeared from the state in 1893. In the 1930's we began to import deer from Wisconsin, and after 30 years of intensive game management we are finally having good deer hunting again in Indiana.

With proper management of the wildlife resource much success can be achieved. The game management program consists of improving the wildlife habitat by creating new and better places for wildlife to live. We must have waterholes and ponds and clearings to increase the wildlife in the woodlands. The farm habitat restoration program provides free seeds, seedlings, and grain to landowners to help increase the wildlife-carrying capacity of their lands. In addition, there are food plot, living fence, and wildlife seeding packet programs. Our main effort in wildlife habitat development is to encourage landowners, for a five-year period, to increase the wildlife on their farms.

The opportunities for development of the fish resources are quite different from those for game animals. Indiana has a tremendous number of natural lakes and at the same time programs in flood control and water resources are developing huge man-made lakes. With proper management these lakes will greatly increase the opportunities for fishing. We know that one acre of water will produce so many pounds of fish per year. Our job is to make sure it is the right kind of fish—that it is bass rather than shad or that it is game fish rather than rough fish. Our goal is thus to provide *quality* fishing opportunities for the public. The proper management of new man-made lakes and the proper revitalization of the natural lakes and streams have become necessary parts of the program.

Indiana now has fourteen state fish and game areas where fishing and hunting can be pursued on state-owned properties. By continuing to develop small fishing areas in the various counties, more fishing opportunities will be available to the public. There are eight fish hatcheries, consisting of 87½ acres of water in 192 ponds, which produce fish for stocking the new lakes and renovated waters. One problem has been that many of Indiana's lakes and streams are not accessible. Consequently, a part of the program of wildlife resource management is to provide public access and to open up thousands of acres of water for fishing and water recreation.

The water resources of the state have received widespread attention from the public. The problem of water resource development has not been too little or too much rainfall, rather it is one of distribution—having the water at the right place at the right time in sufficient quantity to meet the needs of man. The management of water resources is a complicated task and requires the combined planning of the local, state, and federal governments. To properly manage this resource called water, we must gear our program to the long-term future, because nature often has a way of doing the unexpected. For instance, 26 counties were declared flood disaster counties in April 1964 and the following September 59 counties were named drought disaster counties. Twenty-one counties, which were named on both lists, had swung from one of nature's extremes to another in only five months.

Indiana has two major programs of cooperation with the federal government to develop its water resources. One is the Corps of Engineers' program for major river basin development and the other is the upstream small watershed program under the Soil Conservation Service of the U. S. Department of Agriculture. Other levels of government, such as the local communities, have a specific role to play. They must consider their long-range needs. It does communities little good to spend money inviting industries to come and enhance their economic growth when they cannot promise an adequate supply of water. Good water resource programs require teamwork.

Indiana is second in the nation in the per capita usage of ground water. Over 65 percent of its citizens use water that comes from beneath the ground. More knowledge of the earth beneath the surface is urgently needed.

As population grows and industry expands, the problem of water pollution in lakes and rivers will increase. Indiana has accomplished much in the field of water pollution abatement, but much still remains to be done. Our cities and towns have spent almost $400 million and industry has spent another $100 million for this purpose. It is estimated that about $250 million of water pollution abatement improvements are still needed today. In many small communities we need sewers and treatment plants. In some large cities we need to increase the degree of treatment. In others the streams do not have adequate flow in low-flow months to dilute the "properly" treated sewage in an acceptable manner. For every gallon of treated sewage being emptied into a stream there should be from three to five gallons of stream flow. For example, during the summer of 1964 Indianapolis was discharging two gallons to every one gallon of stream flow in the West Fork of White River. Research to increase the effectiveness of treatment methods is needed. Every Indiana community should have modern treatment facilities, and artificial stream flows will have to be provided where treatment is not the sole answer to this problem.

In the past soil resource development has been largely in the hands of the agricultural community. But now the cities are becoming aware of the importance to them of a knowledge of soil characteristics. Such knowledge must be used to locate the foundations of buildings and to design them, to locate sand and gravel deposits nearby, and to plan urban and suburban development. The soil survey has become one of the most important research tools. Unfortunately, much of the state does not have its survey completed, and many that have been completed are now out of date. Indiana's high rank as an agricultural state can be credited to the quality of its soils. The soil and water conservation district programs have contributed much to the progress that has been made, and they will continue to do so.

Many citizens take most of the resources for granted, but air, as a natural resource, is perhaps taken for granted more frequently

than any other. Yet about 133 million tons of aerial garbage
being dumped into the U. S. atmosphere each year and Indiana
receiving its full share. As population grows and urbanization i
creases, air pollution becomes more serious and more difficult
prevent. It is a hazard to the health of our people, as well as d
facing buildings, spoiling agricultural crops, eating away at fabri
and metals, and representing a tremendous waste in valuable r
coverable items, such as the sulfur in sulfur dioxide. Our air
polluted and is becoming more so each day, except in the are
where positive action is being taken.

Indiana, as a state, did not act to protect its air until 1961 whe
the General Assembly passed the Air Pollution Control Act. Th
national Clean Air Act of 1963 now makes federal funds available d
a matching-fund basis to state and local enforcement agencies. On
of our "problem" areas is the northwest corner of the state, an
Illinois has a similar "problem" in her northeast corner. In 196
the two legislatures approved an interstate compact to allow th
two states to work together to solve this mutual problem. Some d
our cities have programs of their own, but the state and the citi
have just started to work on the air pollution problem. One d
the new ideas to speed up control measures is the exemption fro
taxation of all tangible personal property used in industrial pre
vention of air pollution.

Natural resources cannot be separated from natural beauty. Th
value of a scenic view, a scenic highway, and a scenic river must b
given consideration in our natural resources program. We mu
develop but we must preserve. We must utilize but we must cor
serve. A program that takes only one approach will not serv
everyone's needs. And since each person, each group, and eac
special interest has a different idea about how to proceed, goverr
ment must assume the role of leadership—of judging, regulating
and promoting. The demands are great and diverse and the need
are varied, but our planning and concepts must be geared to th
long-term future.

JOHN E. STEMPEL

RICHARD D. YOAKAM

Communications Media

Among the early settlers of Indiana were printers who came to establish newspapers. Trained by John and Fielding Bradford on Kentucky's first newspaper at Lexington, Elihu Stout in 1804 answered the call of Governor William Henry Harrison for a printer to print the territorial laws. At Vincennes Stout began the state's first newspaper, *The Indiana Gazette*, a weekly, in the summer of that year. Burned out two years later, he returned to Kentucky for new equipment, reestablished his shop, and published the first issue of *The Western Sun* in July 1807. The paper survives in today's *Vincennes Sun-Commercial*. The young Abraham Lin-

John E. Stempel, a native of Bloomington and graduate of Indiana and Columbia universities, has been chairman of the Department of Journalism at Indiana University since 1938. He has served on newspapers at Bloomington, Indianapolis, New York, and Easton, Pa. He is a past national president of Sigma Delta Chi and is secretary-treasurer of the American Council on Education for Journalism; he has been an officer or director in several trade and professional associations and in Rotary.

Richard D. Yoakam, a native of Pittsburgh, came to Indiana University in 1957, where he is now associate professor of journalism and radio-television. After taking two degrees at the University of Iowa, he was news editor at WHO, Des Moines, and news director at KCRG and KCRG-TV, Cedar Rapids. He has been active on committees of the Radio and Television News Directors Association and the Radio-TV section of the Association for Education for Journalism.

coln, moving from his Indiana home to Illinois, may have seen his first printing press in Stout's office in 1830. He had been a reader of *The Western Sun,* and its reprinting of Henry Clay's speeches helped to develop his political ideas. The Stout printshop has been restored and now stands on the campus of Vincennes University.

Newspapers soon appeared in the towns along the Ohio River, in the Whitewater Valley, and then farther north as the frontier pushed inland. Some of their early editors were graduates as Stout had been of the Bradford printshop. When Indiana became a state in 1816, two newspapers began publication in the capital at Corydon. In January 1822, six months after the site was chosen for the future state capital, *The Indianapolis Gazette* appeared and was followed a year later by *The Western Censor and Emigrant's Guide,* which became *The Indiana Journal* in January 1825. *The Journal* remained a fixture in Indianapolis until 1904 when *The Indianapolis Star* absorbed it. *The Indiana Democrat* began publication in 1830; its name was changed to *The Indiana Sentinel* ten years later.

When Indian treaties had opened more land for settlement, newspaper publication began north of the National Road. John Scott's *Pottawattomie and Miami Times* was established at Logansport in 1829 and was followed that same year by *The Lafayette Free Press.* By 1835 newspaper publishing reached Lake Michigan with the establishment of *The Gazette and General Advertiser* at Michigan City. Papers were founded at South Bend and Fort Wayne in 1831. By 1840 Indiana had 69 weeklies and four semi- and triweeklies.

One of the more colorful editor-publishers of early Indiana was George A. Chapman, who began his newspaper career in Terre Haute and continued it with *The Indiana Sentinel* in Indianapolis. His use of the rooster and the words, "Crow, Chapman, Crow," on his paper's masthead, along with his rabid partisanship, is credited with giving the Democrats the rooster as a party emblem.

Daily newspaper publication apparently began at Madison in 1835 and at New Albany three years later. *The Indiana Journal* was published daily during the legislative session of 1841 and again for a brief period during the Mexican War, but regular daily publication did not begin at the capital until midcentury. There is no record of Sunday newspapers in the state before the Civil War. *The Madison Courier*, the first daily, was the first Indiana newspaper served by The Associated Press. John Holliday made newspaper history in 1869 when he began publication of *The Indianapolis News* as an afternoon paper despite the warning of friends that such a publication could not really be a news paper, for how could he compete with the morning papers in rounding up the news and setting it into type?

Politics frequently motivated the founding of Indiana newspapers. Party leaders might encourage the establishment of a paper, or a candidate opposing a party machine might found his own. The latter type often lasted only through a campaign. Sometimes newspapers were published during a presidential campaign, such as *The Spirit of '76* published in Indianapolis to support William Henry Harrison in 1840. Early in the twentieth century many Republican newspapers were aided in establishment, in purchase, or even in continuance by the Ball Brothers at Muncie. On the other hand, many Democratic papers were aided financially by Paul Poynter of Sullivan and Walter S. Chambers of New Castle, leading publishers. Political interest has been cited as a factor in the building of John C. Shaffer's holdings, which at its peak included *The Indianapolis Star*, *The Muncie Star*, *The Terre Haute Star*, *The Louisville Herald*, *The Chicago Evening Post*, *The Rocky Mountain News*, and *The Denver Times*. As recently as the early 1930's a group supporting Governor Paul V. McNutt bought the then failing *Fort Wayne Journal-Gazette* to give it a major editorial voice in Indiana.

By the twentieth century most towns that had newspapers, daily or weekly, usually had two, one Republican and one Democratic. If a small town had only one, usually a neighboring town had a paper of the other party. The strong bipartisan nature of Hoosier politics and a favorable legal advertising law that required governmental notices to be published in two papers representing parties with the highest vote in the last general election kept alive dual newspaper situations in Indiana longer than in most states.

Eventually Indiana newspapers faced changing times and economic conditions, and mergers of dailies and weeklies increased in the 1930's and 40's. No longer is political interest a major reason for the newspaper; news and effectiveness of advertising are emphasized today. All but a few Indiana cities have a single newspaper or, in the daily field, a morning and evening paper under one ownership. Some small towns have a Republican and a Democratic weekly under the same ownership but published on different days of the week, making them one semiweekly operation as far as news and advertising are concerned. Since most Indiana dailies grew out of weekly publications, many continued their weekly editions to serve rural subscribers and former residents. But when motor routes replaced the U.S. mail in daily newspaper deliveries, weekly subscriptions fell off, and special weekly editions were discontinued—many soon after World War I and others during the Great Depression.

Indiana's newspaper picture reflects the fact that the state has been essentially an area of small cities and towns. Its only wholly Hoosier metropolitan area surrounds Indianapolis, although parts of the state come within the metropolitan areas of Chicago, Louisville, and Cincinnati. Twenty-eight of the 92 counties have no daily newspapers, and of the 87 dailies, 52 have less than 10,000 circulation. Only 17 newspapers have circulations of more than 20,000. The daily papers—73 evening, 11 morning, and 3 with both morning and evening editions—circulate 1,660,000 copies, and the 17 Sunday papers more than a million. The 216 weeklies, 9 semiweeklies, and 3 triweeklies distribute a half million copies a week. Logan Esarey, an Indiana regional historian, has noted that some 5,000 newspapers were started in Indiana; today 322 remain. As in other Midwestern states, 10 to 15 times as many papers were founded as survive today.

Early in the merger period, in 1938, *The Evansville Courier*, locally owned, and *The Evansville Press*, a Scripps-Howard paper, pioneered a publishing merger. Together they own Evansville

Printing and Publishing Corporation, which provides sales (advertising and circulation) and accounting services and shared mechanical facilities for the two newspapers. The papers also jointly own the Sunday paper, *The Evansville Courier and Press.* The news and editorial departments of the daily and Sunday papers remain completely separate and independent. A similar operation through an agency contract in which one newspaper uses the business and printing facilities of another is in existence at Fort Wayne. These plans reduce plant investment and operating costs.

Indiana newspapers have been for the most part home owned. Only three national chains, Scripps-Howard (originally Scripps-McRae), Thompson (British based), and Ridder, now own an Indiana daily, and one, the Dear group (New Jersey), owns a weekly. Regional groups, such as Federated (Michigan) and Small (Illinois), have come into Indiana, and Indiana owners have ventured into other states. Eugene C. Pulliam, once identified primarily with small-city operations in several states, owns *The Indianapolis Star* and *The Indianapolis News, The Muncie Star, The Huntington Press, The Vincennes Sun-Commercial,* and *The Arizona Republic* and *The Phoenix Gazette. The South Bend Tribune,* with papers at Bloomington and Bedford, also owns morning and evening papers at Hagerstown, Maryland, and four California publications. Ray Barnes of Elwood owns papers in Colorado, Ohio, and Kansas. Other multiple ownerships in Indiana are basically Hoosier groups of two or three newspapers.

Until recently chain ownership in the weekly press usually has meant no more than the publication of two or three weeklies for neighboring communities in the same plant, such as at Rockville, Tell City, and Lawrenceburg. The advent of offset printing a few years ago has resulted in as many as 25 publications being printed in a single plant, as at Connersville and Clinton, but the newspapers usually remain individually owned and edited.

A major exception to the chain of small newspapers was the scheme W. B. Harris developed in the nineteenth century. He published a number of weeklies (seldom more than five in operation at any one time) in his plant at Ellettsville, using the same feature material in each but the local news and advertising from the community served. He continued each paper as long as it was profitable, then dropped it and opened an operation in another town. Altogether he entered 138 publications from Indiana, Illinois, Kentucky, and Ohio for second-class privileges in the post office, perhaps the largest number of entries for one man. He also is credited with originating the scheme of offering Shetland ponies as premiums for subscriptions (he was a partner in a pony farm). His offer was in connection with *Our Boys and Girls*, a magazine for young folks which he developed and built to 35,000 circulation before he sold it. His pony-premium idea was popular with major national publications such as *The Saturday Evening Post*.

Von O. Pinkerton of Marion follows the Harris publishing idea today in the 80 different editions of the monthly *Farm News*, a tabloid newspaper. Each edition serves the Farm Bureau of a county or pair of counties, and carries four pages of general advertising and feature material about farming and homemaking, plus four to eight pages of news of farm events, organizations, and families, and advertising for the co-operative merchandising and services in the county for which it is printed.

Although the number of papers has decreased, more men and women are engaged in gathering and writing news on Hoosier newspapers than when there were 50 percent more newspapers than there are today. The number of newsmen has been further increased by the advent of radio and television. While broadcast news can reach the public faster than the printed word, it does not offer the completeness nor cover the range of topics that the newspaper does. In fact, broadcast news has encouraged newspaper reading. The change in newspaper competition has reduced the dependence of newspapers on sensationalism to gain readers and has encouraged them to wait to print certain stories until they can round out all the facts. On the other hand, there is a tendency to be less prompt in printing news of secondary importance—"If we don't get to it conveniently today, it will still be news tomorrow."

Most newspapers have responded to the one-newspaper situation by providing broader and more objective coverage of controversial news and in many instances have provided space for and encouraged expression of the opinions of those who disagree with the newspaper's editorial voice. At the same time, evidence exists that the editorial voice of many newspapers is not so strong as it once was. Informed critics feel that even an independent newspaper should take a stand on local issues and encourage the publication of opinion in locally written editorials and columns. A number of newspapers do, but too many do not. Until recently broadcast stations had been permitted no editorial position, and the number now exercising the privilege, as WFBM does in Indianapolis, is not yet great enough to provide real editorial discussion in Indiana.

Because of the early commitment of editors to the Democratic and the Republican editorial associations, Indiana developed a state press association later than some states. Weekly editors first recognized their mutual interests and formed their own group. Leaders from these three associations joined in the 1930's to organize the Hoosier State Press Association. Unlike many states, Indiana has brought dailies and weeklies together into a single association, unifying their efforts in legislative matters. The association's principal employee is its legal counsel, and its weekly bulletin emphasizes legal matters as well as social and economic developments. The political editorial associations continue their semiannual conventions primarily as sounding boards for political candidates and party doctrines.

Although Indiana lagged behind in developing a strong state association, it has provided leadership in regional and national newspaper associations. Eight of the presidents of the Inland Daily Press Association, founded 80 years ago, have been Hoosiers. The most recent have been Franklin Schurz of South Bend, the late Stewart Riley of Bloomington and Bedford, and Richard Blacklidge of Kokomo. Mark Ferree, one-time Indiana newspaperman, has been the president of the American Newspaper Publishers Association; Basil Walters was president of the American Society of Newspaper Editors and a founder of the Associated Press Managing Editors Association (organized at French Lick); and Edgar Schergens, publisher of *The Tell City News*, has served as president of the National Editorial Association (now the National Publishers Association), an organization of small-town newspapers, daily and weekly. Many Hoosiers have served as officers and directors of these and other trade associations.

In addition to the newspapers available for a subscription price, Indiana has more than 70 free-distribution weeklies. Most of them provide news and advertising services for neighborhoods in cities (a dozen in Indianapolis, for example) or in suburban areas. Some are "shoppers," distributed free by old-line weeklies to put the community's advertising into every home. The community field is the fastest growing in journalism, and because such papers seldom own printing facilities it offers the easiest opportunity for young men and women to own their own publications.

Indiana also has a number of specialized journals. It is the home of 34 trade and technical publications, 8 agricultural publications, 24 religious publications, 25 scholarly journals, and 17 fraternal periodicals. In the religious field, *Our Sunday Visitor* of Huntington, a Roman Catholic publication, has more than a million circulation, and *The Criterion*, a diocesan newspaper at Indianapolis, is widely quoted.

Even before World War I several Indiana firms published company papers. The number boomed during World War II, because such papers, especially employee publications, were considered essential to the working of greatly expanded industrial plants, and has continued to grow. Beside those for employees, publications are edited for users and recommenders of products, stockholders and the general public, salesmen, and dealers. Eli Lilly, for example, produces publications for employees, foreign trade, research, physicians, veterinarians, druggists, and farmers. More than 60 editors of such publications are members of the Indiana Council of Industrial Editors.

Once the home of a number of foreign-language newspapers, especially German, Indiana now numbers only three: *The Makedonika Tribuna* (Bulgarian), *Goniec Polski* (Polish), and *Nasa*

Nad (Croatian). The trend here is like that elsewhere in the United States. Four Negro weeklies are also published in Indiana.

During the late nineteenth century some colleges in the United States began offering courses in journalism. Indiana University had a course in journalistic writing as early as the 1890's, but the present Department of Journalism dates from 1907, when Fred Bates Johnson, an Indianapolis reporter and son of an editor, began earning his way through law school by teaching journalism. Today's department, with eleven full-time faculty members, is the only department or school in Indiana accredited by the American Council on Education for Journalism. A few years ago the Department of Radio and Television was established and it too is accredited.

After World War I additional colleges and universities began to offer instruction in journalism. Professional programs were developed at DePauw, Butler, Notre Dame, and Franklin, and less complete programs at other colleges and universities. Purdue developed a limited program in agricultural and engineering journalism. Recently it has expanded its offerings, as have both Indiana State and Ball State universities.

DePauw University was the founding site of Sigma Delta Chi, which has grown into an international journalism society with 40,000 undergraduate and professional members. Next year a marker will be placed on the DePauw campus as an historic site in journalism. The Indiana professional chapter recently instituted the Indiana Journalism Hall of Fame with the naming of 15 men, roughly one for each decade of the state's history.

Indiana high school publications long have been recognized nationally as outstanding. Contributing to this reputation have been the Indiana High School Press Association organized in 1922 at Franklin College and the Indiana High School Journalism Institute established in 1947 at Indiana University. This year Ball State began a similar institute. The advisers' section of the press association was the first to develop a high school course of study for journalism and spearheaded the establishment of such courses in high schools and provisions for licensing teachers in the field.

Hoosiers have contributed to the technical development of the press. Important has been the pioneering work of *The South Bend Tribune* in the use of the computer to speed typesetting. At the *Tribune* 8 machines produce more type than 25 machines could under hand operation. The computer also bills classified advertising as it sets it and gives editors a constant check on how much type is available in each news classification. It may soon permit Indiana newspapers to be served by a large, adequate central library. The *Tribune* has also been the proving ground for developments in photographic composition of advertisements and better stereotyping procedures.

Joe Bennett, a printer at Indiana University, developed the first mechanical engraving machine with the help of Indiana University physicists. An electric eye on the Engravograph scanned a photograph and guided a tool etching it in a block of type metal. The machine was never perfected for commercial use, but its principle was the basis of machines later used to make printing plates. Mechanical engraving replaced the cheap photoengraving service developed for small newspapers by the Indianapolis Engraving Company.

In the mid-thirties Paul Shideler of *The Indianapolis News* was a leader in the use of 35mm. cameras instead of the bulkier 4x5 news cameras. Many photographers, after trying the small camera, gave it up because it does not have the tolerance of the larger one. They returned to it when higher speeds in films made pictures less of a problem. The former newspaper and press-service photographer, James L. Mahler, in his work at Indiana University first took sequence-action pictures of indoor sports with available light, now a common procedure.

Color printing in newspapers had its greatest development in the Midwest beginning about 1935, and *The Indianapolis Times* was a pioneer in this development.

Hoosier-born and Hoosier-trained newsmen and editors have made contributions to American journalism. Two great traditions of that journalism are represented by Ernie Pyle, the World War II correspondent killed in action, and Don Mellett, crusading editor slain by gangsters when he fought corrupt government at Canton, Ohio. One of seven sons of an Indiana editor, Don Mellett and five brothers entered journalism; another was Lowell Mellett, an adviser to President Franklin D. Roosevelt.

The list of nationally known Hoosier journalists includes Claude G. Bowers, journalist and diplomat; Edward Price Bell, who while head of *The Chicago Daily News* foreign service at the start of World War I persuaded Lord Grey to tell England's side to the United States in an interview; George Kidd, who covered for United Press Hitler's invasions of Austria, Czechoslovakia, and Poland; Ernest K. Lindley, Paul Leach, Louis Ludlow, and Ray Scherer, long on the Washington scene; Frank Bourgholtzer, NBC correspondent in Europe.

During World War II President Franklin D. Roosevelt selected Byron Price, from Topeka, Indiana, executive news editor of The Associated Press, to head the Office of Censorship and Elmer Davis, from Aurora, a former *New York Times* reporter and pioneer broadcast commentator, to head the Office of War Information.

As managing editor of *The Minneapolis Star*, Basil (Stuffy) Walters, born at Frankfort, early recognized the value of modern editorial research and adapted George Gallup's findings to produce a more readable newspaper; he extended this research as executive editor of the Knight Newspapers. Now in retirement in Indiana he continues as a consultant to many major newspapers.

William Rockhill Nelson, from Fort Wayne, gave Kansas City its *Star* and *Times;* as managing editor, E. S. Beck, from Bainbridge, helped build *The Chicago Tribune* and his successor Don Maxwell, from Greencastle, now is the editor of that newspaper; and English-born but Indiana-trained Norman Isaacs, first at St. Louis and now at Louisville, is a gadfly to American editors.

Today's publishing phenomenon, *The Wall Street Journal*, has grown from an important financial newspaper of 45,000 circulation to a national newspaper of more than 800,000 circulation under the leadership of Bernard Kilgore, born at Albany, Indiana, and a group of Hoosiers brought together by Kenneth C. Hogate, son of a Danville weekly editor. The *Journal* now has a sister pub-

lication, *The National Observer*, a weekly newspaper, with a nation-wide circulation.

The modern press services owe much to the leadership of Kent
Cooper in The Associated Press and Roy W. Howard in United
Press. They broke down the barriers in international news flow
and modernized press association work. Roy Howard, who got
his first newspaper job in Indianapolis when as a high school reporter he skillfully covered a hassle about whether a Negro senior
should sit with the graduating class at Manual Training High
School, and Kent Cooper were reporters on Indianapolis newspapers early in the twentieth century. Barry Faris, who paused in
Indianapolis as managing editor of *The Indianapolis Sun*, was editor of International News Service for several years before its
merger with United Press in 1958. Franklin Schurz, South Bend,
and Eugene C. Pulliam, Indianapolis, are directors of The Associated Press, and Mr. Schurz is currently a vice president.

Hoosier journalists have contributed to the nation's humor.
George Ade's "Fables in Slang" were originally printed in a Chicago newspaper, and John McCutcheon and Gaar Williams became top cartoonists for *The Chicago Tribune*. Ohio-born Kin
Hubbard originated for *The Indianapolis News* Abe Martin, a
Hoosier, whose comments on life a half century ago are as true
today as they were then (The *News* still reprints them). His peers
among newspaper columnists hailed him as the greatest of them all.
Don Herold, an outstanding advertising man and humorist, had
his first job on an Indiana newspaper, as did Strickland Gilliland,
the author of "Off Again, On Again, Finnegan."

Indiana's climate of democracy has greatly aided the development of its journalism. Freedom of the press, guaranteed in the
First Amendment to the United States Constitution, was reiterated
in the state's first constitution in 1816. The principle that truth
should be a defense against charges of seditious (criminal) libel
had been established only a decade before in the United States.
The original Indiana Constitution and its successor in 1851 included this principle. Nearly a century later, *The Indianapolis
News* helped clarify the principle when the United States Supreme

Court decided that the President could not use the federal courts to punish a newspaper for criticizing him. The *News* had questioned certain dealings in the location and building of the Panama Canal. Charges of criminal libel had been filed at President Theodore Roosevelt's behest.

Paul Shideler, chief photographer for *The Indianapolis News*, is credited with establishing the right to photograph the President of the United States in a public place. Secret Service men had attempted to prevent him from photographing Herbert Hoover, when he was entering an Indianapolis hotel.

Although Indiana newspapers and broadcasters have faced most of the legal problems arising from publishing, the legislature and the courts have generally been sympathetic to their need for freedom. As early as 1882 the Indiana General Assembly began to designate specifically which documents required by law were public records. Court decisions have upheld the inspection of records in county and local offices. The legislature may close its sessions under certain conditions but rarely does, and the courts must remain ever open except in juvenile cases. The Hughes Act of 1953 spelled out the principle of open records and open legislative and administrative meetings and provided penalties for officials who disregarded it. Records of payment in welfare cases remain open to inspection (but not publication) largely because of Indiana's opposition when the United States Congress sought to impose total secrecy on such records.

For more than a century Indiana has been one of the few states with a libel retraction law. If a communications medium on being notified specifically of what the complainant believes libelous corrects its statement (within three days for daily newspapers, ten days for weeklies or broadcasters), the complainant, if he insists on going to court, may collect only actual damages (proved monetary loss). Because of this law, relatively few libel cases have been tried in Indiana. The retraction law applies to printed and electronic media alike.

Newspapers have lost on contempt citations when publication clearly interfered with a fair trial but have been upheld in the right to criticize judicial processes, decisions, and actions when the trial proceedings have ended. An Indiana newspaper cited for contemptuous publication is entitled by law to have its case heard by a judge other than the one issuing the citation. This act has been challenged recently in a citation involving comments by James T. Neal, editor of *The Noblesville Daily Ledger*, concerning an order by the circuit court judge there. An appeal is pending.

Another Indiana act makes it unnecessary for a newsman to reveal the source of his information either before a court, a grand jury, a legislative body, or a legislative or administrative hearing. Only 13 states have such a law.

Bar and press, separately and together, are discussing the effect of pretrial publicity of confessions and criminal records and the taking of pictures and recordings in courtrooms, but seldom have Indiana judges interfered with reasonable coverage of news. Newspapers, broadcasters, and press associations are currently discussing with the Federal Judges of the Southern Indiana District a proposal to extend limitations on news photography to areas outside the courtroom. Neither the state judiciary nor the bar has made an issue of electronic reporting of trials or reasonable photographic coverage. Several judges have been willing to experiment to see whether limited use of cameras and recording devices actually impaired the right of fair trial.

The problems of privacy, which have grown extensively with the tremendous development of pictorial journalism, have provided little concern to Indiana media. Only one case involving newspapers has come to trial, and the verdict for the newspaper was not appealed.

In this atmosphere of freedom from Elihu Stout's time on, newspapers in Indiana have felt free to tell the truth fully about government and to criticize freely. Newspaper digging was largely responsible for curbing the excesses of the Ku Klux Klan in the 1920's, and *The Indianapolis Times* exposé of the Klan won a Pulitzer Prize for public service. *The Indianapolis News* received this award a few years later for its campaign to reduce taxes. During the sesquicentennial year, protest demonstrations on campuses at Indiana and Purdue universities and at the appearance of President Lyndon B. Johnson at Indianapolis have put principles of free speech and right of assembly to a test. In each instance Indiana's newspapers, while often highly critical of the positions of those protesting, have upheld their right to speak and peaceably to assemble.

Before long a number of broadcast stations in Indiana will celebrate their golden anniversaries. While this is not a long time compared to the other mass media, the growth of broadcasting in the Hoosier state has been phenomenal, its service important, and its profits satisfying to investors. Broadcasting's development was connected with and stimulated by some genuinely Hoosier preoccupations—the feeling that life was just a little bit better in the small and middle-sized cities of the state, high school basketball, intense interest in "local" events, and a certain swaggering style of independence of action that those who do not know Hoosiers might call arrogance. And the expansion of the industry and its service to the audience mirror the important changes brought about by industrialization and urban growth, most of which occurred within the life span of broadcasting in the state.

Although Purdue University's department of electrical engineering started experimental radio broadcasting in 1910, WBAA, the Purdue station, did not begin as a standard broadcast station until April 4, 1922. Purdue graduated 10 men with degrees in radio engineering the following June. Others were experimenting with this new and exciting gadget also. At Fort Wayne Chester W. Keen, inventor of the transmission bands then used in the Ford automobile, brought from New York enough equipment to put together the city's first broadcasting station, WHBJ. At Indianapolis Francis Hamilton, a graduate in electrical engineering from Purdue, had been assigned the call letters 9ZJ for the station he was assembling in his garage in the fall of 1921. WSBT, South Bend, also claimed 1921 as its starting date.

To Hamilton and Samuel Lewis (Lew) Shank, mayor of Indianapolis, must go the credit for making perhaps the first and certainly the most interesting broadcast by a Hoosier official to the voters. On New Year's Eve, 1921, Hamilton talked Shank into coming to his garage at 2011 N. Alabama Street to say a few words about the prospects for 1922 to what could have been only a handful of crystal set listeners. The two had listened during the evening to stations at Pittsburgh, New York, and Newark, and then to musical numbers over Hamilton's station by Mr. and Mrs. N. C. Hilgenberg. When time came for Lew Shank's remarks, his first words were: "Hamilton, do you mean to tell me people can actually hear me over that damn dingus?"

"Damn dingus" or not, broadcasting caught on fast in Hoosierland. 9ZJ became WLK, as Hamilton picked up *The Indianapolis News* and L. S. Ayres & Co. as co-sponsors. Ayres played records from its phonograph department and opened a radio department in the store to sell sets. WOH came on the air in Indianapolis in March 1922, and *The Indianapolis Star*, with a competitive eye toward the then independently owned *News*, was a co-sponsor with the Hatfield Electric Company, which also sold radio sets.

Quickly other stations appeared around the state: WHBU, Anderson, and WGBF, Evansville, in 1923; WJOB, Hammond, 1924; WOWO, Fort Wayne, 1925; WKBV, Richmond, and WLBC, Muncie, 1926; and WBOW, Terre Haute, 1927. The Indianapolis stations, WOH and WLK, foundered because of the heavy expenses of operations—both left the air early in 1923, but in 1924 WFBM got on the air and is still going strong today. The Merchants Light and Power Company held the license, and on election night, 1924, WFBM began broadcasting at 6:00 P.M.; later in the evening it reported the Coolidge-Davis election returns.

The growth of broadcasting in Indiana was not too different from that of other Midwestern states; in fact, Hoosiers may have lagged behind. The first network (NBC) was formed in 1926, but its radio programs came to Indiana from out-of-state stations; a great family pastime then was bragging to a neighbor that "we got KDKA and WEAF loud and clear last night." Hoosier broadcasters were two years away from network membership. Indianapolis' first network broadcast was, significantly, a sports broadcast, the Dempsey-Tunney "long count" fight in September 1927, carried by two stations. Program schedules were informal and very casual by modern standards. When the stations could find nothing to do, they signed off the air for a while. Broadcast material relied heavily on amateur local talent and local orchestras.

Regular programming and, even more important, regular program forms soon began to emerge. Henry S. Wood, farm editor of *The Indianapolis Star*, joined WFBM in 1926 with ideas for a regular program beamed at farmers and their families. On the daily 30-minute program called "The Hoosier Farm Circle" Wood pioneered many techniques. He talked the station into setting up a glass-enclosed studio at the Indiana State Fair in 1926. He used many amateur musical groups, staged amateur contests on the county fair circuit, and brought the winners in for a state-wide competition at the State Fair. Wood took recording equipment— and in those days that meant a truckload—right into the barnyards and feed lots to record interviews with authentic background sounds. The traditional and almost universal farm broadcast format may have begun with these programs.

Merle Sidener, a former Indianapolis newspaper editor and a principal in the Sidener-Van Riper advertising agency, started another program type with the "Christian Men's Builders' Hour" broadcast from the Third Christian Church every Sunday morning. It became a radio "Sunday school class" which lasted more than 25 years, more than 1,400 broadcasts on WFBM, and it is still heard from time to time over other Indianapolis stations.

The first disc jockey showed up about this time. The idea that radio could serve a morning nonfarm audience—people who wanted the time and the temperature and the weather forecast before going off to school or work—became an instant hit in Hoosierland. These men, particularly in Indianapolis, talked and made jokes, played records, introduced live musical acts, and were involved in elaborate tricks and promotional stunts.

If there is one major program type which runs through the development of broadcasting in Indiana, it must be the sports broadcast, particularly of the Indianapolis 500-mile race and the Indiana state high school basketball tournament. WOWO, Fort Wayne, claims to be the first—in 1924—to broadcast the IHSAA finals and to hold the longest record of consecutive coverage. The Indianapolis 500-mile race broadcasts started in 1925, a series that has continued each May 30 and now plays to what is proudly called "the world's largest radio network."

Across the nation the sports broadcast was one of the earliest non-studio forms. For example, KDKA was reporting the Pittsburgh Pirates' games in 1922. From its beginning, radio understood that one of its strongest assets was its immediacy, its ability to take the listener to the event, and with colorful ad-lib reportage and interviews and commentary by experts provide a new form of journalism—the instant report. That a new form was emerging was recognized very early. My co-author of this chapter, John E. Stempel, helped WFBM broadcasters Blythe and Thomas Hendricks during the 1927 state high school tournament. After sitting before "a squirrel cage" in the rafters of the Butler fieldhouse, he reported his experiences in a Bloomington newspaper under the headline: "For Two Days I Didn't Know Who Got Me."

Although the news broadcast has developed over the years to become radio's most valuable commodity and television's most significant presentation, few of the early broadcasters put much emphasis on news as a program element. The station did cover news events but mostly on a "live" on-the-scene basis. Obtaining a reliable news service on a regular basis became a major problem. Beginning in the 1930's the nation's wire services were pressured by the newspapers, their prime clients, not to sell their service to radio stations. The newspapers became more and more worried about radio competition as the depression deepened and advertising lineage dropped.

In Indiana E. H. Harris, editor of *The Richmond Palladium-Item* and chairman of the American Newspaper Publishers Association, strongly influenced the developments that led to what has been called "The Press-Radio War." He advocated more representation in the ANPA for the nation's smaller papers—those hurt the worst by radio competition. He formed a Publishers National Radio Committee and drew up a statement that went to The Associated Press and ANPA conventions in 1933. The ANPA approved some of Harris's recommendations including:

1. The Association should take legal actions against piracy of news.

2. That all news bulletins broadcast "in fairness to newspapers, should be in the briefest possible form and prepared to whet the appetite of the listener for more news to be obtained from newspapers," and that all national and international news broadcasts should be credited to "all the newspapers of the United States."

3. That newspapers which owned radio stations should tightly control the amount of news on their stations so as not to injure the competition.

Because stations were licensed by the FCC, Harris feared that the federal government might influence news distribution or censor the news on those stations which were also members of The Associated Press. Though such a fear has never been grounded in fact, broadcast stations to this day can only obtain "associate" membership in the AP.

Finally, the wire services and the networks got together with the newspaper publishers organizations and agreed to pool their resources to provide a special service for radio—Press-Radio News. It provided enough news for three or four broadcasts a day, but the movement of this material on the wire was timed to protect morning and evening newspaper deadlines. Since it was not very satisfactory, Trans-Radio-News Service—designed for radio—was born. In July 1936 United Press, seeing potential business going to Trans-Radio, started its own radio news wire. All over the nation radio signed contracts for news from these services, but it was not until 1941 that the AP followed UP with a special broadcast service.

Indiana stations had begun programming regular newscasts in the early 30's. Ken Ellington, now vice president of the Republic Aviation Corporation, was the pioneer newscaster in the Indianapolis area. Regular news reports also were heard in South Bend, Fort Wayne, Richmond, and Evansville. Since many of these stations were network affiliates, the network news reports and their reporters—Lowell Thomas, H. V. Kaltenborn, Gabriel Heatter, Earl Godwin, and Elmer Davis of Aurora, Indiana, to name only a few—had a regular listening public.

In 1937 Gilbert Forbes joined the WFBM news staff as chief newscaster, a relatively new position. For 24 years Forbes was the most believed and most welcomed source of broadcast news in the state. Every state developed a group of men who were "the news voices." People got up to their reports and the end of the 10:00 P.M. newscast was bedtime for hundreds of thousands of persons. Still the reliable reporter of spot news, radio now presented roundups of world events and provided an ingredient that is strangely missing from today's television fare—the commentator on the day's news.

The pattern was to program the news in 15-minute segments around meal time and then just before bedtime—peak times for radio listening. There was little news in between, although some stations did have a mid-afternoon news program, and many, including WFBM and WOWO, broadcast news aimed at the women in the audience in the middle of the morning.

World War II established radio as a primary source of news and information. Some stations sent their own war correspondents to the fighting fronts—for example, WFBM sent Gilbert Forbes—and all vastly increased their coverage of war news. The great network news departments were born in this era. The famous reports of Edward R. Murrow from London, as well as those of scores of other correspondents from the battle fronts, brought the war home to the people of the United States as no communications medium had ever done before.

Radio in Indiana came out of the war an indispensable part of everyone's daily life. It also launched the greatest expansion period in its short history. Between 1945 and 1949 nearly 30 AM stations went on the air; 21 of them are still broadcasting today. Between 1950 and 1955 17 more, which still exist, were added. A number of Indiana cities now found themselves with more than one local station. In Evansville two were added, two more came on the air in Fort Wayne, South Bend got two more, and Gary got not only its first but also its second in a two-year period. Bloomington had three stations in the late 40's. Starting a radio station was relatively easy and not very expensive.

In 1947 something new was added to the radio spectrum when FM radio stations went on the air in Elkhart, Terre Haute, New Castle, and Muncie. Marion, Warsaw, Washington, Connersville, and Evansville got onto the FM band a year later. FM broadcasting equipment was relatively cheaper to buy and to operate and promised static-free reception to listeners. More than 40 FM stations are now on the air in the state; many of them operate along with AM stations. New Castle remained a completely FM market until 1960 when WCTW started an AM sister to its pioneer frequency modulation unit.

FM stimulated educational broadcasting. Indiana University established WFIU in 1950. Other colleges and universities which came on the air with FM stations were Wabash, Evansville, DePauw, Butler, Indiana Central, Ball State, and Notre Dame. The city school systems of Gary, Evansville, Hartford City, Huntington, Indianapolis, Muncie, New Albany, South Bend, and Wabash all put FM stations on the air and used them for educational, in-school, and informational programming during the school day. In 1947 George C. Johnson of Indiana University began a parallel activity, the Indiana School of the Sky, a series of daily programs designed for in-school use at various grade levels. These programs are widely used both by the school stations and commercial broadcasters throughout the United States. Purdue University's WBAA also developed a "School of the Air" series and distributes it by tape to more than a score of stations in the state.

The first television picture in Indiana was seen in Indianapolis in 1939, when local Philco dealers put on a demonstration at the Antlers Hotel. WLS, Chicago, sent a similar demonstration crew to the Indiana State Fair that same year. In 1944 Gerald D. Smith and Marion E. Stevenson put station WXMT on the air in Smith's basement, and the P. R. Mallory Company bought the equipment a few months later. Mallory used the experimental station to test equipment; the "program schedule" was unexciting—all test patterns.

Commercial television did not come to Indiana until 1949 when WFBM-TV went on the air on Channel 6; appropriately, the inaugural program was the first and last Indianapolis 500-mile race to be televised "live" in its entirety. (From 1964 on WFBM-TV has provided the technical and production personnel for a closed-circuit coverage of the race to theater-television installations around the country.) Through the summer of 1949 the station broadcast a limited daily program, including some baseball games from Victory Field, and Gilbert Forbes became the state's first TV newscaster. WFBM-TV engineers also pioneered in another area; they built their own cameras! Under the direction of Chief Engineer Harold Holland, 10 studio and remote location cameras were built from scratch. It is believed to be the only TV station in the country to have built its own camera equipment.

That same summer electronics genius and manufacturer Sarkes Tarzian had his people hard at work building a TV transmitter at Bloomington. WTTV went on the air November 11, 1949, and Bloomington became the smallest city in America with its own TV channel. Because of an FCC freeze on the addition of more channels, during the Korean war, it was not until 1952 that the South Bend Tribune Company added Indiana's third station, WSBT-TV. Evansville became the first Indiana city to have two stations, WEHT and WFIE-TV in 1953. That same year WKJG-TV went on the air in Fort Wayne, and WISH-TV made Indianapolis a two-station market the following year. There are now 17 television stations in the state.

Indiana has been slow to develop educational TV to its full potential, although it is the site of one of the most dramatic experiments in using television for education. In 1959 Purdue and Indiana universities joined with eight other educational institutions in the Midwest to set up the Midwest Program on Airborne Television Instruction. Using specially equipped DC-7 aircraft, the plan was to beam programs from the plane to the ground over a six-state area to a potential audience of five million pupils in primary and secondary schools. MPATI began with seven Indiana schools in 1961 and expanded to more than 1,200 schools in the six states the next year. In 1965 the FCC turned down attempts by the MPATI group to expand the service by adapting more channels to its use, and the program probably will be phased out by 1970. While the initial response was good, the MPATI programs did not receive enough support from school systems, particularly in larger cities like Indianapolis, to make it a self-sustaining operation. Perhaps the most significant contribution MPATI has made is not in broadcasting materials to classrooms but in developing new channels of cooperation and communication in educational circles. And surely MPATI points the way toward future developments; it is a first step toward the use of a satellite to broadcast educational materials not only to the United States but to half the world at one time.

Even before MPATI, Purdue and Indiana universities had begun instruction both in and by radio and television. By 1953 I. U. had courses of instruction and a regular series of daily live programs on WTTV, and was making kinescopes of educational programs for distribution to other commercial stations throughout the state and nation. In 1956 Purdue began a series of foreign language training courses, and I. U. began a series of telecourses that offered college credit to the home viewer who would enroll through the Bureau of Correspondence Study, view the programs, and then take the final examination on the campus.

By 1959 I. U. had started closed-circuit instruction—televised lectures distributed to several classrooms on its own campus, and in 1962 it was linked with Purdue by a unique two-way sound and picture hookup that permitted students on each campus to take courses offered on the other, professors to teach tandem, and even allowed a professor on a campus 100 miles away to pop a question to the nodding student in the back row. The two universities have extended their closed-circuit system to the Indianapolis downtown campus. In the near future I. U. and Purdue will have a state-wide closed-circuit linkage with their regional campuses and perhaps eventually with Indiana State and Ball State universities.

A state-wide educational TV network is much further away. Indiana University will activate a construction permit for Channel 30 in Bloomington in 1966-67. Why Indiana has been slow to develop educational TV stations—it has been one of 16 states without them—is not clear. The 1955 session of the Indiana General Assembly proposed a nine-member board to discuss utilization of educational programs on commercial stations. Nothing came of it. While the MPATI experiment may have slowed other more normal programs and Hoosier educators have not given enough support to the MPATI program, so far they have not demanded other educational TV systems. Educational TV stations will be on the air soon. How much support they will get remains to be answered.

In commercial television Indiana's broadcasters promise that nearly all their programs will be in color, and within the next two years. The color revolution that hit network television in the fall of 1965 swept over Indiana, too. Most stations are now broadcasting color programs from the networks. All managers who answered a questionnaire sent out by the I. U Bureau of Media Research and Services in the fall of 1965 said they intended to have color origination equipment within the next year. Many Hoosier TV stations are also contemplating plant expansion and equipment modernization.

For the other elements of the broadcast spectrum, AM and FM broadcasting, the future is more complex. If in its short history radio went from sports broadcasting to variety programming, from network membership to independent operation, it is now back to its original starting point—more variety and sports broadcasts. Throughout Indiana station managers answering the questionnaire said they will do more sports in the future, that sports broadcasting of all kinds is one of their most popular and certainly most saleable program categories. Some stations even broadcast little league baseball in the summer.

Part of the growth of FM stations in Indiana can be attributed to the need for a nighttime audience for companies operating the many daytime AM stations in the state. Many daytime owners say they have FM stations first on their list of expansion plans, and those who operate FM stations almost unanimously said they will devote more time to sports in the future. Many of the owners see their expansion largely in terms of high school sports, since they believe the colleges and universities charge privilege fees that are too high, and college sports have become a TV staple. The other facet of FM broadcasting which will expand is stereo. By adding a sub-carrier transmitter to their equipment, many Indiana FM broadcasters plan to present stereophonic music on a much expanded schedule. With the growth of the stereo recording market both on tape and disc there is clearly an audience waiting for such service.

Another area of expansion will be news. While not many agree with the former president of CBS news, Fred Friendly, that by 1970 nearly one half of evening prime-time television programming will be in the news and information category, Hoosier broadcasters are almost unanimous in the belief that news programming will expand at the local level. All are doing more news today than they did five years ago, and all see even more news programming in the future. Radio station operators recognize the value of local news; not only is it one of their most saleable programs but it is something they can offer that competes with network TV and radio programming, as well as the local paper, in a favorable way.

The extremely local nature of radio is probably its most distinguishing feature today, and this trend will continue. In one part of Indiana the radio stations bring in special poultry reporting services from Gainesville, Georgia, a prime poultry raising area. In another part of the state special attention is given to Coast Guard reports on conditions on the Great Lakes. The community bulletin board program type is universal. In metropolitan areas radio often concentrates on the mobile and exclusive part of its audience—the automobile driver, and on news of the industrial community. A great change in news programming has been the reduction in the amount of farm news. While some station managers in predomi-

nantly farm areas still think this is an important part of their programming, most of the survey answers indicated a major trend
away from offering farm information. The mass media, better
farm to market roads, and greater educational opportunities have
tended to blur the once sharp contrast between the country boy
and the city slicker. As Indiana has become an urban-industrial
state, as the move to the city has increased and speeded up, information program needs have changed, and the Indiana broadcaster is
clearly aware of this.

In Indiana's northern industrial cities 10 and 20 years ago, the
radio stations programmed some of their broadcast schedule for
ethnic groups in the community. "The Polish Hour," "Polka
Time," "The Slovak Hour," and others were staple programs in
the daily log. Today and in the future, the managers agree, the
melting pot has done its work and the demand for such programs
is disappearing. Some attention is still being given to the Negro
audience, but only one station in Indianapolis says that it will continue to aim a major part of its programming at the Negro. Stations in Indiana's northern cities indicate that they are reducing
this kind of programming and that it will largely disappear.

Radio will continue to try to locate the programming trends as
early as possible and then follow them. The ability to anticipate
what the audience is going to want is one of the main talents needed
by a broadcaster. Robert D. Enoch, manager and owner of
WXLW, Indianapolis—and one of the state's most astute broadcasters—represents one side of what must be one of the most vigorous and never-ending arguments in the business.

> WXLW has made the adult audience its target—catering to the
> 24- to 50-year age bracket—with a music policy designed to please
> and entertain. No "rock," no long-hair, no pure classic jazz, no
> corn hill-billy. Our goals, information and entertainment, and in
> that order.
> . . . Whatever the opportunities are or that the evolution of our
> industry—community changes—political alterations—and business
> alteration demand, WXLW will be prepared to know that de-
> mand and meet it with a changing method of operation. . . . The
> more things change, the more they remain the same. . . .

Others who would agree in part with Enoch are aiming their programming at another part of the audience—the teen-ager and young adult. One station manager said, "Our changeover in programming was complete—from a very weak, sub-standard middle of the road to a very fast, tightly programmed 'rock.' We believe that we made the change at the right time in our area. We are now the only 'rock' station in the market. . . ."

The controversy and argument over kinds of music and programs and the style of presentation is one of the hottest in broadcasting because it hits right at the commercial heart of the matter —the stations sell their time at rates based on audience size. The station operators will always follow trends and styles to provide what they think the audience wants.

As are all stations in the United States, every Indiana station is licensed to broadcast "in the public interest, convenience and necessity." The Federal Communications Commission has never defined what those words mean, but has left it up to the broadcaster to make up his own mind about their meaning and then follow through in his program schedule with a public demonstration of that interpretation. Hoosier broadcasters in their questionnaire answers repeatedly put great emphasis on the kind of philosophical framework for operation that those seven words give the licensee. If there were a list of the good and bad points of Indiana broadcasting, it might look like this:

Unfavorable Points

1. Hoosier broadcasters have sometimes followed others too closely—fads have filled the air without regard to whether the audience really wants them.

2. Hoosier broadcasters have sometimes been slow to realize the needs of their audience in terms of developing an editorial voice for their community.

3. Hoosier broadcasters and educators have been slow to develop a land-based, community-centered educational broadcasting system in television.

4. There are not enough "big thinkers" among the Hoosier

broadcast contingent. Many operations are too narrowly based and conservatively managed to provide the kind of financial expansion future broadcasting will demand.

5. Some Hoosier broadcasters have not had enough interest or resources to carry on research that would provide them with information about whether they are reaching and satisfying *their* audiences' needs. Promotional gimmicks and too much reliance on sometimes poorly structured ratings have sometimes been used in place of local self-analysis.

Favorable Points

1. Hoosier broadcasters have a proud history and a clear future view about their role in news and information programming.

2. Hoosier broadcasters have always provided excellent public service broadcasting in times of crisis and disaster.

3. Hoosier broadcasters have been extremely generous in their support of community advancement and activities.

4. Many Hoosier broadcasters have established and maintained outstanding programs of editorial views, and many exert great community leadership with their editorial campaigns.

5. Most Hoosier broadcasters provide a service that is local in nature and is aimed at their own particular audience in their own particular city.

In these ten points the reader can see the broadcasters as they see themselves. Now for a few personal opinions. Indiana broadcasters in the future must find the resources to increase the power of their radio service to the state. There is only one 50,000-watt radio station in the state, and it must operate on a reduced pattern at night. Although some kind of network news service is available in almost all markets, it is difficult for many Indiana listeners to get a selection of network (i.e., national and international news) services by radio. Southern Indiana listeners often must rely on stations in Cincinnati and Louisville to bring them more than local news in any great quantity. As a parallel thought, local radio stations must expand their own staffs in the area of news and public service programming. In many small stations news is a station-wide responsibility, and each member of the small staff has something to do with it. But as automation makes it easier and more economical to operate many of the technical phases of broadcasting, the broadcaster will have to concentrate his manpower and expenditures in the areas that cannot be turned over to a machine or computer—news and information programming. This will mean that stations must attract and hire a somewhat different kind of person, someone with professional training and skills in broadcast journalism.

At the same time there must be further development of the broadcast station as an editorial voice in the community. Too few broadcasters in Indiana have taken on this important role. In most medium-sized cities there is but one newspaper and some of these do not provide the kind of dynamic community-based editorial leadership that they should. Where this vacuum exists, the broadcaster must step in and provide the leadership. Where there is only one editorial voice, the broadcasters should provide that essential alternate point of view that the democratic system requires. One broadcaster who established a station at Corydon in May 1964 wrote the author: "We feel we have made great strides in getting the name of our first capital city pronounced properly. Heretofore it was 'Cor-don.' Now, more and more of the local population are pronouncing the name 'Cory-don.'"

In a sesquicentennial year this may be the most heartening progress of all. If in two years a broadcaster can re-educate his audience to break a habit of 150 years, then there can be no doubt that the broadcasting industry in Indiana can help push the Hoosier state to greatness by the time we get around to celebrating its bicentennial in 2016.

ALEXANDER M. MOORE

Elementary and Secondary Education

The celebration of the sesquicentennial of the statehood of Indiana provides us with an opportunity to study the challenges and problems that confront us in our program of public education. We can study the original intentions of the founders of our educational system. We can observe the developments in education during the last century and a half as the people of Indiana have struggled to carry out and extend those intentions. We can identify the needs of our contemporary society and determine whether our present educational practices are adequate to prepare young people to meet those needs. We can use these investigations in choosing those trends in our history that should be fostered, and those that should be halted. Our proper use of this anniversary observance will be to re-examine our history, survey our present problems, and make decisions about our future actions.

Nowhere is such an examination more needed than in the field of public elementary and secondary education. In our society we have assigned to our public schools the responsibility for preparing all our young people for the civic activity and the jobs which they

Alexander M. Moore, a native of Indianapolis, has been principal of Crispus Attucks High School since 1957. He has degrees from the University of Chicago and Butler University and has done graduate work at Indiana University. He is very active in Indianapolis civic and educational organizations.

will have to perform when they are adults. Other social agencies, such as the family, the church, the peer group, and the private and parochial school systems share in the nurture of our young people. The public school system, however, has been given the ultimate responsibility for the proper preparation of young people for the demands and expectations that modern American society imposes upon all adults.

We look to the past in this examination and ask the difficult question: "What were the ideals and motivations of the people who participated in the development of public education?" We then look at our contemporary life and ask the even more difficult question: "What are the real demands that a democratic society places on adults and how can our public schools meet those demands?" This latter question is so difficult that we often approach it indirectly by asking ourselves: "What are the big problems in public education today?"

The answers come from a wide range of concerns. Some of these concerns are basic, some are symptomatic, some are trivial, and some are even illusory. Some are engrossed in the mechanics of school operation instead of drawing attention to the fundamental philosophical decisions which must be made. Any list of the problems in education therefore will include those on the nature of the curriculum (which is basic), on the amount of secondary school credit to be given for a certain course (which is trivial), on the state of our competition with the Russian educational system (which is illusory), and on the size of school districts (which is a question of mechanics). There are as many different lists of problems as there are observers who comment upon them. The important task is to distinguish secondary problems from basic ones and then to draw up a list of priorities among the basic problems.

One list of problems suggested to me included the following:

1. Athletically minded and anti-intellectual school boards
2. Refusals to provide adequate school funds
3. Resistance to federal aid for education
4. Inadequate training for teachers

5. Lack of library and laboratory facilities
6. Injection of partisan politics in school reorganization issues
7. The teaching of religion in the public schools
8. The relationships of public, parochial, and private schools in the uses of publicly provided facilities and funds
9. The dropout problem

The public secondary school system is plagued with an over-emphasis upon varsity athletics in many school corporations. This obsession comes from our failure to keep in mind the basic purposes of the public schools in Indiana. Therefore we fail to recognize when an activity, such as varsity athletics, becomes diverted from its genuine educational purposes and adversely affects the entire educational program. Varsity athletics was added to the school program as a device to motivate boys to remain in school, as an extension of the physical education program, and as a means of indirectly teaching the standards for certain group behavior. It has now become an autonomous activity devoted to providing a glamorous recreational spectacle for the public. Too many people who deplore this development propose mechanical suggestions for reform instead of basic ones. The real issues in the problem of over-emphasis of athletics will be faced only when there is a serious examination of the basic purposes of public education and an evaluation of every activity in the schools in terms of those purposes.

The degree to which many school boards are "anti-intellectual" will be diminished when the basic intellectual purposes of education are examined and accepted.

The problems of adequate funds (including the hysteria that arises from a fear of funds coming from our national government based on our federal taxes) and of adequate facilities are caused by confusion over the real purposes of the public school. Taxation and the expenditure of public funds in a society as affluent as ours is entirely a matter of public decisions about the kind and size of the public programs that we wish to foster. Some objectors to school budgets may be expressing a fear that we cannot afford the proposals but many more are really questioning whether the proposed educational activities are legitimate and necessary ones. Once again this reaction emphasizes the need of constant attention to the purposes of public education and the procedures necessary to carry them out.

Similar comments must be made about the inadequacy of teacher training. Inadequacy for what? Many discussions center around the number of hours of college credit to be required in educational methods versus the number of hours in the subject to be taught. These discussions are often carried on without a systematic examination of the tasks we expect teachers to perform and their historical and philosophical justifications.

The presence of partisan politics in school reorganization issues is all too evident in our state. The final recourse for all citizens who are concerned about this intrusion is to indicate, clearly, why political partisanship is an "intrusion." This again brings up the question of basic issues.

The sharing of public resources with nonpublic schools and the teaching of religion in our schools are both subject to final settlement only in terms of our assumptions about the responsibilities of the public schools and the best methods of meeting those obligations.

The dropout problem concerns the reasons why at least 30 percent of our youth fail to continue their formal education until they receive a high school diploma. We have read and heard an enormous number of explanations and suggested nostrums. A few observers are insisting more and more that we examine certain questions: "What should be the content of the educational program which requires twelve years of formal schooling that can be recognized finally by a high school diploma?" "Why should all people in this state have these complete experiences?" "How do we effectively offer these experiences to young people?" These are the questions which must be answered. We often exert great intellectual effort to devise ways of restraining the withdrawal of young people from the school without examining the nature and the objectives of the school itself. The essential explanation for the "drop out" is that the child, when he has the opportunity to make a choice, no longer sees as much meaning for him in the school program as he does in some other alternative activity. When we can be sure of the value of our educational program for everyone and the efficiency of our instructional devices, we will no longer witness any sizable withdrawals by young people from our schools.

This emphasis upon the primary importance of an examination of purposes and procedures does not imply that the tactics of our fight for good education will not be concerned with incidents, personalities, and persuasions. It does predict the failure of any campaign for good education which avoids consideration of these fundamental issues. We must examine them in terms of our values and intentions, the history of our efforts, and the needs of the present.

The most significant area in the examination of a school is its curriculum—the organized, planned educational activities that are conducted by the school. They constitute the school's reasons for existence just as the distribution of power is the reason for government or the distribution of material goods is the reason for business. We need to focus our attention first upon the curriculum. When we master the difficulties inherent in the school's educational activities, we will be able to find solutions for all the other dilemmas of public education. The curriculum in the elementary and secondary schools of Indiana should provide general education for all, effective vocational education for all, and the kind of moral education that is acquired through racial integration.

Always present in any educational system are learning experiences that all students are expected to acquire. These experiences, which are called "general education," are considered to be so basic, so natural, and so necessary that the schools must guarantee that they are acquired by all students. Almost the entire curriculum in the elementary grades consists of certain experiences that all children must share, but the secondary school levels have only recently become a part of the required educational experience for all youth. The curriculum of the secondary school still reflects a wide variety of learning experiences that are "elective" rather than required.

The general education programs in elementary and secondary schools highlight our primary purposes in public schools, and the length of compulsory school attendance and the subjects required of all students reveal the framework within which we operate.

An early State Board of Public Instruction listed as required subjects for the elementary schools in Indiana: reading, writing, spelling, and the four fundamental processes of arithmetic. An early license law added orthography, geography, and grammar. The teaching of "good behavior" was specified by a law in 1865. Physiology, U. S. history, and German (upon demand) were added in 1869. These subjects taught to all students in elementary schools were expected to develop literacy and good citizenship.

These subject labels are still found in the elementary curriculum, although the contents have changed considerably in response to the increasingly complex demands of society. Instruction for literacy has developed from rote spelling drills and orthography to linguistic grammar and a wide range of readings from the literature of many countries. Instruction in mathematics has developed from simple exercises in addition, subtraction, multiplication, and division to "modern math," which stresses the use of mathematical symbols as a means of communicating ideas and analyzing simultaneous relationships among several variables.

Instruction for good citizenship has developed from simple precepts on behavior to courses in geography, U. S. history, social studies, health, and physical education. The entire range of social studies now includes local and world history and studies drawn from anthropology, sociology, and economics. Young students are now given instruction in phases of economic geography and demography instead of mere descriptive geography. Expanded courses in the arts, music, the practical arts and crafts, and other languages besides English are now offered in the elementary school as additional experiences that can promote the mastery of literacy and good citizenship.

Literacy has come to mean not only the recognition of verbal symbols but also the development of high levels of reading comprehension of varieties of writings, the development of literary tastes, and the encouragement of creativity. The growing use of the label "language arts" (instead of spelling, grammar, etc.) symbolizes this change of content and emphasis. Citizenship has come to imply not only the memorization of simple data and a few precepts but also an understanding of the background of our political life and the kinds of influences that affect our political decisions. The use of the term "social studies" (instead of history, geography, etc.) indicates the intention of developing this kind of broad and integrated understanding of the problems of citizenship.

These objectives have been clarified in our minds by the use of sophisticated evaluative devices. We no longer assess achievement in the elementary school by the scores that children receive on memorization tests; we now use standardized tests that require children to use their capacities for analysis and judgment in addition to memory. We require that the elementary school program prepare children for at least one year of secondary school experiences. We emphasize acquiring concepts and generalizations in order to interpret the meaning and usefulness of collections of information. The program of general education in the elementary school does not correspond to the popular images of the "little red schoolhouse," the "3 R's," or "McGuffey's Reader," yet the objectives are similar to those of the traditional program recalled by these phrases. The demands of present-day society, the inclusiveness of the enrollment in elementary schools, and the expansion of our knowledge of pedagogy, however, require different and more complex curricula.

High schools were organized in Indiana in the 1850's. Their curriculum has had a different history from that of the elementary schools, which had the objectives of literacy and good citizenship for all children from the beginning. Indiana high schools did not begin with such clear and self-contained objectives for all youth. Instead, the State Board of Public Instruction in 1869 decreed the "harmonizing of the high school courses of study to that of the University." The earliest requirements for admission to the freshman class of the state university included orthography, reading, geography, grammar, arithmetic, U. S. history, composition, word analysis, plane geometry, elementary algebra, and elementary Latin. High schools offering these subjects were commissioned by the state. Graduates from these schools were assured admission to the state university.

Just as the task of educating for literacy and good citizenship had been assigned to the elementary schools in Indiana, the task of preparing young people for civic leadership and professional activity was assigned to the university. The "general education" program of the university was focused upon the development of leadership and profession skills and grounded in the "liberal arts," which included grammar, rhetoric, mathematics, languages, history, and philosophy. All university students, regardless of their special interests, were required to enroll in these subjects. Since they began with the general assumption that their students were preparing for college, the high schools emphasized the liberal arts. The first secondary schools in Indiana were tuition-supported county seminaries with limited enrollments and courses that usually included geography, natural philosophy, chemistry, astronomy, geometry, algebra, logic, moral philosophy, Latin, and French.

The students in the early secondary schools tended to be those who were academically able, well-motivated, and college-oriented. There was no compulsory school attendance in high schools until 1897, and it was 1901 before school attendance was made compulsory up to the age of sixteen. These laws, and the liberalization of promotion policies, meant that all the fourteen- and fifteen-year-olds who had finished the elementary grades entered the freshman classes in high schools.

High schools, faced with a comprehensive range of student interests and abilities, were required to become "comprehensive" in their curricular offerings. The first response to this demand was to develop a range of "elective" subjects in addition to the traditional liberal arts courses. The diversity of individuals was to be matched by a well-nigh chaotic diversity of curricular offerings. Those students who were not preparing to enter college were permitted and encouraged to enroll in these electives, often to the exclusion of liberal arts courses.

Only small budgets and small school populations kept Indiana from following the practice in some states of developing specialized —"academic" and "vocational"—high schools based on the assumption that the "vocational" school could not also perform the "academic" function. This led to a tendency toward dual school systems with a segregation of pupil population based upon the European concept of high school education as both a class privilege and a vocational function. There was also a widespread feeling that the "academic" school could not offer instruction in the "vocational" courses because of limitations of staff background and facilities. Any separatist tendencies in the task of secondary education-for-all began to wane in Indiana in the last few decades. Indiana high schools tended to incorporate as much vocational teaching as possible. The remainder of this task was assigned to apprenticeship programs, beyond-the-high-school trade-training programs, and independent training programs often under nonpublic school sponsorship.

Our state, in response to a number of influences, has now developed the educational philosophy that the secondary school is neither vocational nor class conscious in its primary objectives. Its chief function, and the one which is to be shared by all of its students, is not a preparation for college but the provision of liberal education. Neither starting nor ending at the stage of formal schooling, liberal education has become the primary goal. There are "educational primitives" who still attempt to establish dual school systems which deny the need for any common educational experiences at the high school level. There are stereotyped reactions that violently oppose any reminders of "culture" and rationalize these prejudices by extolling "work" and the "use of the hands" as if these were dissociated from intellectual activity and from the elite of society. These dissenters are more vocal than numerous, although they are occasionally in the centers of decision-making on educational policy.

Despite these reactions, the prevailing, though often inarticulate, trend is toward "comprehensive" high schools. Accepting the complete gamut of individual differences found among the young people in the community, the comprehensive high school teaches a common core of essential educational experiences to all students and extends beyond this core with a variety of educational programs corresponding to the varieties of pupil interests and abilities. This common core is found in liberal education. Although it has sometimes been confused with a traditional college-preparatory curriculum or has been described very vaguely, liberal education does have a fairly precise meaning expressed in the answers to two questions: "What kind of education helps a man during his non-working hours?" "What kind of education helps a man make wise political choices?"

The alternative of "work" in the use of our waking hours is not a "leisure" devoted to a "recreation" that turns out to be mindless distraction. The alternative is "re-creation" or an opportunity to examine the unique concerns of man and to use his uniquely human qualities. Most "work" unfortunately affords little opportunity for these pursuits. As the average hours of work per week diminish, all of us are being given the time for the kind of recreation that can provide value-seeking and creative activities. This is a revolution which we have not yet fully comprehended. Liberal education must always be directed toward preparing men for this kind of leisure.

Liberal education must also prepare men to make wise political choices, and this function extends beyond the elementary school objective of "citizenship," which is often confined to various aspects of law-abiding behavior and patriotism. American civilization has produced a need for a citizen who can go beyond obedience and patriotism to political decision-making. This need has been emphasized by the expansion of the suffrage, our political contests which represent choices among the many interpretations and applications of commonly held ideals and loyalties, the increasingly complex social order, and the inevitable major intertwining of government into every facet of American life.

This need necessarily requires that the secondary school provide a liberal education to all youth while they are still compelled to attend school. Hence, the reappearance of a non-vocational liberal education that has become the general required core of learning experiences for all high school students. The subjects labeled English, science, mathematics, history, and the arts can contain the understandings and skills that promote a liberal education. Going beyond the mechanisms of team teaching, programmed learning, closed-circuit TV, nongraded classrooms, etc., into reorganization of content (such as in "modern math"), the curriculum revolutions are making these subject areas the effective sources of a sound liberal education. It includes the study of the social organization, ideologies, beliefs, and heritage of our culture; the significant value-systems, and the methods of determining and applying values; the various "strategies of inquiry" by which men seek truth and understanding, that is, scientific methods, social analysis, logic; the use and understanding of the principal means of communication among men, such as verbal, musical, mathematical, artistic, etc.; and the abstractions and generalizations that represent intellectual activity.

When general education was extended to the all-inclusive secondary school, not only was the curriculum revised but the necessity for an organized guidance program in the schools became apparent. At first, these programs emphasized vocational information and were limited to the non-college-bound student, but when colleges began to vary their curricula, they were extended to provide information for the college-bound. The most recent development has been the creation of general guidance programs. The State Department of Public Instruction now requires that each high school have a ratio of students to counselors that will permit the individual counseling of each student. Elaborate testing and record-keeping systems have ben developed to provide the information about each student that a professional counselor needs. Special services (social work, psychological therapy, etc.) have become accepted parts of the guidance systems in the high schools.

In the past the rigidity of the compulsory attendance laws obscured the need for such guidance programs at the elementary school level, since the enforced continued presence of each child concealed the possibility that he was not really absorbing the general education set before him. The high schools were affected by the expiration of compulsory attendance midway through the average student's career. The large number of dropouts dramatized the failures of the school program. When we finally recognized that it was imperative for all children to receive the full four-year program of general education in the high school, we could no longer be complacent about dropouts nor identify them as the inevitable rejects of a selective system. Retention of all children in high school until graduation depends upon the development of a meaningful and effective education. Such a mass educational system demands individualization of instruction in order to understand each child. It does not mandate a tutorial system, but it does require the specific information provided by a good guidance system and the special professional skills that are the outgrowth of the new curricula. This is the challenge of general liberal education that is rapidly being met in the school systems of Indiana.

The philosophical basis of vocational education stems from the assumption that there are two distinct kinds of students—those with a mechanical or technical orientation and those with a professional or intellectual orientation. Believers in this dualism accept this differentiation as inescapable. The contrary viewpoint recognizes that there are natural inequalities among persons but stresses that they are quantitative, not qualitative. All human beings have approximately the same qualities of intellectual powers but the quantity of their productivity will vary. Children of more or less ability should be expected to acquire different amounts of the same kind of education. Many educators point out that the usual vocational education, or "job training," is both undemocratic and unjust and represents a threat to democratic educational practices, because it tends to prepare the job-trained individual only for his technological requirements but not for his social responsibilities. Any scheme for vocational education that limits itself to the current technology may become a futile example of social predetermination. It must not perpetuate past distinctions but instead prepare youth for the potentials of the future in a democratic industrial system.

The path of vocational education in Indiana might be indicated by three signposts: apprenticeship programs, simulated programs within the schools, and general education. As in other parts of the country, the craft unions in Indiana first had the task of preparing young people in their areas of work, and most work skills were obtained through an apprenticeship either within the family or upon the job. This system began to decline with the increasing variability of occupations and the appearance of work skills in the industrial world which did not require long periods of observation and practice under the supervision of master craftsmen. The new altruistic child-labor laws also caused the withdrawal of competitive child labor from the labor market.

At the present time vocational education is influenced by the primary importance of general education and the effects of automation. Specific skill-training courses are still found in regular high school programs, but we now realize that we cannot teach a replica of all occupations in the curriculum. Vocational educators are beginning to emphasize training in those skills and attitudes that are most broadly representative of several occupational areas and to try to identify areas in which rapid changes are least likely to occur. One example of the effects of rapid change was the installation of courses in key-punch operation in high schools at the time that data-processing centers were beginning to develop new procedures that eliminated key-punching from the sequence of essential skills. Most people will work in four or five occupational areas within their lifetimes. Programs in vocational education must emphasize those essential skills which can be found in all job areas regardless of the shifts to different occupational groups. These skills include the understanding of the basic physical properties of motors, the basic requirements found in service and distributive occupations, some manual training, and such necessary attitudes toward work as cooperation, integrity, and punctuality.

Alongside these programs in high schools there are separate organizations, institutions, schools, and regional centers where more extensive training in specific skills can be obtained. The financial support of the federal government has enhanced these separate programs as have the specific pressures brought to bear in many localities for certain kinds of workers. These skill-training programs will be concentrated on post-high school and adult retraining; consequently, they will disappear from the secondary school.

Another area of great activity in vocational education is in the three accredited work-experience programs—distributive education, diversified cooperative education, and office experiences—which provide young people, while attending school, with paid and supervised work experiences in the basic skills and attitudes needed in specific areas. The programs in exploratory teaching, library experiences, and other work experiences for students during school time contain some of these elements. These work assignments do not compete with the regular programs or divert children away from the general education programs of the high school. In the future, combinations of these various programs are likely to prove to be among the most fruitful sources of vocational education, since the advantages of the apprenticeship program will be combined with the pattern of general education in the schools. Not only do these programs emphasize the general skills, understandings, and attitudes that are found in various occupations, but they also provide realistic experiences that cannot be duplicated within any high school building.

Racial integration in the public schools obviously concerns the education of Negroes. Other ethnic groups and social classes might be considered, but this is the crucial problem that public policy must solve. The nature of the original educational programs for Negroes in Indiana can be represented by two specific instances:

A private seminary known as the Union Literary Institute was established by abolitionists in 1846 for Negroes and was long known as "Nigger College." It had an interracial board of directors, but its student body was all Negro, although its charter asserted that it was open to all without distinctions of race, color, rank, or wealth. The Literary Institute differed from all contemporary seminaries in that it stressed student labor as an essential part of its curricular program rather than academic education. This emphasis was found only in a seminary committed exclusively to the education of Negroes.

One hundred years ago there was not an elementary school in Indianapolis for the Negroes who had just been freed from slavery. Therefore the Disciples of Christ, a religious denomination, decided to provide education for some of the Negroes who, by the accident of war or the aftermath of previous conditions, were living in the center of Indianapolis. The church established a small private seminary in a residence that was turned into a one-room schoolhouse for Negroes from ages six to twenty-three. It was located on the grounds that later were purchased for the construction of the first public elementary school in Indianapolis for the instruction of Negro children.

Legal regulations enacted in the middle of the nineteenth century made it clear that the state felt no obligation for the public education of Negroes. The justification for this attitude recorded by one committee is worthy of being quoted: "It is better that no privilege be extended to them [the Negroes], the tendency of which might be to induce a vain belief that the prejudices of the dominant race could ever be so modified as to break down the rugged barriers that must forever exist between their social relations."

By 1866, however, the school examiners in Indiana urged that the requirements and the benefits of the public school system be extended to Negroes. On May 13, 1869, the General Assembly enacted a common school tax to provide funds for the education of "the colored children of this state." The schools were to be separate from those for white children, however. In 1877 permissive integration was allowed in those school corporations that were unable to provide separate facilities.

The practices in educating Negroes in Indiana can be characterized (not too uniquely) as being those of segregation, discrimination, and second-class educational goals. They stemmed partly from the "border-state" atmosphere in Indiana during the Civil

War era. The term "integration" represents a reversal of all three of these practices and has been fully acknowledged by only a small number of people.

The struggle against segregation in Indiana public schools was climaxed with the passage of the law in 1949 that forbade the deliberate practice of segregation in the assignment of pupils or staff to specific schools or classes. Within the allowed seven-year period following this law, Indiana abandoned the deliberate separation of Negroes in schools. This process was accelerated by the impact of the Supreme Court decision against school segregation in 1954.

Prior to 1949 in Indianapolis, for example, 98 percent of the Negro school population was concentrated in eight elementary schools and one high school. The high school (Crispus Attucks) was opened in 1927 by the action of a Ku-Klux-Klan-dominated board intent upon extending school segregation practices up through the high school level. Practices of segregation extended into the publicly supported colleges and universities of Indiana through implied quotas, restrictions to certain curricula, nonavailability to Negroes of campus housing and boarding privileges, rigid segregation in social activities, and irrational restrictions in certain sports and co-curricular activities. Such practices in the higher educational institutions and in the few white elementary and secondary schools that had some Negro enrollment helped to erect rigid walls around the Negroes and made an anomaly out of their physical presence with whites in a common building or on one campus.

The implementation of the 1949 law required an abandonment of the obvious assignments of pupils by color. It called for the "soft pedaling" of the assumption that Negro teachers could only be assigned to predominantly Negro classrooms. The statistical result in Indianapolis in fifteen years has been a change from eight all-Negro elementary schools to eighteen elementary schools that are 90 percent or more Negro, and from one all-Negro high school to one all-Negro and one 75-percent-Negro high school. This is a numerically discouraging result that is everywhere labeled as "de facto" segregation. The primary, though not exclusive, cause of this social frustration of legally established public policy is the continuation of the housing segregation which affects the neighborhood district policy of pupil assignment.

The neighborhood school system is an example of social engineering. The "neighborhood" itself is the result of the arbitrary delimitation of boundaries which may be defined honestly, but they are not inevitable or irreplaceable. The capacity of a projected school building or the line of a public transportation facility can alter a seemingly obvious decision about the boundaries of a school district. Decisions about the relative importance of these various factors may be made publicly and consistently, but they are arbitrary decisions. There is no *natural* school district. The argument is a specious one that professes adherence to the spirit of the 1949 law but at the same time claims an inability to stop the "natural" effects of the neighborhood system. Segregation *in fact* continues in the public school systems of Indianapolis and most of Indiana. The increasing mixture of staff and students does not negate the hard fact that actually segregated school buildings have increased.

The processes of discrimination were most evident in the legally segregated systems of the pre-1949 era. Facilities and class sizes were the most glaring evidences of the discriminatory treatment of Negro schools. The post-1949 attempts at special schools have shown the beginnings of a process that is full-blown in other states. "Special" schools become predominantly Negro schools with deficiencies in facilities and services. The "inner-city" schools tend to show the same racial predominance and the same glaring discrepancy from the norms in facilities and services. There are few examples of inner-city schools which are equal, and none that are superior, in facilities and services to suburban schools. One liberal observer in 1963 looked at an $8 million suburban high school plant in Marion County and at the then totally decrepit all-Negro inner-city Crispus Attucks High School. He expressed his indignation, not from envy or dislike of the suburban school, but from a disbelief in the incredible social immorality and political stupidity that could tolerate the simultaneous existence of such wide differences in facilities in the same county. Until inequalities are abolished, or are occasionally found to favor the predominantly Negro school, discrimination will still proclaim its undeniable presence in the public school education of Negroes. Inequalities will exist so long as there is segregation in the schools.

The third practice in the education of Negroes in Indiana—second-class educational goals—is even more insidious and widespread. Many social pressures have made it impossible for the bigot openly to bar Negroes from any level or branch of education. There are many, however, who share some version of John Calhoun's confidence that no Negro could learn Greek. Sometimes this bigotry is disguised under positive assertions that Negroes have a monopoly of excellence in certain fields, such as vocal music, religion, track, basketball, popular entertainment, etc. The prejudiced nature of these purported acknowledgments of Negro superiority in a particular field is illustrated by the bland statement in an Indianapolis newspaper during World War II that Negro soldiers had shown superior endurance to the travails of jungle warfare and also, incidentally, to the rigors of the Arctic. Whether clothed in negative or positive statements, these allegations about an entire group are unfounded and illogical. The most pervasive assertion of all, despite a flood of research to the contrary, is that the Negro has a lower and narrower intelligence than the white man. The basic error in these statements is the assumption that "Negroes" are a "kind" of people, identified by a skin coloration (that actually runs the gamut of pigmentations), for whom some common characteristics can be identified. An assertion that all Negroes can sing is as repugnant and false as an assertion that all Negroes are of low intelligence. An examination of these statements reveals one peculiar consistency in educational practice; they are always justifications for second-grade instruction.

The elimination of bigoted practices rests upon the realization by policy-makers and teachers that there are no homogeneous social groups. If all Negroes and whites were lined up according to measured amounts of any criterion (I.Q., achievement, personality, musical aptitude, manual dexterity, abstractive qualities, criminality, courage, etc.), the people labeled Negro would be scattered among the whites from one end of the continuum to the other. A good device for detecting the often subtle practices of discrimination is to plot the distribution of Negro students by any criterion—I.Q., achievement scores, teacher grades, aptitudes, occupational interests, or participation charts—being measured in the school population. If the distribution curve of the Negro students is significantly different from that of the white students, the observer is seeing the symptoms of discriminatory practices. Some of these practices may stem from nonschool sources, but they, along with the ones that can be attributed directly to the school, should be examined to determine how the school can mitigate their effects. Any random sampling or distribution study of large groups should reveal that Negro characteristics are as normal as those of whites. This dictum is rarely stated and even more rarely accepted.

The education of Negroes in Indiana must be in an integrated situation for the benefit of the Negro and the white child. Both will live in a world that will be integrated in the final acknowledgment of the richness of human brotherhood or fused in the nuclear explosions of doggedly held hatreds. The integrative process requires the elimination of segregation, discrimination, and second-class expectations from the instructional programs for Negroes, and for other minority groups.

All citizens need to be informed of the historical development of our educational programs. All citizens need to be convinced that all children, regardless of presumed social or academic characteristics, must be able to experience general, vocational, and integrated education in the public schools. Secondary schools must be organized as comprehensive high schools, and they must use the best-developed professional skills to teach children who have all kinds of academic abilities and interests. The greatest loss suffered by "the culturally deprived" is their meager participation in the worlds of experience revealed in English, mathematics, science, social studies, history, and the arts. The schools that enroll any of these young people must be equipped to provide the intensive programs needed to counteract their deficiencies.

Vocational education must be placed in a proper perspective in relation to general education and be directed toward work-experience programs. It must be relieved of any class or racial implications and recognized as a part, but not all, of the educational experience for all young people.

Integrated education must be recognized as an urgent necessity for black and white children and not just as a desirable experience. The schools have a responsibility to provide this kind of education regardless of the obstacles of the present social situations. The greatest obstacle to the desegregation of schools is found in segregated housing practices. These practices may be destroyed legally in the next decade, but the schools should not wait for this eventuality. The pupil assignment system based upon the neighborhood school district concept will have to be replaced by a system of assignment not subject to this pressure. The public must combat the subtler evidences of segregation, discrimination, and second-class practices in the education of Negroes. The public must accept the fact that integrated education is a pedagogical necessity and a moral obligation.

These, then, are some of the unfinished tasks in education that this sesquicentennial celebration, with its focus on the past and the promise of the future, has revealed to us. Caleb Mills challenged not only his contemporaries but also the inheritors of his zeal and vision when he said: "Let every pious man and good citizen give his countenance, patronage, and influence to the enterprise of elevating common schools to the highest point of improvement and then they will be good enough *for everyone* and prove rich blessings *to all.*"

ELVIS J. STAHR

Higher Education

Indiana's educational history began before Indiana became a state, even before the Indiana Territory was carved from a large land area of the Midwest. The far-seeing members of the Congress of the Confederation wrote into the Northwest Ordinance of 1787 a then novel provision, intended to ensure educational opportunity for all who made their homes in the Northwest Territory. The Ordinance declared: "Religion, morality, and knowledge being necessary to good government and the happiness of mankind, schools and the means of education shall be forever encouraged." In subsequent years various Acts of Congress began to give substance to the intent of the Ordinance's authors with provision in 1804 that a township be reserved from sale for the use of a seminary of learning and with a stipulation in the Enabling Act of April 1816, which provided for the admission of Indiana as a State of the Union, that an additional township be reserved "for the use of a seminary of learning to be appropriated solely to the use of such seminary" by the legislature of the State.

A native of Kentucky, Elvis J. Stahr graduated from the University of Kentucky, going on to Oxford University to study law as a Rhodes Scholar. After serving as an infantry officer in World War II, he was made dean of the University of Kentucky College of Law and later became Provost of Kentucky. The University of Pittsburgh named him Vice Chancellor in 1957;

It remained for the framers of Indiana's first Constitution to incorporate a specific commitment to educational opportunity, a duty which they performed so admirably that their words are still quoted far beyond the borders of the state. They wrote: It shall be the duty of the general assembly, as soon as circumstances will permit, to provide by law for a general system of education, ascending in a regular gradation from township schools to a State university, wherein tuition shall be gratis and equally open to all." One hundred fifty years later it is difficult to realize that the circumstances which would permit carrying out such a directive were far off—that in 1816 not only the wilderness but also the preoccupations of the majority of the pioneers had to be conquered before a graduated system of education through the university level could be established. Relatively few years had gone by since George Rogers Clark had wrested Fort Sackville at Vincennes from the British for the Virginia government which had sponsored his expedition. In the decades following Virginia's cession of this area in 1784 to the government of the American Confederation, the settlers who came down the Ohio and up from Kentucky faced the exigencies of clearing land, fighting Indians, and securing the essentials of existence. The entire family was pressed into this struggle, its sights set on a home and the simple life of a settlement.

Yet some of the pioneers, particularly those who came to the Midwest with a religious mission, were determined that minds as well as bodies should be nurtured during the development of the new territory. Eight years before Indiana gained its Statehood, a

---

in January 1959 he became President of West Virginia University; and in January 1961 he was selected by the late President John F. Kennedy as the Secretary of the Army, serving until he became the twelfth President of Indiana University in July 1962. He has assumed numerous important responsibilities in educational organizations at the state, regional, and national levels. Currently, he is serving as chairman of the Commission on Federal Relations of the American Council on Education, as a member of the executive committees of the National Association of State Universities and Land-Grant Colleges and of the Institute for Services to Education, as a trustee of the Argonne Universities Association and of the Committee for Economic Development (CED), and in June 1966 was named to a three-year term on the board of directors of the Council for Financial Aid to Education.

Presbyterian minister by the name of Samuel Scott founded a private school in what was then the governmental seat of the Indiana Territory, Vincennes. His school became the nucleus of the first public institution in the Territory when two years later Vincennes University was founded in accordance with provisions of the Indiana Territory Act of 1806, which authorized the incorporation of an institution "to be called and known by the name or style of the Vincennes University" and, for its support, granted to a board of trustees the disposition of the seminary funds in Gibson County reserved by the Congressional Act of 1804. Governor William Henry Harrison, later ninth President of the United States, was the first president of the board of trustees of the Territorial university at Vincennes and he along with the Reverend Mr. Scott was largely responsible for the full activation of the University in 1810, the second university to open in the Northwest Territory.* Neglect of the institution by both its trustees and the legislative authorities caused its progressive decline in the next 15 years, until in 1825 it was converted into a seminary, an action later declared illegal. Meanwhile the State Seminary at Bloomington, established by action of the General Assembly under date of January 20, 1820, pursuant to the first State Constitution, began to draw to it some of the backing and funds that its struggling predecessor in Vincennes had lacked. In 1822 the land reserved for the support of Vincennes University was confiscated by the State for the support of Indiana Seminary, and although restitution was made eventually, other factors operated to promote the eventual emergence of the seminary in Bloomington as *the* State University.

Meanwhile, a number of county seminaries and academies established by towns, cities, and religious denominations had developed into institutions of higher education. A grammar school founded in 1827 at the request of the Presbytery of Salem was chartered as Hanover Academy in the following year and five

---

* The Ohio University at Athens had been founded by the Territorial legislature of Ohio January 9, 1802.

years later became Hanover College.* In this same year of 1833 a convention of nine Presbyterians, five of whom were ministers, founded a college which combined with the Crawfordsville Teachers' Seminary (opened in 1830) to gain a charter in 1834 as "Wabash Manual-Labor College and Teachers' Seminary," finally assuming the name Wabash College in 1851.** The Indiana Baptist Manual Labor Institute (1836) developed into Franklin College in 1844. Between 1816 and 1850 24 county seminaries and 37 private academies or seminaries were incorporated. The genesis of these preparatory schools belongs to another chapter of Indiana education. What presently concerns us is the variety of forms in which higher education became available to Hoosier citizens between the time of the founding of the first two public universities and the turn of the century. It took almost 50 years for another state university to come into existence and meanwhile the "college movement" had hit Indiana.

The impetus for establishing all of the early private institutions was religious. Ministers and missionaries, like the Pilgrim Fathers, wished "to advance learning and perpetuate it to posterity, dreading to leave an illiterate ministry to the churches after our present ministry shall be in the dust." That an "illiterate ministry" might well be their bequeathal unless education could be provided was evident from the more than 82 percent of school-age children who were not attending school, from the one seventh of the adult population which was illiterate, and from the ranking of the state in lowest place among the free states in "popular intelligence and means of popular education," according to Dr. Joseph Tuttle, President of Wabash College from 1862 until 1891. The principal obstacles which higher education faced during these years were

* Sources disagree on the dates of founding of several Indiana colleges and universities. Most of the dates cited in this chapter agree with those which appear in *American Universities and Colleges*, Allen W. Cartter, ed., American Council on Education, 9th ed., 1964.

** Students literally built their classrooms and performed the routine chores of maintenance in part payment of their educational expenses at these manual labor institutions.

poverty and indifference on the part of the populace and bitter sectarianism among the supporters of higher education. By 1850, Hanover, Wabash, Franklin, DePauw (Indiana Asbury University, 1838), Concordia (1839), St. Mary-of-the-Woods College (1846), the University of Notre Dame (1843), Taylor University (Fort Wayne Female College, 1846), and Earlham College (Friends Boarding School, 1847) were engaged in instructing students. In the next quarter century Evansville College (Moores Hill Male and Female Institute, 1854), Butler University (North Western Christian University, 1855), St. Mary's College (St. Mary's Academy, founded in 1844 in Michigan, moved to Notre Dame in 1855), Valparaiso University (Valparaiso Male and Female Academy, 1859), and St. Meinrad College (Saint Meinrad Seminary, 1861) had opened their doors. Of these, four were founded by Orders of the Roman Catholic faith, four by Methodist Congregations, two by Presbyterians, and one each by the Baptist, Disciples of Christ, Lutheran, and Society of Friends persuasions. Other denominations which built colleges in Indiana before 1900 included the Mennonites, the Church of the Brethren, and the United Brethren. Among the institutions that had their start in the period from 1875 to 1900 were Tri-State College (1884), Oakland City College (1885), Manchester College (1889), Saint Joseph's College (1889), Saint Francis College (1890), Goshen College (1894), and Huntington College (1897).

Many of these church-established schools prospered while others were slowed by factionalism and misfortune. Indiana Asbury University (DePauw) and the University of Notre Dame attracted large student bodies including some students from outside the United States. Several institutions survived disastrous fires. Hanover College split into two schools and Franklin College was twice forced to suspend its operation. Still the experiences of these schools differed little from those of the public institutions, which also had their religious controversies and their crippling setbacks from fires, and they supplied educational opportunity to hundreds of young Hoosiers in their regions and to out-of-state students as well.

Meanwhile the two State universities had grown unequally. Vincennes University, permitted to languish for 15 years and then converted into the Knox County Seminary, opened again for university instruction in 1853 after recovery of its land endowment through successful litigation against the State. By this time the establishment of other colleges, the removal of the seat of government to Corydon and then to Indianapolis, and expansion of the frontiers farther and farther north had withdrawn from Vincennes and its University the vitality of its earlier years. Although Vincennes University was later described as a "vigorous academic school," its instruction was thereafter confined principally to the first and second collegiate years. The Indiana Seminary, however, which had been authorized in 1820 and opened to students in 1824, grew despite a catastrophic fire, a "faculty war" so intense that the board gave the college up for dead and did not meet again for two years, a prolonged attack upon Eastern academic imports, and an equally long period of sectarian intrigue. Then in 1869 and 1870 two more institutions were added to the State system of higher education.

The Morrill Act, passed by Congress in 1862, granted lands to each state for the establishment and support of colleges with the specific assignment of teaching the agricultural and mechanic arts and military tactics. The State of Indiana accepted its grant in 1865, and subsequent gifts of land and money determined the location of the institution at West Lafayette and its 1869 chartering as Purdue University in honor of a substantial donor. Of course, the choice of a site north of Indianapolis reflected the by then sizable population growth in that area. Various delays postponed the opening of the University until 1874.

Prior to the State's acceptance of the Morrill Act grant, the General Assembly had enacted a law in 1864 establishing a State Normal School for the "preparation of teachers for teaching in the common schools of Indiana." The city of Terre Haute gave lands and funds toward the establishment there of the Indiana State Normal College, which opened in 1870. Two unusual features of the Normal College had their origin in its function: From the first the College was coeducational; and its students were asked "to teach, if practicable, in the common schools of Indiana for a period equal to twice that spent as students in the school." Since 1965, it has been Indiana State University.

By these two State additions to the higher educational system Indiana's young citizens were at last enabled to obtain preparation in most of the fields needed for the pursuit of their careers. Until the opening of Purdue, technical training had been available only through the engineering departments of some of the private colleges and in the College of Engineering of the University of Notre Dame. The incorporation of the Terre Haute School of Industrial Science in 1874 marked the first instance within the state of a private school planned for the sole purpose of providing education and training in the mechanical and engineering professions. The school was the realization of a dream long held by a Terre Haute citizen, Chauncey Rose, whose energies and munificence in this cause were given permanent recognition by the renaming of the school Rose Polytechnic Institute (1875).

There had also been an urgent demand for the training of teachers. Most of the college graduates had sought teaching positions in the seminaries and academies, and the common schools were thus left to the instructional mercies of the untrained. What these "mercies" could be the historian James A Woodburn recorded only too vividly: "It has not been two decades since men applied for positions at the teacher's desk in Indiana who thought the 'metropolis of Illinois was corn, wheat, and rye,' and that Shakespeare and Virgil were American poets." A number of independent normal schools came into existence as a result of this situation, with arrangements designed to accommodate the multiple needs of teachers temporarily away from the classroom. Students were admitted for any period of time at any period of the year and they were free to choose their courses as they wished. These schools served a useful function at a time when a little teacher education was less dangerous than none. The emergency nature of the undertaking ensured substantial though fluctuating enrollments in the normal schools. The Valparaiso Normal School, for instance, which opened in 1873, boasted an attendance of 4,000 by 1888, making it the largest normal school in the United States. The Central Normal College and Commercial Institute, established at Ladoga in 1876 but moved two years later to Danville, had an annual enrollment of nearly 1,000 by the end of ten years of operation. A somewhat smaller school, The Southern Indiana Normal College and Practical Business Institute, was founded at Mitchell in 1880. In addition, many of the counties began offering a "summer normal" and the county superintendents performed yeoman's service in their conduct of the compulsory county institutes to supplement teachers' training; yet, by the end of the century the majority of teachers were still not college graduates.

This, then, was the state of higher education at the beginning of our present century. Institutions of various kinds and sizes were accessible to the young people of Indiana, relatively few of whom were able or motivated to attend them. Educational, religious, governmental, and community leaders had produced this opportunity through ingenious financial planning which included, besides the gift of public lands, the sale of stock, assessment of the members of a religious sect, private philanthropy, a public lottery, the sale of "perpetual" scholarships, fund drives, and, in the case of public institutions, taxation. Most of the colleges and universities taught the classical languages and literatures, English language and literature, French, German, chemistry, physics, and philosophy. Music and art were frequently offered in the denominational schools as was mental and moral philosophy. A course in law was available at three of the denominational colleges, two of the normal schools, and at Indiana University. Purdue introduced agriculture, veterinary science, and pharmacy while Indiana University, along with the normal schools, provided training in pedagogics. Engineering was among the curricula of several denominational and normal colleges and universities, Purdue and Rose Polytechnic. It was even possible to elect courses in business education and preparatory classes in medicine. Just how broad and deep these studies were varied with the institutions, as it does today, but the range of subjects assured some possibility of individual preference for specialized or general education.

A word should be said about the education of women. There

were several female seminaries, the earliest of which seems to have been Monroe County Female Seminary (1833). Butler University appears to have been the first institution in the state to open on a coeducational basis (1850), followed soon after by Earlham in 1859. Soon after its founding, Franklin College admitted women students. Vincennes University had established a department for women in 1856 which was later incorporated into the University (1870), the same year that a coeducational Indiana State Normal College began instruction. Meanwhile, Indiana and DePauw universities opened their doors to women in 1867; Hartsville University admitted women at about the same time, and Purdue University was coeducational from its beginning. Often only one or two young ladies braved a masculine stronghold of the "higher learning" for the first few years, unless commercial or pedagogic courses were available. Nonetheless, the principle of coeducation was well established in Indiana at the dawning of the twentieth century.

Now, in the sixty-seventh year of the new century, as the state reflects on her history from the vantage of her sesquicentennial year, the educational progress of her first five or six decades under conditions exceptionally adverse seems remarkable and suggests comparison with developments in these recent decades when the climate of education has been favorable. In contrast to the low state of literacy 60 years before the beginning of the twentieth century, the situation 60-odd years into the 1900's is almost reversed. Attendance at public schools is mandatory for young Hoosiers up to age 16, except under unusual circumstances, and 95 percent of the teachers are college graduates. As a consequence, the literacy rate is now approximately 99 percent.

And what of the colleges and universities founded during those early years of Indiana's history? The survival rate has been striking. A few of the denominational colleges have succumbed; the independent normal schools have been vulnerable; but in general changes have not been in the direction of disappearance so much as of combination or of operation under different auspices. Student enrollments and faculty staffs have grown and the quality of both has improved.

Meanwhile, although the pace of establishment slackened, new institutions continued to appear on the scene. The fourth State college, at first simply a branch of Indiana State Normal College, extended the State system to its eastern section. Ball State Teachers College (Ball State University since 1965) was the Eastern Division of the Normal College from 1913 to 1929. It then became an independent unit, concentrating on the preparation of teachers. Other additions since 1900 include Indiana Central College (1902), Fort Wayne Bible College (1904), St. Benedict College (1914), Anderson College (Anderson Bible Training School, 1917), Marion College (1920), Fort Wayne Art School (1921), Indiana Institute of Technology (Indiana Technical College, 1930), Marian College (an outgrowth of St. Francis Normal School, founded in 1853, 1937), Bethel College (1947), Grace College (1943), and Christian Theological Seminary (1952). Side by side with these developments has come the establishment of regional campuses by Indiana, Purdue, and, recently, Indiana State universities. Beginning with an Indiana University Extension Center established in Indianapolis in 1916, branches of State universities are now to be found in most of the state's larger cities, as will be noted later. And mention should be made of the developing plans of Indiana and Purdue universities to bring together the various Indianapolis programs of both institutions to form a large educational complex adjacent to and including the big I. U. Medical Center.

The present healthy state of higher education in Indiana could easily be attributed in such a summary view as these pages present to an overriding concern for education among the state's leaders and citizenry, but such an impression misrepresents the struggles that have preceded every advance and the continuing necessity to remind each generation of its obligation to maintain and improve upon its educational heritage.

What encouragement and support Indiana's private citizens and public representatives have given has required the leadership of able educators, whose successors are now confronted with a situation that is at once encouraging and crucial: the dramatic increase of the teen-age population; the growing belief that college education is essential for later optimum employment in this Age of Science and Technology; and the re-emergence of the federal government as the important source of funds for higher education, which it had been initially in the establishment of Vincennes, Indiana, and Purdue universities. The surge of students seeking admission has pushed the capacities of the private institutions and forced major expansion of the public universities; and the impact of federal funds increasingly affects facilities, teaching, scholarships, equipment, research, and areas of program development.

The enrollment picture in Indiana for the 1965-66 academic year contrasts dramatically with the sparse attendance of the mid-nineteenth century. The student population (of which little more than a third is female) in Indiana's thirty accredited and seven additional colleges and universities places it ninth among states in the nation. It is worthy of notice that none of the top eight states has less than eighty institutions. Yet less than 50 percent of Indiana's high school graduates entered college in 1963, and of all Indiana students attending college, more than 16 percent went to out-of-state campuses. About 62 percent of the undergraduate students who enrolled in Indiana schools last fall were at State institutions, in contrast to the situation several years before when the majority of such students were in the private colleges and universities. The shift came about with the somewhat greater expansion of the faculties and facilities of the State institutions, including their development of regional campuses, in response to demands for greater and more widespread opportunities. The State institutions have long enrolled more graduate students than the private universities; at present 81 percent of the students taking graduate work in Indiana are at the State universities.

It should be a source of pride to Indiana citizens that their state is one of the few of the top ten which are not educational debtor states; that is, in the exchange of students fewer Hoosiers are educated in other states than the number of their counterparts who are attracted to Indiana institutions. Part of this "balance of trade" reflects the out-of-state undergraduate enrollments of regional or national and church-related private institutions and the graduate enrollments of both the private and public universities; part is the result of the influx of students from bordering states, particularly Illinois. These nonresident students constitute a sizable economic asset, not only bringing considerable income to the state while they are in college* but also furnishing much of the out-of-state support after they have graduated. Additionally, they introduce a desirable cosmopolitan element into Hoosier student bodies with their differing backgrounds, experiences, and orientation. When out-of-state young men and women choose Indiana campuses for their collegiate education and are in turn chosen by Indiana colleges and universities through their selective admission practices, it means an import of above-average students to the halls of our Hoosier institutions.

Indiana's ability to handle the massive enrollments of college students in the postwar years has been due in no small part to the instrument of cooperation among the public and private institutions which had been forged in 1944. At that time, as the result of a conference called by the Post-War Planning Committee, the Indiana Conference of Higher Education was founded voluntarily by 33 privately supported, church-related or state-sustained colleges and universities of Indiana. Developed to deal with the problems attendant upon the assimilation of veterans seeking to realize the educational benefits of the G. I. Bill after their service during World War II, the Conference has sponsored studies, resolved conflicts, and participated in planning among its members, all with a view to assuring the accessibility of college education to the maximum number of Hoosier youth—an accessibility that combines the level of education an individual desires with the kind of institutional orientation (e.g., small or large, male or coeducational, liberal arts or multiple-programmed) that he seeks.

In 1960 the Conference adopted The Indiana Plan which made explicit not only this objective of accessibility but also such additional aims as maintenance of a balance in main-campus under-

---

* A prominent Arizona banker recently estimated that each student enrolled in a college contributes about $3,000 per year to the area in which the institution is located.

graduate enrollments between the private and public institutions, utilization of existing facilities before new ones are encouraged, minimizing of destructive competition between institutions or groups of institutions, and promotion of the effective use of both the tax and the privately donated dollar. During its existence the Conference has grown to 37 members and has established wide areas of mutual trust.

Other circumstances have contributed to the spirit of cooperation among Indiana's public and private institutions. With the student demand so large, the active institutional rivalry of the Depression years for the limited numbers who planned to enter college has relaxed. Similarly, the contest for financial support is less intense. Among the State institutions a formula for a joint legislative request, mandated by the General Assembly, has eliminated a great deal of the special-pleading and divisiveness that previously had attended each school's endeavor to satisfy the needs of its own budget.

In another distinctive venture of cooperation some of the private colleges and universities banded together to form the Associated Colleges of Indiana.* They hoped by combining to strengthen the appeal of their individual members for financial support. The Association, first of its kind in the country, has achieved many of its initial objectives and is now expanding its outlook to embrace joint endeavor beyond financial support.

Meanwhile enrollments, which now increase by the thousands annually, have boosted the operating costs of the public institutions and their requirements for capital funding. The amounts requested of the legislature for support have risen proportionately, but the need to advance programs and meet the national competition for faculty has forced the public institutions into broadening the base of their financial support through stepped-up alumni solicitation and active seeking of foundation and federal grants and private gifts. The experience of recent years seems to prove that the efforts

* Anderson College, DePauw University, Earlham College, Evansville College, Franklin College, Goshen College, Hanover College, Indiana Central College, Manchester College, Rose Polytechnic Institute, St. Joseph's College, Valparaiso University, and Wabash College.

of private and public universities, rather than competing for the same private monies, result in enlisting more donors in the total educational cause. The Council for Financial Aid to Education reported a ten-year national increase by 1963-64 of 214.8 percent in gifts to higher education. Evidence of this kind explodes the myth of the limited philanthropic dollar. The private institutions continue to gain support for their basic needs in view of their distinctive contribution to the totality of higher education, while the public universities seek different sources of philanthropy to give them the flexibility and leverage they must have if they are to keep moving away from a state of mere adequacy toward a position of competitive excellence.

In addition to the pressures of enrollment expansion on the educational budget, the developing demand for graduate and professional training has affected the costs of higher education. Sixteen Indiana colleges and universities have graduate or professional degree programs and some have both. The talented and experienced faculty who teach at this level and the equipment these instructional programs require constitute an expensive item, but there is abundant evidence of the economic advantage and social necessity of having these doctoral and professional programs. Increasingly, advanced training is requisite for the problem-solving and decision-making of today's complex society. The so-called "knowledge explosion" has placed a premium on focused, graduate education. Just as the American educational effort has responded to the challenge of "Sputnik," so individual states have reacted to the exciting promise of scientific and technological advances with strong encouragement of research and development and implementation of education to the highest level of student capability. Federal and foundation grants have helped underwrite some of the attendant costs, but the essential encouragement of graduate education depends upon far-seeing leaders. Today Indiana has an opportunity to emulate the foresightedness of the State's founders by providing for the highest level of education needed to secure a manpower pool of top personnel for industry, government, finance, education, and the professions.

During recent years various attempts have been made to analyze conditions which produce a thriving economy. Analysts have observed that wherever there are large concentrations of resident scientists and researchers, the economy seems to benefit. The comment has been made that one Ph. D. will generate employment for ten engineers, and ten engineers will generate employment for 150 technicians and skilled workers. To an appreciable extent the post-Korea experience of the Midwest in failing to attract its proportionate share of federal research and development contracts illustrates the interrelatedness of highly trained manpower and the economy. Indiana has been one of the Midwest states which has lost many of its doctoral specialists in science and technology to East and West Coast industries and institutions. A pressing challenge, therefore, in Indiana's sesquicentennial self-appraisal is to discover how to retain and make productive use of its brainpower in the pattern of more prosperous states. With a conviction of its necessity and the same fervent optimism and strong determination to build for the future which the State's founders exhibited by providing for the education of a largely illiterate constituency, Hoosier leadership can help ensure Indiana's emergence from the Midwestern "brain drain" by consistent promotion of advanced graduate and professional training within the universities, among qualified students and throughout the public attitude, including especially the business community.

Twelfth most populous state in the nation, according to Census Bureau estimates in 1964, Indiana stood seventh in production of Ph. D.'s that year, fifteenth in the number of its engineers, twelfth in the number of its scientists, and fifteenth in the number of its industrial research laboratories. Yet 23 states received more substantial amounts in NASA contracts (Indiana's portion was 0.1 percent of the total), and its share of Department of Defense Prime Research and Development contracts (1.0 percent of the total) tied it with North Carolina in fifteenth place. The colleges and universities are producing advanced graduates and professional men at a pace that could satisfy practically all of Indiana's needs, were the people of the state convinced of the asset which lies within their summoning. Similarly, the research capability of the colleges and universities has been tapped, not mined. There is a gap between the expert knowledge available and public understanding of how that knowledge can serve non-instructional needs. Some use has been made of it through consultantships to educational corporations, government, and industry. Some has been developed through such institutional operations as Purdue's McClure Industrial Park, Indiana University's Aerospace Research Applications Center, and the University of Notre Dame's Lobund and Radiation Laboratories. More lies well within the compass of imagination, but it will require desire, searching, ingenuity, and co-operation on the part of citizens and institutions alike to weld this potentially dynamic relationship.

The underdevelopment of research services should not overshadow the fact that from the very beginning higher education has responded impressively to the needs of the state. Besides preparing teachers, lawyers, doctors, dentists, businessmen, engineers, and other specially trained personnel, the institutions have rendered continuous public service. Agricultural extension was an early and exceedingly valuable example of this, to which in more recent years have been added various other forms of adult education, frequently supplied through the regional campuses of the State universities. Of late the importance of this resource has been given emphasis through what has been termed the rapid obsolescence of knowledge. With technology advancing at a spectacular rate and new data becoming available daily, the terminus of education has become less related to the traditional span of formal schooling and more to the extent of an individual's active employment. Knowledge and training acquired during the first two decades of life are now subject to displacement. Although this altered environment has not yet affected many of the senior members of our society, in the decade ahead it will be less and less possible to maintain a professional posture without frequent resort to continuing education, supplied in large measure by the faculties of our educational institutions, who themselves must constantly update their knowledge and lead in pushing back the frontiers.

The regional campuses of Indiana, Purdue, and Indiana State

universities and the Calumet Campus of St. Joseph's College, which have the primary function of making undergraduate education accessible to students who otherwise might not be able to attend college, are also a ready source of continuing education. Indiana University regional campuses are located at Gary and East Chicago (Northwest Campus), Indianapolis, Kokomo, South Bend (South Bend–Mishawaka), and Jeffersonville (Southeastern), along with a new Fort Wayne campus shared with Purdue. In another cooperative arrangement, Indiana University operates the Eastern Indiana Center with Earlham College and a Southwest Center with Vincennes University. Besides the Fort Wayne campus, Purdue maintains campuses in Hammond (Calumet Center), Michigan City (Barker Memorial Center, soon to be incorporated into a new campus at Westville), and Indianapolis. Through host-guest arrangements, programs of both Purdue and Indiana universities are available on each other's regional campuses. Indiana State University has recently added to the state network a campus in Evansville, and a New Albany addition to the Indiana University Southeastern campus is in the planning stages. The regional campuses have reflected the enrollment pressures experienced generally with the result that their programs are now being rapidly extended and their facilities enlarged. They give every indication of becoming increasingly vital, undergraduate arms of the State universities while their roles as cultural and adult education centers grow correspondingly.

Technological developments in the area of mass media could provide a new source of continuing education and probably hasten the popularity of coordinated training and practice in an occupation. During the next decade, for example, educational television may well become an important instructional tool both on campus and off, though as yet there is not one educational television station in the state and few Indiana institutions have sought the requisite financing for such a project or even for closed-circuit television instruction. It is quite conceivable that persons as diversely employed as scientific technicians, lawyers, pharmacists, farmers, teachers, plant managers, doctors, and others could be benefited by programs designed to report the developments in their particular fields. That this need is realistic can be gathered from the summary of a recent study: "The Department of Labor predicts that the average youth of today will probably shift occupations some five times over the 40 years he spends in the labor market. A life of continuing occupational adjustment will mean a life of continuing education to meet changed or additional educational requirements." If people come to accept instruction by television as a means of enlightening their vocations and broadening their cultural understanding, the character of higher education in the next quarter century will vary markedly from the past. It is to be hoped that such a change would not be so closely related to occupational demands that the fields of the humanities with their bank of man's past experience, wisdom, and creativity and his current thought and performance would be neglected, for these can be as important to the lives of Hoosiers as vocational knowledge is to the plying of their trades.

The concept of education by broadcast (or even closed-circuit) television is in many ways merely a new aspect of a long-time educational practice called extension service, conceived and initiated following the land-grant college Act of 1862, mentioned earlier. Other services that have been supplied to the people in their locales by colleges and universities range from consultation, advice, and lectures to performances by musical and dramatic groups. More frequently, Hoosier citizens are invited to the campuses of the various institutions for clinics, seminars, institutes, conferences, and cultural attractions throughout the year. These embrace uncounted opportunities, from labor education to executive development; from coverage of the latest dental and medical treatment to actual diagnostic and therapeutic services; from seminars in hospital accounting to information on aerospace research spin-off; from updating of teacher education to use of the new communications media—the list is lengthy and constantly being renewed and revised. Citizens who avail themselves of these services increase annually, but the many who are not free to leave their jobs or families or who lack the initiative or resources to attend constitute a vast majority of the state. Progressive development of media from their present early stage to bring the advantage of the classroom and the stage directly to Hoosiers promises the most significant educational exploration since the missionaries and educators came from the East to create a desire and facilities for education among the indifferent pioneers in the new State of Indiana.

Within the last decade or so the creative and performing arts have developed impressively on many of the campuses. Talented student groups present concerts, plays, and dance programs on their campuses throughout the academic year, and sometimes go on tour, in both cases attracting audiences from surrounding areas as well as locally. The Indiana University Opera Theater has gained steadily in stature in the past two decades. And the frequent appearances of artists of national and international renown at the various university auditoriums add significantly to the position the campuses are attaining as the state's cultural centers.

Higher education has assumed responsibility not alone for undergraduate, graduate, professional, and continuing education in the state. It has concerned itself as well with the quality and methods of instruction in Indiana's elementary and secondary schools. In addition to the training of teachers and the endeavors of the public and private institutions to improve the content of courses in the state's schools through the updating of teacher education, there have been new and important developments such as the Indiana Language Program, operated under the office of the State Superintendent of Public Instruction through an advisory committee, and headquartered at Indiana University. The program has been concerned not alone with added training for language teachers but also with revision of curricula, establishment of standards and requirements for language instruction within Indiana's high schools, overseas experience, and even experimentation in the efficacy of various methods of teaching. As a result, more students are studying languages than ever before in Indiana's history, equipping themselves for the realities of an adult experience no longer likely to be restricted to an English-speaking world.

Further provocation to improvement among high school students has come from higher education in the form of advanced placement and credit programs which encourage students to earn college credits through tests in a number of fields before they become freshmen. The new seriousness and related superiority of today's high school students are evident in the growing numbers of students who gain advanced placement through these examinations.

College-sponsored programs reach into the high schools also through faculty members assigned to coordinate the work in high school courses with the correspondent college fields; through music clinics; through science institutes for outstanding high school science students, and through study and recommendation of curricular revisions in various secondary fields. The impact of all these programs has narrowed the division between high school and college in much the same way that graduate programs have affected undergraduate work. Increasingly, education in Indiana—as elsewhere—is moving in the direction of a continuum, from the first years through a graduate degree, and students receive encouragement from many sources to continue as far in this continuum as their capabilities permit.

A part of the effort which has been described as "human conservancy"—the conservation of individual talents through their full development—is the relatively new interest in the post-high school, non-degree field. A State Department of Vocational and Technical Education, created by the 1965 General Assembly, is engaged in coordinating previously established agencies, including the Indiana Vocational Technical College. This latter has been a "paper college" until very recently when a president and vice president were appointed to head it and it assumed control of a training school, founded earlier by the Indiana General Education Commission. To help meet the urgent need for such training while giving it a higher education component within the concept of the educational continuum, Indiana University established recently a Division of General and Technical Studies. The Division will absorb current associate degree programs in nursing and the allied health fields and will initiate new ones, in cooperation with others, where asked to help meet unfilled local needs. Purdue University has been expand-

ing its technical, non-credit, and degree programs in a similar response to industry's need for increased manpower trained beyond
the high school level. A notable example is its new College of Technology, which will offer curricula on all Purdue campuses.

Greatly enlarged enrollments and services amplified in the many
ways sketched here inevitably require expanded staff and facilities
and this expansion produces financial pressures. The capital investment in higher education throughout the state is enormous, easily
beyond the billion dollar mark. When to the operation of the private and public colleges and universities are added the associated
enterprises which supply textbooks, equipment, food, utilities, and
like maintenance needs, the "knowledge industry" is seen to be a
major part of the state's economy. Institutional costs mount, as do
those of any other industry, with rising labor and materials costs.
The shortage of the academic equivalent of skilled labor has special
implications for colleges and universities which, though producing
unprecedented numbers of doctoral graduates, cannot increase the
supply rapidly enough to meet the demand. Thus, the price of adequate staffing is now more than at any previous time a serious problem of the state's colleges and universities. For the nationwide
competition for academicians affects the retention of present faculties as well as the recruitment of new members; and so delicate is
the quality of excellence that the loss of several key professors in
a department or failure to attract some of the better candidates
among the new entries into the ranks can alter the capability of that
department to draw top-quality students, to produce vital research,
or to contribute to the overall stature and usefulness of the institution. Industrial competition has its counterpart in the academic
market!

Among smaller schools stature is a key determinant in the quality of students and faculty attracted by an institution. Stature has
an additional significance for larger schools because it frequently
influences the number of fellowships, federal grants, and foundation awards won by a university. Few universities choose to ignore
these opportunities for program development and enrichment,
graduate student support, faculty salary subsidies, equipment addi-

tions, and similar contributions to the academic operation. In fact, the extent and strength of a university's research function may be almost wholly dependent upon such outside support.

This situation has created a relatively new requirement in the organization of most American (and Hoosier) universities. It has been necessary to assign to some office the responsibility for keeping itself informed of available grants and contracts; for circulating the information among the faculty; for assisting in the preparation of proposals; for coordinating interdisciplinary projects that need funding; and for screening and facilitating proposal submissions to agencies and foundations. A by-product of this operation is the stimulus it provides to active participation in the mining of knowledge and adapting the store of present knowledge to the use of underdeveloped segments here and abroad. Furthermore such offices occasionally initiate cooperative research ventures with other institutions in the state or region when the requirements of a proposal exceed the capabilities of a single school.

The alternative to an active search for strengthening support funds, private and public, by the colleges and universities of the state is an inevitable surrender to second-class status; and, as go the institutions, so goes the state, if the experiences of the wealthiest to the poorest states can be instructive. Faced with an inadequately competitive budget, an institution's administrators must decide to hire in the national market less talented or less trained faculty members than it seeks and needs or it must raid the faculties of sister, less-favored institutions nearby, robbing those institutions of their top men. The spirit of the Indiana Conference has militated against such a practice within Indiana—in fact the existence of the Conference has probably facilitated the recruitment of faculty for the smaller schools from the graduates of the larger—but the basic problem is very real, placing the management of the faculty shortage high among the factors which will determine Indiana's progress during at least the early decades of its next half century.

A brief word should be inserted here concerning the supposed neglect of teaching in the larger institutions of the state. It is true that the multiple public and private demands upon universities, often directly connected with institutional support, do require research activity, but such a stimulus to continued learning by faculty members can only have a beneficial effect in the classroom. Research scholars have current findings to report to their classes, thereby enlivening textbook exposition and involving students in the research process—an advantage that should be weighed against the lessening of extracurricular student-faculty contacts. The realities of the present situation must be faced, for, as Cornell's President James Perkins asserted in one of his Stafford Little lectures at Princeton University recently, "the university can never again run on the assumption that it commands or can command the full-time interest and attention of all its faculty."

Among the sources of institutional support, the income from student fees and tuition forms a substantial part, especially in the private schools. It has been the laudable ambition of practically all the schools in the state not to price education out of reach of qualified students. While even state-supported education has never been strictly "gratis and equally open to all," educators throughout the long history of the state have resisted the increase of costs to students, although they have not been averse to a differential rate at the public institutions for out-of-state students. This higher rate represents a compromise between the State's defensible position with regard to underwriting the education of other states' students to an extent equal to its own, and the educational advantage of having state students associate with those from a variety of different backgrounds and experience. Were education confined to the classroom there would be less reason to desire a cosmopolitan student body. But students learn much from each other; many will be engaged in regional, national, and even international contacts through their interests or their employment, and restriction of their collegiate associations to students whose environments and outlooks have been similar would hobble Hoosier students at the very time when education should be freeing them from the limitations of their individual experiences.

As institutional expenses have risen, fees and tuition have had to be increased to a degree that appears to be prohibitive for many competent high school graduates. The Indiana Conference tackled this problem a year ago, originating and backing a scholarship plan which was given legislative implementation by the 1965 General Assembly. The program is administered by a State Scholarship Commission, appointed by the Governor, chaired by Samuel R. Sutphin, and empowered by the Act to award annually as many grants as available funds will provide to students who are deterred by financial considerations from attending a college—or from attending the college of their choice. At least two qualified students from each county are to be among those designated to receive these scholarships. Providing up to $800 each, applicable only to tuition and fees, the scholarships are renewable through satisfactory performance for three additional years unless a degree has been received in the meantime. A scholarship winner may choose to seek admission at any accredited or approved institution in the state. By appropriating one half of a million dollars for this purpose in the first biennium, the State recorded a truly noteworthy accomplishment that sets the stage for the educational advances which the next 150 years in Indiana may produce.

The State support of higher education, as distinguished from the attitudinal and overall support of the system of colleges and universities throughout the state, has specific reference to the biennial appropriations of the General Assembly for operation and capital improvements of the four State universities: Indiana, Purdue, Indiana State, and Ball State.* These appropriations represent the State's constitutional obligation, first recorded in 1816, to provide education through the university level for its qualified citizens who seek collegiate course work. The comparative measure of Indiana's support of higher education among the states of the nation is obtainable from a reading of the per capita amount appropriated. The Indiana ranking on the basis of per capita appropriation rose slightly from twentieth nationally in 1956-57 to nineteenth in 1964-65, but then in 1965-66 when many states improved their support, Indiana's ranking slipped to twenty-first,

---

* Vincennes University, though not a State institution in the same sense as these four, also receives some State assistance.

although the per capita appropriation increased from $16.64 to $18.48. The State of Indiana's 98 percent increase in appropriations to her public universities for operating purposes over the last six years, and her 27 percent gain over the last two, compare unfavorably (and disquietingly) with the fifty-state average gain of about 117 percent for the six-year period and 39 percent for the two years.

State support of higher education is now customary in all of the fifty states, although the tradition of great private universities in the East has deterred assumption of adequate public responsibility there. The dominance of the private universities in the East has also affected cooperative movements in the region, it seems. Asserting that "universities now find that close collaboration is a stark necessity," Dr. Perkins in his Princeton lectures chided the Ivy League "that this group of distinguished universities does not have any collective weight to exert on matters of educational importance to the area in which they live," as does the Midwestern organization of Big Ten presidents. He was referring to the Council of Ten, formed in 1951 with Herman B Wells of Indiana as its first chairman, which grew out of an earlier informal organization of presidents of thirteen Midwestern universities. The history of collective discussions and actions among the heads of leading institutions of the area extends back into the last decade of the nineteenth century when the Intercollegiate Conference of Faculty Representatives*—now popularly known as the "Big Ten," or sometimes as the "Western Conference"—was formed by an action of seven Midwestern universities. The Council meets semiannually and while it customarily reviews the athletic program of

* Presently composed of the University of Illinois, Indiana University, the University of Iowa, the University of Michigan, Michigan State University (replacing the original membership of the University of Chicago), the University of Minnesota, Northwestern University, The Ohio State University, Purdue University, and the University of Wisconsin. Indiana's other two State universities, Ball State and Indiana State, along with Butler University, DePauw University, Evansville College, St. Joseph's College, and Valparaiso University constitute the Indiana Collegiate Conference and enjoy a spirited athletic rivalry.

the Conference with the Conference Commissioner, it is joined by the president of the University of Chicago for most of its agenda, on exchanging views and information on institutional problems of the eleven universities and exploring avenues of effective cooperation in educational activities. Although financial support differs between the private and public members of this group of institutions, many common concerns have gained useful airing in the Council and more recently also in the Committee for Institutional Cooperation (CIC), a body sponsored by the Council and composed of an administrative representative, typically an academic vice president, from each of the ten universities, plus Chicago. They have worked out over 40 cooperative ventures including a research project in oceanography designed to solve some of the major problems associated with the Great Lakes, an interdisciplinary program to initiate a concerted attack on economic problems in the Midwest, and the Traveling Scholar Program by means of which a graduate student of one CIC school can receive a part of his training at another. A central library depository, associations for joint astronomy and high energy physics research, a policy-making body for the Argonne National Laboratory, and a consortium for administration of an international studies grant have been implemented by the Conference membership or a part of it.

Other forms of organized inter-institutional cooperation extending beyond the state borders could be cited, but the Indiana Conference of Higher Education is the outstanding cooperative endeavor within the state, one of the first if not *the* first of its kind anywhere. The founding of the Conference has already been described. Continuity of organization is assured for the Conference by two permanent officers, an Executive Director and an Assistant Secretary-Treasurer, while the presidency is elective and alternates among the presidents of the member institutions. The Conference's Committee on Inter-Institutional Cooperation is an action agency which has had a history of successful projects, among them the annual conference on programs for superior students. Just recently the Committee illustrated its data exchange possibilities by compiling a report on the foreign study programs of the various members. Of fifteen institutions with their own foreign study programs, twelve have programs for study abroad during the academic year, and nine have summer study or travel tours for credit. Sixteen members participate in the Indiana Intercollegiate Study Project which offers programs in England and Mexico during the summer.

The Conference provides a ready instrument of joint action, demonstrated recently in its promotion of the State Scholarship Act; of joint proposals, illustrated in the Regional Education Laboratory proposal—now extended to out-of-state participants—and the Peace Corps Project with the Chilean Institute of Rural Education; and of joint programs such as the Non-Western Studies Project. The Conference has also sponsored a national meeting and can be even more enterprising in the use of its combined interests to attract otherwise unobtainable projects and programs. For despite all of its accomplishments, its potential is greater than anything yet realized, and its members might well find in the challenge of this sesquicentennial year's accounting new goals for progress. In such areas as uniformity of admission and degree standards, facilitation of credit transfer, intermural faculty exchanges, curriculum coordination, sharing of expertise in proposal-preparation, inter-institutional circulation of data, experimentation in teaching aids, development of an electronic communications network, formation of consortia to administer grants or advance research—in these and many more ways the Conference can eventually lead to a vitalization of the state's higher education resources. A full measure of good faith must underlie the developments of the decades ahead, but the very existence and record of the Conference augur well for the state's educational capability of the future.

Groups of persons who perform similar functions for the various colleges and universities also help draw their institutions together. Among these are the Indiana Association of Women Deans and Counselors, the Scholarship Association of Indiana Colleges and Universities which sponsors financial aid conferences for high school personnel, the Indiana College Personnel Association, the Indiana College Public Relations Association, the Indiana Association of Collegiate Registrars and Admissions Officers, the Indiana Group of the National Association of Educational Buyers, and the Indiana Association of College and University Business Officers.

The four State universities enjoy good relations with each other and enter numerous cooperative projects. In order to facilitate the exchange of information among themselves which can make even more cooperation possible while guarding against unnecessary duplication, they recently organized the Committee on Academic Coordination of Indiana's Four Public Universities, composed of one representative from each. They have also demonstrated the beneficial result of their working together in projects such as the Cooperative Program for Teacher Education. The CPTE venture, as it is called, represents firm institutional commitments to offer in northern Indiana a sequence of graduate courses which may apply toward the master's degree at any one of the four State universities. Initiated in 1963, this service to teachers has been successful enough to encourage its extension to other areas of the state where there may be a similar need.

Another statewide development resulted from the passage by the Congress in 1963 of the Higher Education Facilities Act which called for a state commission to administer federal matching grants. The Indiana Advisory Commission on Academic Facilities was appointed by Governor Matthew E. Welsh in 1964 with Dr. Herman B Wells as its chairman and with fifteen nonacademic members. The Commission in fiscal 1965 advised the award of $6,026,900 in grants to 13 institutions for the construction of academic facilities whose total cost exceeded $27 million. Now Governor Roger D. Branigin has given the Commission an additional assignment, the administering of Title VI of the Higher Education Act of 1965, providing financial assistance for the improvement of undergraduate education. Thus begins the reaping of benefits from the actions of the "Education Congress" by the state's public and private institutions.

In surveying and summarizing the present status of Indiana's higher education certain trends are quite clear. First, the colleges and universities have opened wider the avenues of communication and cooperation among themselves. This is a distinctly healthy situation amid the complex array of circumstances which attend the management of educational institutions today, with the pressing demands for multiple public services and the triple pressures of population growth, rapid technological and scientific development, and the equally accelerated pace of the discovery of new knowledge. In the decades ahead it seems likely that Indiana higher education will continue to promote a cooperative solution of problems which confront all of the state's institutions, a fraternal relationship between the stronger and weaker schools, and alliances to meet challenges beyond the capability of a single institution.

The second contemporary characteristic is the widespread search for a broader basis of support induced by the need to meet the above-mentioned pressures and the competition for faculty. The traditional sustaining sources are even more essential than before, but they are unlikely to swell rapidly enough to meet the immediate needs. Foundations and the federal government offer this likelihood, and thus there is a premium on the development of successful approaches to obtain funds.

A third characteristic, again influenced by the triple pressures, is the view of formal education as a continuum and of education itself as a lifelong process. In this respect educators are realizing and enhancing the concept of the State's founders to provide education to the limit of an individual's capabilities. But educational opportunity is not truly available as long as qualified students are prevented by financial circumstances from taking advantage of it. The State Scholarship Program is an important move to extend opportunity, and also of intrinsic importance in this extension of opportunity are the regional campus development and the potential growth of media for instantaneous communication.

A fourth characteristic is the expansion of the concept of what an education should include. Long ago the "classical course" of the first schools gave way to additional arts and humanities courses, teacher education, professional training, and similar reflections of the needs of the people. The two most recent developments have been a widening acceptance of a curricular responsibility in the areas of international relations and foreign study and the quite different responsibility for the post-high school, technical, non-degree program. Both represent the responsiveness of the Indiana educational system to contemporary conditions, which include a need for a pool of workers trained in the basic areas of the new technology and of a citizenry with an understanding of the nation's neighbors, drawn closer by advances in communications and transportation.

Finally, higher education in Indiana as elsewhere is beginning to mine more fully its intellectual resources. The unknown has yielded layer by layer to intensive investigation and, by analogy, much that has been accepted as unknowable seems to present the possibility of discovery. The research activities in Indiana's institutions are an important component of the nationwide search for new information.

The path from illiteracy to literacy and beyond has been difficult but successful. The pathfinders have been leaders throughout Indiana's history who have envisioned benefits for this state comparable to those anywhere else in the nation. Their faith in education through all the gradations up to and including the university level has been instrumental in bringing Indiana to its present stature. Ignorance and indifference are no longer the antagonists. The one great challenge for Indiana is to adopt the conviction and urgency of its founders and developers without reservation, for what the generations have gained posterity can advance. Indiana faces the future in a position of hard-won strength. Its place in the future depends upon a reaffirmation of faith in the historical imperative of Indiana's founding fathers:

> Whereas the independence, happiness, and energy of every republic depends (under the influence of the destinies of Heaven) upon the wisdom, virtue, talents, and energy of its citizens and rulers;
> And whereas science, literature, and the liberal arts contribute in an eminent degree to improve those qualities and requirements;
> And whereas learning hath ever been found the ablest advocate of genuine liberty, the best supporter of rational religion, and the

source of the only solid and imperishable glory which nations can acquire;

And forasmuch as literature and philosophy furnish the most useful and pleasing occupations, improving and varying the enjoyments of prosperity, affording relief under the pressure of misfortune, and hope and consolation in the hours of death;

And considering that in a commonwealth where the humblest citizen may be elected to the highest offices, and where the Heaven-born prerogative of the right to elect and to reject is retained and secured to the citizens, the knowledge which is requisite for a magistrate and elector should be widely diffused.

EUNICE CARMICHAEL ROBERTS

Hoosier Women

The distinguished French historian, Alexis de Tocqueville, who traveled widely in this country when the state of Indiana was just 15 years old (the year of its sesquidecennial anniversary), wrote in his famous series of books *Democracy in America*: ". . . and if I were asked, now that I am drawing to the close of this work, in which I have spoken of so many important things done by the Americans, to what the singular prosperity and growing strength of that people ought mainly to be attributed, I should reply: To the superiority of their women."

The reader may ask, "Why a separate chapter on women? Are not women, as citizens of the state, automatically included in all other chapters?" They are indeed. For one significant fact, they

Eunice Carmichael Roberts came to Indiana University in September 1952 as Assistant Dean of the Faculties and Director of Women's Educational Programs. The title was changed in 1959 to Assistant Dean for Undergraduate Development for Women's Educational Programs. For seven years, she was Dean of Student Personnel and Head of Modern Language Department at Eastern New Mexico University in Portales, New Mexico, and from 1948 to 1952 she was Dean of the College, Lindenwood College, St. Charles, Missouri. Currently, she is serving on the National Board of Directors of the Girl Scouts of the U.S.A. and is Chairman of the Governor's Commission on the Status of Women.

constitute more than one half the population of the state. Nevertheless, much that is to be said about the state as this sesquicentennial anniversary is celebrated applies in a somewhat different
way to women, or has implications for women that are somewhat
different from the implications for men. Of course, anything to
be said of significance about women obviously is significant for
families, which include men and children; and any important facts
about a group which constitutes more than half the population of
the state is significant for the state.

If further reason is needed for making some comments about
women as a special group, it is found in that basic document, the
Constitution of the State of Indiana, which provides for apportionment of the state into political districts on the basis of "the number
of *male* inhabitants" of voting age—thus automatically excluding
women and therefore making them a separate group. Subsequent
legislative action has not been so exclusive, however, and in recent
decades this wording of the constitution has not made a difference
in fact in political districting. It may be hoped that before the state
celebrates another important anniversary, the constitution might
be amended to make it fit into the twentieth century.

In this chapter I shall examine some of the facts about Hoosier
women and the implications of those facts for the state, and some
of the facts about the state which have special implications for
Hoosier women. It is obvious that in the space provided I cannot
comprehensively examine in detail all significant aspects of the
matter. I have therefore chosen certain areas to discuss in general
terms and have reluctantly omitted much detail (including statistical data), and excluded from discussion other areas that might
be of interest.

There are more Hoosier women than Hoosier men. They now
live longer than Hoosier men. This was not the case 150 years ago.
Men outlived women. A stroll through any old cemetery will reveal
many family lots containing the graves of a man and his two (or
even more) wives. Women also live longer than the women of
their mothers' and grandmothers' generations, and much longer

than they did when Indiana became a state. This latter fact is true of Hoosier men also, but women gradually but steadily caught up with and then passed men in longevity, so that now, on the average, Hoosier women outlive Hoosier men by about seven years.

A larger percentage of women (almost all) marry now than in earlier years, and they marry at a younger average age. Although there is some evidence that this trend is changing, each of them now averages more children than the mothers of recent decades, but not as many as did the early Hoosier women settlers (although they raise to maturity a larger percentage of those they bear). They have their children in a shorter span of years, so that the youngest child is likely to be born while the mother is still in her twenties, and launched in school while she is in her early thirties. When this fact is considered in conjunction with the well-known facts that Hoosiers now buy from outside sources many services and materials which used to be provided or prepared in the home; that they have mechanical devices which decrease the time required and increase the efficiency in the performance of many tasks necessary in the home; that they and their children wear clothing that affords much more freedom of action and requires less time in its care; that they live in vigorous health to a greater age than ever in the past—the question is inescapable: What do Hoosier women do with the 35 to 45 years they can anticipate after their children are in school, and when only a portion of their time is required to carry out the necessary mechanics of operating a home?

More than one third of Hoosier women are in the labor force; that is, they work part time or full time at paid jobs outside the home. More than one third of our labor force consists of women. More than one half of these working women are married. Few of the married women workers have small children (they remain in the home while the children are small, and this is good), but many of them have children in high school or older. In fact, many of our Indiana youth are able to afford a college education only because Mother has gone back to work to help finance it. Women work at *all sorts* of jobs in all occupational fields, although they are concentrated in larger numbers in certain fields. Almost all Hoosier women are working or have worked from a few to many years, and social scientists estimate that of all young women in school today in this country, nine out of ten will probably work an average of twenty-five years at paid jobs. Not only are many families economically sound only because the woman works (in fact, more than one tenth of the family units is headed by a woman), but the sound economy of the state depends upon the contribution to the labor force of Hoosier women. For example, the whole educational system would collapse if all women teachers were removed —indeed, even if just the married women teachers withdrew.

Although it may appear to be so obvious as not to need mention, it should be remembered that the work Hoosier women do in the home (whether they also work outside or not) is *work* and is an essential contribution to the economy of the family and of the state, and that it has a *monetary* value even though this fact seldom appears in statistical tables.

What of the more than half of Hoosier women who are not in the labor market? Many of them are in school, for more of them are going farther in school than was formerly true. Further, there is a real explosion of a new development in education. Large numbers of "young mature" married women are returning to college or to other training programs after they have started their families. Of those out of school but not married, essentially one hundred percent are in the labor market. Therefore, our nonworking, nonstudying women are almost all married.

The contribution these women make to the state involves complicated intangible factors which do not lend themselves to statistical analysis. Nevertheless, it is clear that there are differences between the way they make their usefulness socially effective and the way earlier generations of Hoosier women participated in the life of the state.

A brief look at the past is needed to understand the significance of the current situation. The pioneer Hoosier woman gave almost all her time, energy, thought, and strength (and from an early age) to helping carry on the necessary work within the family circle. But this was much more than just "running the house" and bearing and raising the children, time consuming and difficult (often even dangerous) as these were. It involved work outside to help keep the small family farm or business functioning, sometimes even including helping clear land and protecting with firearms the safety of the family. She received no wages for this, but she was, in a true sense, a very real partner in the total enterprise, which was establishing and maintaining a home and providing for its sustenance; that is, its *economy*, which was primarily "in kind" rather than in money. She was managing the house, bearing and caring for the children, *and* helping earn the living, as well as helping to build a state in the wilderness. Often she was the only teacher her children had in the fundamentals of the "three R's," and also in religion, singing, arts, and crafts. De Tocqueville devoted several chapters to discussing the enormous (and astonishing to him as a European) contribution of women to the development and progress of this country, concluding that they were essential partners, far beyond their roles as wives and mothers, in that progress. He found them just as charming, but quite different, from European women.

It should be noted that the pioneer Hoosier man's contribution to earning the living, to the economy, both family and state, was also primarily "in kind," in what he did and what he produced, rather than in wages or salary earned. If pioneer Hoosier woman's economic participation was essential to the development and progress of the state (and it certainly was) and if she was a fully participating partner in an economy which was based primarily on something other than wages and salary, why should it seem surprising to some that she should continue to make a similar contribution—to manage the house, bear and care for the children, and also to participate in earning the living—in the context of the twentieth century in which family and social economy is primarily based on wage and salary checks?

Only one or two developments in the sequence of changes in the roles women have fulfilled can be mentioned. In the early decades of this century married women were doing little outside the house and its management that contributed money directly to the economy of the family. Nor indeed were unmarried women (and there were more of them), for they were likely to be the unpaid baby sitters, nurses, seamstresses, and household aids in the homes of parents or unmarried brothers. Servants were plentiful and did not cost much. With increasing population, the beginnings of urbanization, better communication, roads, and transportation, there had developed for women considerable social life. Organizations began to be formed, at first purely social, or dilletante, or church connected. "Good works" became so much a pattern that the expression "Lady Bountiful" became entrenched in our vocabulary.

As organizations matured and more women achieved higher levels of education, changes began to appear—changes which have significance today. The Indiana Federation of Women's Clubs today has an on-going study program, a Latin American exchange fellowship program in cooperation with Indiana University, as well as other scholarships and contributions to community programs. That uniquely Indiana organization, Kappa Kappa Kappa (Tri-Kappa) has much social activity, but also has a very substantial scholarship program that has helped thousands of Indiana girls and boys finance their educations at college and graduate school, as well as a program in support of Indiana artists that, through exhibit and purchase every year, has publicized the work of Hoosier artists and has developed a substantial collection of their works. It would be difficult to measure the influence for progress in Indiana of the varied contributions of the Indiana State Division of the American Association of University Women (Indiana was one of the early states to organize the AAUW) through its fellowships programs, support of legislation for education and libraries, and development of adult education programs, to name but a few of its activities. The Indiana Federation of Business and Professional Women's Clubs maintains a program of scholarships, an active committee on legislation, and was one of the influential organizations in support of the appointment of an Indiana Governor's Commission on the Status of Women. (Indiana was the fourteenth state to have such a commission. There are now at least

48 states which have commissions.) The League of Women Voters covers the state with educational programs, study groups, and the distribution of nonpartisan informational materials to aid voters.

The above examples provide only the very sketchiest suggestion of the contributions being made to the progress of the state by Hoosier women through organizations. Other groups could have been selected as examples, and much more could have been said about any of the groups mentioned. It would be grossly inaccurate to write off with the smile induced by a Hokinson cartoon the current value of the constructive work of thousands of Hoosier women through scores of organizations. They provide a channel for education and civic participation for many of our non-working women, as well as for working women, which goes far beyond the mere giving of baskets of food to the poor at Thanksgiving and Christmas. By and large, the women's organizations tend now to identify social needs, study their various ramifications, seek the causes of social problems, and develop socially constructive approaches toward meeting the needs and solving the problems. A recent example is the role they have played in many Hoosier communities in launching Head Start programs.

There is emerging a rather new development nation-wide, and widely exemplified in Indiana, of volunteer and unpaid work by women, often on a semiprofessional or even professional level, and in a wide variety of fields. These volunteers provide services needed by Hoosier communities but often not covered by public funds. These educated or trained women, who do not need to earn money but who have a sense of moral responsibility to return some dividend to the society that provided them the opportunity for education, feel a deep sense of personal satisfaction in volunteering for community-improvement projects. Examples of this sort of volunteer work are teaching English and citizenship training to foreign immigrants, tutoring children at community centers in poverty areas, performing auxiliary services in hospitals, and serving as part-time professional workers in social agencies, such as family counseling centers. It is doubtful whether Indiana, or any other state, for that matter, has any real conception of the tremendous debt it owes to volunteer women for their very real and professional-level contributions to the economic, social, and cultural progress of the state. Unquestionably there is vastly more of this type of volunteer contribution to Hoosier society by women than by men.

Many Hoosier women are actively participating in politics, especially at the precinct level. Many a recent political campaign has owed its success, in part, to the work of women. If space had permitted, I should have liked to add a section on politics and to challenge Hoosier women to seek participation at a much higher level than most of them do, as well as at the "grass roots" level. It is the state's loss that they do not.

To complete the analysis of who Hoosier women are, it must be granted that Indiana has its share of nonproductive, noncontributing women who spend their days largely in bridge playing, shopping, and TV viewing and who are worth little to their families or to society. While there are statistics on working women (that is, job-holding, money-earning women) and women in school, it is impossible to provide numerical statistical data on the relative distribution of the others in the population. It is my judgment (perhaps an "educated guess") that more women are now making more substantial contributions to the economic, political, social, and cultural progress of the Hoosier state than at any other time in this century.

Who, then, are the Hoosier women? They are more than one half the population of the state. A scant minimum are "free loaders" on society. They work before they are married and before their children are born, and then again some time after their children start school. More than one third are in the labor force, one tenth head family units, one half the wives help earn the family living. They marry—more of them than of the women in their mothers' generation, and at a younger age than their mothers. They have children—more than their mothers and grandmothers, and they have them in a shorter span of years. They do relatively little outside the home while their children are small, but after children are in school they go back to work, or to school, and they participate in community affairs constructively and significantly. They educate themselves—to a higher level than their mothers.

Although the more than one half million women working in Indiana constitute over one third of the labor force, they earn considerably less than one third of the income. One important reason for this is that a larger proportion of women workers than of men are only part-time employees, and most statistical data are given in terms of annual earnings. Some writers, in discussing relative earnings of men and women, do not take into account this distortion in statistical tables.

This does not tell the whole story, however. When the facts concerning full-time workers only are considered, there is still a substantial differential between the earnings of men and women. For example, information prepared by the Bureau of Labor Statistics of the U. S. Department of Labor shows that the average income of full-time men workers in Indiana in 1959 was $5,452, while for full-time women workers the average was only $3,118, or 57 percent as much as that of men.

Another significant factor in the difference in the earnings of men and women is that women tend to be concentrated in the lower paying job fields. These fields, where unskilled, untrained workers are concerned, tend to be intrastate occupations and not covered by the Federal Minimum Wage Law. The 1965 Indiana General Assembly enacted a state minimum wage law which is now in effect and which covers most of the occupations not covered by the federal law. Since the state law affects so many women, it is hoped that it will decrease somewhat the differences in earnings of men and women at the lowest wage levels.

Further up the economic scale, women workers with moderate or even fairly high levels of training or education are also concentrated in the lower paying of the occupations above the unskilled level, often even below their real competence. They have a virtual monopoly of the positions in secretarial, stenographic, typing, and bookkeeping fields. Many are factory operatives. Perhaps as a result of the movement of industry into the state, there was an increase of two percentage points of factory jobs held by women in Indiana between 1940 and 1960, while the percentage of such jobs held by women decreased nationally.

Finally, there still remains some discrimination against women on the part of some employers. There still exist in Indiana some businesses which maintain different pay scales for men and women for the same sort of work carried out with the same level of competence and efficiency. The new federal "equal pay" law, which has been in effect less than two years, should help to correct this situation where it exists in businesses that come under interstate commerce regulation. Indiana is one of the twenty-one remaining states which do not have a state "equal pay" law. Enactment of such a law would serve to reduce further such unfair discrimination against women in wage scales as still exists. Some employers are hesitant to hire women or to promote them on the same basis men are hired and promoted. Unquestionably there has been a gradual erosion of these discriminations, and the time may not be far distant when they cease to exist. When that time comes the state and its potential for progress will be the major beneficiary.

To discover the reasons for the still-existing discriminations is difficult. The easiest explanation, and possibly the most accurate, is to say that women are relative newcomers in a world of paid work outside the home which is, and has long been, a world dominated by men. When men first began to go away from home in large numbers to earn pay checks, women did not have the conveniences that they now have to make it possible to get away from the house for hours at a time, so they did not follow men into the new work patterns. Perhaps men resent, or even fear, consciously or unconsciously, women's incursion into what they have regarded as their domain. Research in *attitudes* of employers shows that there are some who believe that women possess some characteristics which make them less good risks than men as employees. They find it difficult to support these beliefs with facts— they just have always "*known*"—and considerable research exists to refute most of these opinions.

Another characteristic of women workers is that few of them, in proportion to their numbers in the labor force, are in high-level positions in management, administration, and policy forming, and their proportion in such positions seems to be decreasing in the last two or three decades, rather than increasing. Complicated factors are involved here and one cannot be certain what all the reasons are. The interruption most women face in their work careers for child bearing and rearing plays a part, as it does to some extent in the salary levels they are able to reach. This would not apply to single and childless women, however, nor would it in any case account for a decrease in the proportion of top-level positions held by women.

Even in public school education, which employs more women than men, there has been a decrease in the proportion of women administrators. For instance, in the academic year 1954-55 in the Indianapolis public elementary schools 63.5 percent of the principals were women; in 1964-65 only 42 percent were women. The actual number of women principals decreased by 14.7 percent. The number of men principals increased by 100 percent. The number of men assistant principals increased by 260 percent in the same period, while the number of women assistant principals remained almost the same (up from 11 to 13). Parallel illustrations can be found in much of business and industry, although the numbers of women involved are proportionately smaller.

Undoubtedly, discrimination has some influence and more in some fields than in others, but it is possible that anticipated discrimination that in fact would not be encountered is an important factor in deterring women from preparing for or seeking high positions. I have talked with many women in positions of substantial responsibility in a variety of fields in business and the professions and have yet to find one who felt she had been handicapped in her advancement because she was a woman.

Possibly American society discourages competent women from striving for the top in personal achievement of substance—from the image advertising projects of the happy little housewife, always young and beautiful, in her glamorous split-level house, whose chief concern is to hold her man by using the right dishwashing detergent and shampoo, to uninformed counseling of girls and young women by parents and schools. Most of the girls in school now are going to work many years, and yet the goal placed before them by their parents may be, by implication if not explicitly, just to find the right man and, having worked a year or two, get married—period. This is most unrealistic, but if this is the vision of the future presented to her, why would a young woman prepare herself for anything but a routine, stopgap job? Even school counselors, who as professionals in their field should be aware of the probable life pattern the girl's future holds, are not always realistic. This sort of counseling, which Dr. Conant reported he found too often in his study of high schools, says to the bright girl who wants to take a course in mathematics, "Oh, you don't want to take that. You'll just get married. Why don't you take a course in personal development?"

Some of these reasons probably account for the small number of women who enter the top professions. The facts in Indiana parallel those in the rest of the country in this regard. We have far fewer women doctors, lawyers, and dentists, for example, than many other countries in the world. And yet women who do practice medicine, law, and dentistry are successful and find the practice rewarding and well adaptable to marriage and family life. The late Dean John Van Nuys of the Indiana University School of Medicine reported that just as high a percentage of Indiana women recipients of the M. D. degree as of the men were successfully engaged in practice in the years following graduation.

More than one half of Hoosier women in the labor force are married. A majority of these have children, but most of their children are in school or are grown and away from home. For those with schoolchildren still in the home there is no evidence, except at the lowest economic levels, that there is any harmful effect created by the mother working (and at the lower levels the mother may well have no other choice but to work). There is substantial evidence that whether the mother works or not has no relationship to the well-being and development of the children. Research seems to show rather that it is the kind of person she is and the affectional security that exists in the home that have the significant influence.

Hoosier women work because their families need the money, which is the same reason men work. The single woman, of course, is supporting herself, and this is different from the situation several decades ago, when she was likely to be dependent upon her parents or a married brother. Many single women are supporting or helping to support one or both parents. Married women are working to help pay for the children's educations, to help pay off the mortgage on the house, or to raise the standard of living for the family. An element of personal satisfaction is often involved, of course, but the old notion that women work "for kicks," for glamor, or for "pin money" is simply not borne out by the facts.

The average age of the Hoosier woman worker is higher than it was a few years ago. In the 1930's her average age was in the late twenties; it is now over 41. A very few take only a short maternity leave to have their babies. Most drop out of the labor market for 10 to 15 years and go back to work only after the children are started in school. The single woman is likely to pursue an uninterrupted work career, and this is not unusual for the childless married woman as well.

Women in Indiana average more years of formal education than men; the average is barely more than ten years, however. A larger proportion of girls graduate from high school than of boys. More girls than boys rank in the upper grade percentiles of high school graduating classes. At the level of higher education women students' grades usually average above those of men students. Indiana University was one of the pioneer institutions in the United States in making higher learning available to women. Women students were admitted to the university in 1867 on an equal basis with men—earlier than at any other major university in the country—and they were attending classes as non-degree candidates some thirty years before that. (It is said that the diploma was presented to the first woman graduate at the base of the platform steps for fear that, if she went up the steps to the platform as did the men graduates, there might be an unseemly glimpse of her ankles, which might induce titters from her male classmates.)

In spite of these and other facts, fewer of the most intellectually able Hoosier girls go on to college than the boys. This is undoubtedly a loss for the state. The liberally educated mother contributes more effectively to the cultural atmosphere of the home, and to the cultural development of her children and of society. The daughters *and the sons* of college-educated mothers are more likely to go on to college than if the mother is not a college woman. The state needs, perhaps as never before, well-educated young people to assume their inevitable roles in the leadership of the state. These young women are going to be a substantial part of our productive labor force, and the level of their contribution to the progress of the state may well be determined by the level of their education. Psychologists have learned that women's intellects are just as good as men's (although their interests vary sometimes).

This is not to suggest that all young people, men and women, ought to pursue a college education. It is to suggest that society loses, as well as the individual and her family, when a fine intellect goes untutored and undeveloped to its highest potential. Undoubtedly, chapters on education in this book will discuss the new developments in the state for the establishment of post-high school programs of special sorts, terminal curricula with specific occupational goals, technical training, refresher courses, etc. It is to be hoped that those responsible for planning and launching such educational programs will not overlook the fact that women unquestionably are in the labor market to stay, and that their interests, as well as those of men, will be met in courses offered.

Some of the areas which had to be omitted in this discussion but which deserve thoughtful consideration are: Hoosier women in politics; Hoosier daughters of distinction; women in the professions in Indiana; civil rights of Hoosier women; legal barriers to women in Indiana (there are some); Hoosier women in creative fields—literature, art, music. My purpose has been to present some information new to some readers; to enhance awareness of the

CORBIN PATRICK

Literature and the Arts

Literature and the arts have profited in many ways by the cultural boom that has shaken the land since the state of Indiana was only 100 years old in 1916. It is possible to believe there has been as much progress as change, and reason to hope the ground has been prepared for great leaps forward in the next half century.

Indiana crossed over the great divide separating its "golden age" from modern times in 1916, the year that James Whitcomb Riley died. Every county seat town had its chautauqua and its "opera house" for occasional use in that misty time, but the citadel of culture in this broad area was at the end of the interurban line in Indianapolis. Here was the greatest concentration of halls and theaters, like the old and lamented English, that procured for the state the most luminous actors, musical artists, and touring orchestras of the day in a seemingly magnificent procession. It was the home of a publishing house, Bobbs-Merrill, that shared the distinction of the state's prestigious authors in literary circles. It was headquarters city for the painters who founded the still influential

Corbin Patrick, a native of Tell City, Indiana, and a graduate of Butler University, has been writing on the arts for *The Indianapolis Star* since 1927. He also contributes a column to the editorial page five days a week.

Brown County school. The presence of figures celebrated in all the liberal arts quickened its cultural impulses.

The transformation we recognize in 1966 did not take place overnight. It was gradual, 30 years in the making. It was stimulated by the automobile, improved highways, the great depression of the 1930's, rising costs that made commercial sponsorship of cultural attractions in obsolescent auditoriums increasingly prohibitive, and the dispersal of urban populations.

These were among the contributing factors in the most significant change that has occurred, the rise of the great universities as centers of creativity as well as learning, to provide a sheltering palm for both art and the artist, whose place, while respected, has never been made secure in our affluent society. The condition of the writer and artist who cannot follow their professions without supplementing their incomes, usually by teaching, is among the most vexing problems we have to face, despite a burgeoning economy. But their presence, whether as faculty members or "in residence," to stimulate the hearts and minds of students by their companionship and example, has brought within sight Goethe's ideal of the cultural life: "One ought, every day at least, to hear a little song, read a good poem, see a fine picture, and, if it were possible, to speak a few reasonable words." The ideal can be realized more completely today in university towns like Bloomington than almost anywhere else in the country.

While the period has been notable for many brilliant individual achievements, emphasis has been on the building of strong institutions that give promise of enduring, even though some of them stand on wobbly financial bases. Several of the most flourishing were depression blooms.

The people of the state capital take pride and satisfaction in the fact that they have successfully maintained the Indianapolis Symphony Orchestra, organized in 1930 on a cooperative basis by unemployed musicians under the leadership of the late Ferdinand Schaefer. Undaunted by annual deficits that became more considerable as time went by (it earned approximately 60 percent of a budget in excess of $500,000 during the 1965-66 season), they raised it to a full professional status in 1937 when Fabien Sevitzky became its musical director and have seen it forge ahead during his tenure and that of his successor, Izler Solomon. The composer and musicologist, Deems Taylor, was gracious enough to mention it among the ten orchestras he considered the country's best in the 1950's and other erudite critics, sampling its work on the extensive tours it makes every year, have been favorably impressed.

The depression years also contributed powerfully to our cultural expansion in other ways. The need for public works to relieve unemployment resulted in the building of the splendid Indiana University Auditorium at Bloomington and the spacious Edward C. Elliott Hall of Music at Purdue, which have become models for performing art centers across the country. In a time when private concert managements were faltering elsewhere, they brought to the state the most distinguished orchestras, ballet companies, vocal and instrumental musicians, and playacting groups available in the national and international markets. For twenty years after 1941 they enjoyed a fruitful association with the No. 1 company of the Metropolitan Opera House in New York, which visited no other campuses on its annual spring tours. The relationship was broken only because rising costs forced the Met to limit its tour engagements to week stands.

But it was long and intimate enough to inspire the Indiana University Opera Theater, an adjunct of the I. U. School of Music, as vitalized by Dean Wilfred C. Bain, which Hoosier enthusiasts are pleased to believe is the finest thing of its kind in the United States. Staffed by experts, many of whom were lured to academic life from the Met itself, it presents an opera production in East Hall on the Bloomington campus every possible Saturday night of the school year. Its graduates are singing now in many of the world's great opera houses and it has the potential of becoming a regional company of the first importance. It's a radiant new jewel in our state heritage that should be handled with loving care.

The most comparable development in this area of the performing arts is that of the Butler University Ballet, a fine young collegiate company that gives beautifully staged entertainments under professional direction several times a year in the university's new Clowes Hall. It's no wonder the Hoosier has become extraordinarily fond of opera and ballet, once regarded as the most exotic of musical experiences. The cult is growing. The I. U. Opera Theater now has its own ballet affiliate. Allen County has a Fort Wayne Civil Ballet, partly independent of schools.

While the audiences have widened, there has been a subtle change in musical taste over the years. We are in the age of the spectacular. There is perhaps more interest in sounds than in music. It can be seen in the comparative neglect of the recital, which enabled a virtuoso to be heard at full length rather than as an accessory to an orchestral or choral performance. Before anyone ever heard of audiophiles, recitals were a major part of a season's musical fare.

We are thinking back to the late 20's and 30's, when the Indianapolis Maennerchor entertained graciously in the building that now houses the downtown branch of the Indiana University Law School. It issued cards of admission addressed to "Mr. —— and Ladies," a courtly gesture no present-day entrepreneur could afford. Announcements for the 1928-29 season, of which the Maennerchor provided a good share, promised the Indianapolis public recitals by Joseph Szigeti, Gertrude Kappel, Myra Hess, Georges Enesco, Hulda Lashanska, Elly Ney, Roland Hayes, Paul Koschanski, Sophie Breslau, Emilio de Gorgoza, Rudolph Ganz, Louise Homer, Fritz Kreisler, and Sergei Rachmaninoff, to name a conspicuous few. Three visiting orchestras were on the program—the Cincinnati, the Minneapolis, and the New York Philharmonic.

Today we have less variety, but more orchestras, most of them home based. The American Symphony Orchestra Society grades them by size of their budgets. An orchestra spending about $250,-000 a year is "major," one financed below that figure "metropolitan." In addition to the major Indianapolis orchestra, the state has one in the metropolitan category, the Fort Wayne Philharmonic, which continues to flourish under the direction of Igor Buketoff. That is not the total of Indiana's resources, however. Indiana University has a complex of orchestras specializing in concert and opera performances. Cities from South Bend to Evansville, Richmond to Terre Haute, and Muncie to Lafayette pride themselves on this possession. Large and small, they have pretty much the same problems—underpaid musicians (when they are paid at all) and deficits that often threaten to become unmanageable as seasons grow longer and costs mount higher.

The Indianapolis orchestra in 1965-66 had a 28-week season, with a weekly minimum wage of $111.50. Because it played 115 concerts in the season, its earning potential was near capacity. The musicians have their hearts set on the goal of a 52-week season, so that they will not have to seek other employment, often in other fields, during the off-months. The merit of their case is recognized. Blessed are the fund raisers.

The complexity of the situation was suddenly dramatized when the musicians of the Indianapolis Symphony Orchestra declared a strike in the spring of 1966, partly on account of expectations raised by reports the orchestra would receive a handsome grant from the Ford Foundation under its program of assistance to American symphonies. The grant, when announced, was handsome indeed, $2,-000,000 toward an endowment fund, with the stipulation that an equal sum be raised locally in the next five years. A supplemental, nonmatching grant amounting to about $160,000 a year also was announced to help stabilize the orchestra's finances during the fund-raising period. But the implied promise of a better tomorrow did not bring immediate peace between the orchestra's musicians and its board of directors. Agreement had not been reached two weeks before rehearsals for the 1966-67 season were to begin. It was realized that even a $4,000,000 endowment fund was only priming the pump.

The public today has not come to accept the necessity for tax support of the arts of the kind and extent accorded education, industry, and agriculture. It has been limited to grants for specific purposes, like the Indianapolis Symphony Orchestra's school and municipal concerts. But government has given the arts substantial indirect subsidies resulting from tax laws that favor or encourage gifts from large estates. This has contributed greatly to the building of institutional strength in the past three decades.

Almost every city and town of size in the state counts among its assets a museum that is bulging with paintings and sculptures received from private collectors. And many Indiana homes are richly adorned with art objects, both traditional and contemporary, that will be donated to public museums when they can provide for them adequately. Expansion is the order of the day. Among the most promising in the year of the Indiana sesquicentennial is the plan to build a new John Herron Art Museum at Indianapolis. Only a small part of the treasure it possesses can be displayed at any one time in the present antiquated building, which is rendered largely useless in the summers by lack of air-conditioning. Preliminaries have been started toward building a modern new museum within the next few years. Among the favored sites under consideration is the proposed jointly operated Indianapolis campus of Indiana and Purdue universities.

The Herron, during the tenure of Wilbur D. Peat as director, increased its acquisitions and organized many important exhibitions, some of which have circulated nationally. Museums with select collections, including a surprisingly extensive representation of moderns, are cultural assets of Indiana University, Evansville, Fort Wayne, Lafayette, Ball State University at Muncie, the University of Notre Dame, Richmond, South Bend, Terre Haute, Nashville, and other state schools and cities.

The Hoosier Salon holds one-man shows by Indiana artists throughout the year, as well as a prize exhibition each winter that includes work of artists resident in the state and native Hoosiers working in all parts of the country. Other notable annuals include that of Indiana Artists Club and the Herron's Indiana Artists Exhibition, at which they display their expertise in all the latest modes and media. While the rural landscape still is most characteristic of Indiana art, the state has both painters and sculptors who are "contemporary" in composer Easley Blackwood, Jr.'s definition of the word, "right now." Repeated, but usually short-lived, attempts have been made to give the contemporary artist a showcase for his work at least comparable to that of the Hoosier Salon, the latest being the Talbot Gallery at Indianapolis. Every county seat town has its art league or club to further the cause. Art shows have become conspicuous side attractions at shopping centers, theaters, and dry cleaning establishments. Art is practically everywhere. And painters, especially, have become as numerous as poets were in Riley's era.

The problem of the gifted artist is gaining the recognition he merits, a task rendered doubly difficult by the local and regional nature of the occasional shows to which he can submit entries with reasonable expectations. The struggle to gain attention beyond his own area undoubtedly accounts for a good deal of the gimmickry in such developments as "pop" and "op" art. The Indiana artist today might be assisted in winning recognition beyond his own backyard if a competent group were to hold a statewide competition and send its choicest items to a New York gallery for an annual exhibition, much as the Indianapolis Symphony Orchestra plays occasionally in Carnegie Hall to increase its national reputation. The celebrated nostalgia of the Sons of Indiana living in exile there might provide the motive power necessary for such a venture. The fame of the Brown County School was established largely in this way, when the annual exhibitions of the Hoosier Salon were held in Chicago under the sponsorship of that city's Indiana Society.

In a sense, the artist today is to the new frontier what the Indian was to the old frontier—the only good painter is a dead one. Reverence of tradition is still a Hoosier trait, even though it has acquired a tinge of sophistication. Life for the sculptor is further complicated by the decline of the monumental in both public and private building, as witness the vacant niches for statuary in many of the state's middle-aged structures. He will come into his own, perhaps, with the dawn of a new heroic period. It does not seem to have begun to break.

The spiritual malaise reflecting the materialism of the times can be glimpsed by the unaided eye in much of the severely functional architecture that has replaced nobler edifices in recent years. The urban scene has been marred, too, by the scarred back and sides of older buildings, never meant to stand alone, that were left exposed when adjoining buildings were demolished. As long as they stand thus, there should be a demand for a new school of exterior decorating, for which the state's artists might apply. They have become a more conspicuous blemish than parking lots or junkyards.

On the other hand, there has been much fine, imaginative work in the architectural design of smaller buildings now lining the streets that link old urban centers with suburbia. Many of the new shopping centers, too, have a touch of distinction, and the more thoughtfully conceived new homes thankfully ignore Le-Corbusier's dictum that "a house is a machine for living in," despite their complete assortment of modern conveniences. There has been real progress, too, in preserving and restoring historic mansions and public buildings of more than ordinary interest, and the realization that proper maintenance is half of the battle.

The current trends in architecture can be studied nowhere better than in the complex of state buildings between Washington and Ohio, Capitol and West streets in downtown Indianapolis. Buffing its limestone exterior has restored much of the pristine dignity of the old Corinthian Statehouse. Its rear faces the strictly functional state office building, which could easily be converted to industrial leases. The office building is flanked by the classic elegance of the Indiana State Library and the sparkling blend of the contemporary and traditional in the building of the Indiana Employment Security Division. Some may find significance in the fact that the state's tallest structure is not Indianapolis' new 26-story City-County Building, but a gas tank.

While it's time for another survey, it seems unlikely that production of books by Hoosier authors has diminished since 1950, when a study by John Moriarity, director of Purdue Libraries, showed they turned out more best sellers during the first half of the twentieth century than writers of any other state. And writing is still, perhaps, the most honored of the professions among a people who continue to glory in the fading memory of a literary golden age. But changes of emphasis and attitude have occurred. There is a growing tendency among intellectuals to dismiss the more celebrated Indiana novelists of the old school as popular entertainers and to give more credit to comparatively neglected masters from Edward Eggleston to Theodore Dreiser, William Vaughn Moody, David Graham Phillips, and others, who made direct contributions to what has become the mainstream of American literature.

A balance should be struck, of course. Pride is justified in the accomplishments of Booth Tarkington, James Whitcomb Riley, Gene Stratton Porter, Charles Major, George Ade, Maurice Thompson, Meredith Nicholson, and others of their illustrious company, who entertained well in the genteel tradition of a day when people read as avidly as their grandchildren watch television in this advanced age. It is well to note, too, that a later generation finds social value to a degree in Tarkington's *Alice Adams* and *The Magnificent Ambersons*, both of which were sufficiently distinguished to win him Pulitzer Prizes.

While every other Hoosier, to this day, is a born storyteller, the most conspicuously brilliant works of recent years have been in the field of scholarship, history, biography, and the humanities. Towering examples are Herbert J. Muller's far-reaching search for our philosophical roots in *The Loom of History*, *The Uses of the Past*, and his splendid trilogy on freedom; James Randall's authoritative works on Lincoln; Kenneth P. Williams' monumental *Lincoln Finds a General*; and R. Carlyle Buley's sweeping account of pioneer life in *The Old Northwest: Pioneer Period, 1815-1840*, which received the 1951 Pulitzer Prize in history.

Buley's achievement calls attention to one advantage Indiana writers enjoy over painters and others who create in areas still reserved to individual initiative. They have access to trade channels that occasionally recognize merit and take risks on their behalf that lead to recognition. And even when the big publishing houses fail them they have powerful friends at home. The first edition of Buley's *The Old Northwest* was published by the Indiana Historical Society. The trade edition was brought out after it had won the Pulitzer Prize. State writers also have an influential aid in the university presses, notably the Indiana University Press, which commands increasingly wide interest for many important publications that do not have immediate commercial appeal. That influence is spreading. The Indiana University Press, in conjunction with the publishing arms of seven other American universities, including the University of Notre Dame Press, recently has opened a London office.

If there is not a readily identifiable Indiana school in fiction today, there is no lack of activity by novelists who are native or resident Hoosiers, many of whom write affectionately of things seen or remembered in their home state. A future generation of super-readers may penetrate the fugue-like structure of Ross Lockridge, Jr.'s epic *Raintree County* to find that it captures more of the color and feeling of Indiana life in the tumultuous middle decades of the nineteenth century than any other book we have. To list all the writers who are making, and have made, important contributions in this field would be to trip over names. We can mention only a few to indicate the scope and variety of their work. The old tradition, filled with nostalgia for a pleasant way of life, is continued admirably in both the fiction and nonfiction of William E. Wilson. The problems of people in relation to an increasingly mechanistic world have been the concern of Kurt Vonnegut, a master satirist. The versatile Joseph A. Hayes has been equally successful in writing popular dramas and novels. Rex Stout has kept millions of devotees of detective fiction bemused for years. Marguerite Young's Proustian novel, *Miss MacIntosh, My Darling*, not only was the heftiest published in 1965 but was also among the most widely discussed.

These serious times have not produced a humorist to succeed George Ade and Kin Hubbard, or a people's poet to fill the shoes of Riley. But they have given the country two of its best song-writers—homespun Hoagy Carmichael, a disciple of Riley in his line, and the haut monde composer, Cole Porter, each representative of Indiana in his own way. The fact is that Indiana's song-writers, including Paul Dresser and others equally illustrious, had a following as large and loyal as its novelists in the golden age, although few of them were closely identified with the state during their productive years. When families and friends gathered around the piano to sing a generation ago, the program was almost sure to include Albert Von Tilzer's "Take Me Out to the Ball

Game," J. Will Callahan's "Smiles," and J. Russell Robinson's "Margie," to recall three memory gems.

In recent times the state has produced such gifted literary poets as Barris Mills, Samuel Yellen, Lionel Wiggam, and Ruth Stone. Libraries of the nation are well stocked with outstanding books for children and young adults by skilled and industrious Indiana writers.

While it hardly is the primrose path to fame and wealth that it was at the turn of the century, the quality of authorship in the state today probably is higher than it has ever been. Excellence of the work submitted annually since 1951 for the Indiana Authors' Day awards at Indiana University is evidence of this. There were 50 nominations for a possible 5 awards in 1956.

Despite the boom in the performing arts, it has not been a happy time for serious composers and playwrights. The concert repertoire has become standardized, and that of the American theater, still dependent on popular taste and the chaotic conditions that prevail in the New York production channels, has stagnated. While concert audiences remain notoriously hostile to new music, contemporary composers receive their principal support from the intellectual elite at the universities and from orchestra conductors who insist on seasoning each program with a first performance. This practice, however, is largely self-defeating, since the same work seldom gets a second hearing. Despite these difficulties, Easley Blackwood, Jr., an avant-garde composer who received his early training in the state, has established an international reputation.

While concertgoers prefer old, familiar music, there is almost no general support from playgoers for drama that has stood the test of time—even the celebration of the 400th anniversary of Shakespeare's birth in 1964 was slight outside the festival centers. The demand is for late comedies and musical shows, with revivals in favor only when they have nostalgic appeal. Thrillers and plays that plumb the new psychiatry for shock values have a certain vogue. But dramas with a glint of light for our time are usually set in past ages, like *A Man for All Seasons* and *The Crucible*, leaving the audience to draw its own parallels. The result is that playgoers who would refresh their acquaintance with the classics or study firsthand the new trends in experimental drama are forced to rely more and more on the university theaters and the efforts of struggling nonprofessional groups like Indianapolis' Morris Street Players. Still, there is unprecedented activity in supplying the public with the light entertainment it seeks.

The increase of activity has been especially pronounced in Indianapolis since the opening of Clowes Memorial Hall at Butler University in 1963 provided it with a suitable home for the performing arts, a facility that had not always been available after the English Theater was closed in 1948. It brought to the city a splendid variety of concert and cultural attractions and most of the touring Broadway shows, besides providing permanent quarters for the Indianapolis Symphony Orchestra. Its greatest achievement to date has been the premiere engagement of the newly formed Metropolitan Opera National Company in a series of 11 performances between September 20 and October 2, 1965. The 2,200-seat house was virtually sold out for the entire run. Its success has been complicated, however, by its comparatively small seating capacity in a day of rising costs, when money can be lost much faster than it can be made, and the profit margin allowed local management even on "hits" is thin at best. Whether it can maintain its starting pace would seem to depend greatly on the continuing goodwill of subscribers to a guaranty fund or some other form of subsidy.

Perhaps the cost factor accounts in part for the remarkable growth of summer theaters, operating in tents, barns, or outdoors, in the past 20 years. There is one of repute within easy driving range of most Hoosier communities today. Indianapolis in recent years had the fully professional Starlight Musicals and the Avondale Playhouse, both employing guest stars to appear with resident companies, to give it a variety of light entertainment in July and August. Indiana University operates the Brown County Playhouse and the showboat *Majestic* on the Ohio River during the summer months. The Purdue University Theater supplements its student casts with professional guests, summer and winter. The Wagon

Wheel Playhouse at Warsaw, the Enchanted Hills at Syracuse, and the Shawnee at Bloomfield are among other established theaters doing their part to make Indiana summers pleasant for Hoosier theatergoers.

The "little theaters" of a generation ago, while they cultivate dramatic art less enthusiastically, still exist in expanded forms to amuse a wider public. The Indianapolis Little Theater of 1914 observed its 50th anniversary as the Booth Tarkington Civic Theater in the 1964-65 season by reviving eight comedies reminiscent of the period. Some, like the Richmond Civic Theater, which celebrated its 25th season in 1965-66, have enlarged the cultural life of their communities. Richmond today has a symphony orchestra that was first a small ensemble organized to support the actors in the production of musical shows. While its primary purpose is to organize a series of road-show attractions, the Broadway Theater League of Evansville has made a unique contribution by sponsoring an annual playwriting contest with a guaranteed production for the winner.

A sustaining program of the performing arts in years to come may depend on the further development of embryonic repertory groups like the Indiana Theater Company, the Indiana University Opera Theater, and the Butler University Ballet, all of which have begun to move in wider orbits. There may be the seed of a renaissance in the training and experience they are giving their young performers. They may become the educational base for regional companies in opera, drama, and the dance that will be at least as well founded as major symphony orchestras are today.

Perhaps the brightest feature of our Hoosier heritage in literature and the arts is the challenge it presents. The field is wide open and there is plenty of room at the top. We await the next half century of the state's cultural history hopefully, in the spirit of Adolphe Brisson, a French critic who once exclaimed in *Figaro*: "We needed reassurance, ideals, panache, and then there came Cyrano! Our thirst was assuaged."

Where is our Cyrano?

REYNOLD E. CARLSON

Recreation and Parks

What people do in their leisure is at least as important to society as what they do in their work. In pioneer days, when work hours were long and the few leisure hours were home-centered, a society was burdened with very few responsibilities for recreation. That situation no longer prevails. Most people have more free time today than their predecessors ever dreamed of, and there is the promise of far more in the future. Leisure has become a two-edged tool which can either destroy or bring enrichment to life. Which edge of the tool will fashion our future may well depend upon the provisions which society makes for recreation and for education in the use of leisure.

Herein lies a challenge to Indiana. It will take serious and dedicated planning to realize a better society through recreation. The concept of recreation must be expanded to encompass not only sports and games but all those leisure activities engaged in primarily for the satisfaction they give—music, literary activities, arts and

Reynold E. Carlson, at Indiana University since 1947, served as chairman of the Department of Recreation and Park Administration from 1962 to 1966 and received the university's Lieber Award for Distinguished Teaching in 1963. A former president of the American Camping Association and office-holder of numerous national professional organizations, he is co-author of *Recreation in American Life* and *Outdoor Education*.

crafts, outdoor recreation, social activities, dancing, and drama. Moreover, the programs of recreation must encourage activity and creativity, participating rather than watching, and being involved rather than being entertained. Such programs should not only help to lessen such social ills as delinquency, mental illness, poor physical health, boredom, and ignorance, but should touch every life with the positive benefits of personal satisfaction and fulfillment.

In many respects Indiana lies in the "averages" for the nation. It is average in its recreation development, excelling in some respects and lagging in others. It presents to the nation the image of a state outstanding in four completely different facets of recreation: the 500-mile race, basketball, state parks, and professional training for recreation leadership. Indiana graduates are scattered throughout the country as administrators of important park and recreation programs and directors of professional curriculums in colleges and universities.

These strengths are balanced by unfortunate weaknesses. Indiana has been sleeping while other states have garnered the lucrative tourist business. It is a standard joke that Indiana ranked forty-eighth among the states in tourist promotion until Alaska and Hawaii attained statehood; then Indiana became fiftieth. Although this rank is now being improved, most travelers still regard Indiana merely as a space to be crossed en route from one place to another. Another of Indiana's recreational weaknesses lies in its unevenly developed community programs. There are several outstanding community recreation programs under highly qualified leadership, but the number of cities having year-round diversified programs is few. Other weaknesses and strengths will be discussed in the pages that follow.

In early Indiana, recreation pursuits were largely those associated with a pioneering and farming culture. Libraries and books were scarce. Social activities centered around the home, tavern, or church. Boys and girls found their pleasure in the work of home and farm, helping with farm chores, and creating with their own hands various articles needed by the family. Hunting and fishing were pastimes for boys and men, sometimes pursued to the neglect of farm work.

Work and recreation were not as sharply distinguished in these early rural settings as they are today. The work at home and on the land was often difficult; but the drudgery was relieved by the satisfaction of making things with one's own hands, working with animals, and being near to the earth and its changing seasons. Community gatherings were frequent. Neighbors would work together to put up a house or barn, husk corn, shear sheep, or make maple sugar, each man giving labor that would be repaid with labor in turn. When work was finished, the group might sing, play games, or—religious scruples permitting—even dance. Quilting bees, shooting matches, or spelling bees also enlivened the social life. Weddings gave excuse for two-day festivals. Manners were rough and brawling frequent. Cultural opportunities—music, dramatics, and art—were relatively meager. Although sports as we know them did not exist, holidays such as the Fourth of July were celebrated with foot races, wrestling matches, and tug-of-war. There might be feasting and drinking, with wild turkey, venison, bear, corn bread, preserves, hard cider, and whiskey on the tables.

Following the Civil War, the mode of life changed rapidly. The soldiers brought home many sports and games, such as baseball, previously unfamiliar. Cities began to grow, libraries expanded, and public education became widespread. Leisure was more plentiful, and with it came a demand for recreation and the acceptance by society of its responsibility for providing it.

The recreation movement had four more or less separate origins. One lay in the conservation of forests and wildlife; another in the establishment of parks; a third in community recreation provided by public recreation departments, voluntary agencies, and schools; and a fourth in commercial recreation. As time went on, these four movements drew closer together, though even today there is not as close cooperation in some areas as would be desirable.

The first white men found about nine tenths of Indiana covered with hardwood forests, among the finest in the world, including giant sycamores, oaks, and tulip poplars. Here resided, in abundance, elk, bear, deer, wildcats, timber wolves, wild turkeys, and numerous species of small fur-bearing animals. Great herds of bison crossed from the Illinois prairies to salt licks in Kentucky, beating out with their hooves wide trails, used by the Indians and early settlers and still followed by sections of modern roads.

There was no thought of setting aside land for recreation when the forest seemed inexhaustible. Each man, concerned for the immediate livelihood of himself and his family, set out to clear the land as quickly as possible. He must have felt nothing but satisfaction as he toppled and burned the huge trees that had stood for hundreds of years. Unfortunately, much of the land that was cleared, especially in the hills of southern Indiana, became eroded after a few years and was soon abandoned. As the years rolled on, forests were felled at an accelerated rate. Between 1880 and 1897, forest land was reduced from 4,335,000 to 1,500,000 acres. Fish and game and their habitats suffered similar depreciation. Some species were hunted to extinction. Bear, elk, and panthers ceased to roam in the Indiana woods; and wild turkeys and passenger pigeons became extinct. With industrialization, coal mining stripped much of the land, scarring it with barren pits. Waters pouring through the pits eroded them still further and picked up chemicals deadly to all fish life.

Not until late in the nineteenth century did alarm over the widespread destruction become strong enough to cause protective steps to be taken. Laws to protect various species of wildlife were passed. In 1881 the office of Commissioner of Fisheries was established, and in 1899 its jurisdiction was extended to birds and animals. Attempts to restore losses through artificial propagation were undertaken in the twentieth century. In 1930 game preserves were established to restock fields and woodlands, a measure which passing decades proved to be less effective than restoration of habitats.

Of the state's fine stands of virgin timber, only a few scattered remnants still stood by the twentieth century. One of these was preserved with the establishment in 1916 of Turkey Run State Park, which, with McCormick's Creek State Park, established a few months earlier, marked the beginnings of the state park system. Indiana, though slower than California, New York, Michigan, and Minnesota in setting aside its first state parks, progressed rapidly when the system was once established. Under the vigorous leadership of Richard Lieber, the state park system soon became known as one of the nation's finest. With areas chosen to perpetuate different types of native terrain, the state park system grew to 16 parks and memorials by the 1930's. Indiana bore for many years the questionable distinction of being the only state that charged admission to its parks, its philosophy being that parks should be as nearly self-supporting as possible. Today over half the states have followed Indiana's example by adopting some type of fee system in their parks. The fee policy made possible the original development of the parks, but in recent years, the income from fees has not been enough to provide needed improvements and to keep pace with park advances in other states.

Recreation offered in the first state parks was that of quiet appreciation of natural beauty. There were few conveniences for visitors. Indiana pioneered in offering naturalist services in state parks. The Indianapolis Nature Club sponsored naturalist services at McCormick's Creek State Park in 1923 and 1924, and the following year the Division of State Parks made naturalist services a permanent part of the state park program.

As the twentieth century progressed, with cities becoming more congested, working hours shorter, automobiles more numerous, and roads better, crowds besieged the parks; and the need to make provisions for public use became acutely felt. When the depression of the 1930's struck, Indiana was ready with plans to use federal government aid in developing inns, exhibits, naturalist services, picnic and camping grounds, and hiking trails, with the result that Indiana emerged from the depression with some of the finest state park facilities in the nation.

The need for timber reserves rather than recreation dictated the creation of a state forestry board in 1901 and the first state forest in 1903. Most of the land acquired by the state was cut-over timberland or eroded farm land, unattractive and uninviting. After years of planting, protection, and management, it became apparent that these poor lands were becoming superb recreation resources. Increasingly they were used for picnicking, hiking, hunting, fishing, boating, and camping, in a few cases rivaling even the state parks in popularity.

Various divisions of state government which had been concerned with conservation, including forests, parks, and wildlife, were united in 1919, when the Department of Conservation was established. Recreation thus became a responsibility of the Department of Conservation.

The federal government was slower than the state government to accept responsibility for either conservation or recreation in Indiana. The depression-born agencies of the 1930's were the first of the great federal programs affecting recreation in the state. The W.P.A. and the N.Y.A. brought recreation facilities and leadership to many sections of the state and included the training of recreation leaders. The C.C.C., supervised by the National Park Service and U. S. Forest Service, improved the state parks and forests to such an extent that, in the opinion of many, the development of these areas was advanced by as much as twenty-five years. The National Park Service at this time set up two recreation demonstration projects which later became state parks (Versailles and Tippecanoe River). In 1935 the U. S. Forest Service set up plans to purchase 677,000 acres of timberland and eroded agriculture land as the Hoosier National Forest, to be operated not only for timber production and watershed protection but also for recreation and wildlife management.

Indiana in 1859 became the first state to authorize community use of school facilities, but at first the only areas for recreation were small playgrounds in connection with the schools. Nor did the first public parks (Indianapolis received one in 1866) have much provision for active recreation, for they were regarded primarily as reserves for the enjoyment of natural beauty. The mounting demand for recreation resulted in several state laws in the early twentieth century permitting local communities to set up recreation programs administered by park departments, recreation departments, or public schools. Playgrounds and parks, with play apparatus and equipment, and a number of fine community centers were established. Cities were authorized to establish departments of recreation in 1925. Two years later counties were given authority to establish county parks.

Where park departments and recreation departments were separate, cooperation was sometimes difficult to achieve. The Indiana Park and Recreation Association, established about 50 years ago, was one of the few professional organizations in the country to serve both parks and recreation from the beginning. The complete coordination of parks and recreation was not to be realized until mid-century.

Voluntary organizations preceded governmental agencies in recognizing the need for community recreation. Neighborhood houses and boys' clubs appeared late in the nineteenth century. The Young Men's Christian Association, first of the large national youth-serving organizations, was established in 1854 in Indianapolis, only three years after its first appearance in the United States. The Young Women's Christian Association reached Indianapolis in 1895.

In the second decade of the twentieth century, the Boy Scouts, Girl Scouts, 4-H Clubs, the Camp Fire Girls began to spread. In the years that followed, these organizations came to be regarded as important supplements to the schools.

The turnvereins, gymnastic associations of German origin, were introduced in the United States at an early date. One of these became the first physical education teacher-training institution in the state and one of the first in the nation. Founded in Indianapolis in 1866, it is now operated as the Normal College of the American Gymnastic Union, a division of Indiana University.

Indiana's many industries began providing recreation for their employees at least as early as 1909. Baseball was the most popular activity, with bowling a close second. Industrial recreation grew rapidly until the depression, with basketball, horseshoes, and golf added to baseball and bowling. Libraries, musical and dramatic activities, and amateur circuses were popular. Although curtailed during the depression, recreation sponsored by both management and unions expanded during and after World War II.

Tourist recreation, overlooked by the state government until recently, was a commercial interest from early days in Indiana. Such places as the French Lick-West Baden area, Martinsville, Sulphur, Trinity Springs, and Dillsboro were developed for the supposed curative values of their mineral waters. Though a hotel existed at French Lick as early as 1840, the first part of the twentieth century witnessed the heyday of the spas. Attracted by gambling as well as the waters, the fashionable and wealthy, famous and infamous flocked to the resorts. The resorts declined in the 1930's, probably because of changing public tastes and the depression. Today most of them are closed. The French Lick Hotel, refurbished, modernized, and under new management, is a notable survivor.

Family and individual effort are and probably always will be the leading sources of recreation. Commercial activities run a close second. Public and other nonprofit agencies fill the gap to provide those things that people cannot readily provide for themselves or buy commercially but that are considered to have social value.

About 1.6 percent of the land area of the state is in public lands, mostly forests of southern Indiana. A study directed by Walter Stone and published in 1962, *Recreation in Indiana* (Indiana State Board of Health), showed that there were also under the jurisdiction of federal, state, and local governments 387 children's playgrounds, 926 baseball diamonds, 733 softball diamonds, 103 outdoor and 15 indoor swimming pools, 45 golf courses, 224 football fields, 1,119 basketball courts, 516 picnic grounds, 231 recreation buildings, 778 gymnasiums, and 173 social rooms. These figures include school facilities. Some of the schools permit use of their recreation facilities by the public; others do not.

As measured by minimum standards of the National Recreation Association and the Indiana Governor's Committee on Recreation,

Indiana can reasonably well meet current needs for playfields, playgrounds, baseball fields, auditoriums, and gymnasiums but is seriously deficient in tennis courts, golf courses, and rooms for indoor games, reading, arts and crafts, and club meetings. Swimming pools, especially indoor pools, are so scarce that schools can rarely include swimming instruction in their physical education programs. None of the facilities is considered adequate for the needs of the population anticipated by 1970. The gross acreage for recreation under the jurisdiction of local governments—approximately 28,000 acres—is less than half of the acreage that will be needed by 1970.

Since World War II, the state government has encouraged local governments in the establishment of recreation programs in several ways. The State Board of Health provided consultation services to communities for several years. A Governor's Advisory Committee on Recreation functioned from 1946 to 1963, when a Recreation Council was created within the Board of Health, with a State Director of Recreation to promote community recreation. In July 1965 a new Department of Natural Resources replaced the Department of Conservation and the Flood Control and Water Resources Commission. The Recreation Council was transferred to the new department and renamed the Outdoor Recreation Council. Thus most of the state agencies concerned with recreation were united under one department, a move which was intended to coordinate efforts.

There are today well over 30 state parks and memorials in the state park system. Their great variety is exemplified by the Dunes, with their shifting sands and unusual flora, Clifty Falls with its falls and scenic view of the Ohio River, Versailles with its new man-made lake, Turkey Run with its small grove of virgin timber, and Pokagon with its beautiful lake setting and winter sport facilities. Camping, swimming, hiking, and sightseeing are outstanding recreation activities in the state parks. The naturalist services, which include guided tours and lectures, are among the finest in the nation's state parks, although lack of a permanent year-round nucleus staff has hampered their development.

Indiana's history has left rich recreation resources in the form of historic sites and buildings, old trails, and roads that annually attract thousands of visitors. While many of these historic treasures are now designated as state parks or memorials, others are preserved or merely marked by private individuals and associations. The fascinating old river towns such as Rising Sun, Madison, Jeffersonville, and New Albany, with their fine old buildings along the Ohio River, attest to the importance of the river as a highway in the colorful early days of the state. The George Rogers Clark State Memorial and the Indiana Territory State Memorial preserve some of the flavor of the old territorial capital at Vincennes. South of them on the Wabash lies the New Harmony State Memorial, site of the Rappite and Robert Owen communal societies. A new state park that will give recognition to this significant area is under way.

Abraham Lincoln's boyhood in southern Indiana (1816-30) is commemorated by the Lincoln State Park and the recently established Lincoln Boyhood Memorial operated by the National Park Service. North of Lafayette is the Tippecanoe Battlefield State Memorial, site of a memorable Indian battle, and near Mitchell is Spring Mill State Park, which centers its major attraction around a reconstructed village of the early nineteenth century. There are memorials to such distinguished persons as Wilbur Wright, Gene Stratton Porter, and T. C. Steele. Memorials also preserve part of the old Whitewater canal and Goshen church.

The Indiana state park system, at one time rated among the first three in the country, is still highly regarded. Since World War II, however, the state parks have had a difficult struggle to keep abreast of the heavy demands placed on them. During the fiscal year of 1963-64, an attendance of over four million visitors was recorded. The system has been largely self-supporting, and very probably the people of Indiana have come to expect the parks to pay their own way to an unjustifiably great extent. The income has not been sufficient to provide for expansion and upkeep. Only recently, through allotments from the cigarette tax, direct legislative appropriations, and the potential income from the federal Land and Water Conservation Fund, does it appear that the state park system may receive the financial support that may enable it to resume its place as one of the best in America.

The state's 13 forests contain about 126,000 acres. Camping and picnicking facilities are being enlarged as pressures for use of these areas increase. All state forests are open to hunters during the hunting season. Several small lakes provide fishing and boating.

State fish and game properties include numerous hunting and fishing areas, many of which have boat ramps and one of which has a campground and picnic area. Simple outdoor enjoyment as well as fishing and hunting is offered on these lands. The Fish and Game Division has leases on private lands for hunting and fishing and maintains 85 public fishing sites. One of the duties of the division is issuing hunting and fishing licenses and enforcing fish and game laws.

The state universities are deeply involved in recreation. The Department of Recreation and Park Administration at Indiana University and the Division of Recreation Leadership at Purdue University offer professional preparation in recreation leadership, and Ball State offers a Boys Club curriculum. Purdue's Agriculture Extension Service (now the Cooperative Extension Service) in 1936 became the first in the nation to offer field service in recreation to rural communities. Indiana University's service to communities, begun in 1945, was the first in the nation apart from that of the Agriculture Extension Service. The universities serve communities and state agencies in organizing and evaluating recreation programs, in conducting training institutes, and in making surveys.

The Great Lakes Park Training Institute, conducted each February at Pokagon State Park by the Department of Recreation and Park Administration at Indiana University, draws an annual registration of over four hundred park and recreation leaders from coast to coast, including the United States and Canada. Established in 1947, it is the first of such institutes conducted by various state universities in the country. Its impact upon park and recreation developments is beyond estimation. Garrett G. Eppley, first chairman of the Department of Recreation at Indiana University, has directed the institute since its beginning.

Other state agencies are also concerned with recreation. In recent years the state's mental hospitals have made recreation programs under professional leadership a part of their therapeutic programs. The state institutions for delinquents are also expanding their recreation programs. The State Commission on the Aging and Aged is interested in recreation for the elderly, and the Indiana Arts Commission is awakening the state to the importance of the arts. It is to be hoped that the state will give attention also to other aspects of community recreation.

The U. S. Forest Service now has jurisdiction over 125,000 acres in the Hoosier National Forest—a far cry from the forest of 677,000 acres envisaged when the purchase was planned, but the increase in land prices has in recent years limited acquisition. The forests are open to hunting and fishing. Picnic and camping areas have been developed. The recreation area supervised by the Forest Service at the new Monroe Reservoir contains a launching area, picnic grounds, and camp sites and will eventually include a public swimming area. In 1957 the Hoosier National Forest had 82,000 visitor-day users; by 1963 this number had increased to 180,000.

The transfer of the Lincoln Boyhood National Memorial in 1963 from the state to the nation gave the National Park Service its first holding in Indiana. A new visitor center has been constructed, and the numbers of visitors are increasing. Additional areas in the state are now under consideration by the National Park Service.

The U. S. Army Corps of Engineers is another federal agency active in Indiana's recreation development. With locks and dams on the Ohio River, six reservoirs either completed or near completion, and several more reservoirs under consideration, the much-needed recreational waters for Indiana are well on the way to realization. Though the Corps' chief concern is with flood control and navigation, its impounded waters are heavily used for boating and fishing. The Corps generally turns over to other agencies the development and operation of recreation areas on the shores of the reservoirs. At the 11,000-acre Monroe Reservoir, for example, public recreation lands, with the exception of those administered by the U. S. Forest Service, are the responsibility of the state Department of Natural Resources.

Through the years various state enabling acts have defined the ways in which local communities might conduct tax-supported park and recreation departments. In 1955 a comprehensive park and recreation law created a liberal basis for future developments, making it possible for cities and counties to establish joint park and recreation boards individually or in combination with other cities and counties and to cooperate with school boards in providing park and recreation facilities and services. The law provided for bipartisan boards, employment of professional personnel, and financing through municipal, county, and school funds. The law as amended in 1965 expanded bonding power for park and recreation purposes, permitting a flexibility hitherto unknown in the structure of public recreation programs.

Thirty-one communities in Indiana have year-round recreation programs. Surprisingly, three cities of over 30,000 population—Kokomo, Anderson, and Terre Haute—have no year-round tax-supported programs under professional leadership, although many smaller cities, including nine of under 10,000 population, afford such programs. Sixty-one counties have public summer recreation programs, generally limited to children's playgrounds and boys' baseball.

A few communities in Indiana, among them Fort Wayne, South Bend, and Evansville, are nationally known for their exceptionally fine provisions for community recreation. There are some excellent public community centers that have been constructed with private funds. Outstanding are the Honeywell Memorial Center in Wabash and the Whiting Community Center in Whiting. In Columbus, local industry has provided remarkable facilities, including the Donner Center with its large swimming pool, Lincoln Center with its artificial ice skating rink, and the new Otter Creek golf course.

In general, Indiana's tax-supported local recreation programs have not developed along broad lines. They place emphasis on sports and games. Although these activities should comprise a major part of a community program, other areas, such as arts and crafts, music, dramatics, and outing activities, should receive greater attention.

Commercial recreation meets many of the needs of Indiana people. The economy of the state is bolstered by recreation, for a vast number of businesses thrive on recreation expenditures. They range from businesses purveying recreation, such as bowling alleys, pool halls, racetracks, skating rinks, taverns, dance halls, professional sports, movies, and theaters, to those supplying products used in recreation such as automobiles, sporting goods, boats, television sets, and radios. Stone's survey indicated that there are over 6,000 commercial recreation facilities in Indiana, among which bowling alleys, 233 in number, and indoor theaters, 189 in number, are the most common.

Some of the commercial attractions in Indiana especially worthy of mention include Santa Claus Land (an amusement park); the shops, restaurants, and galleries clustering about the art center of Nashville; and the lake resorts of northern Indiana.

Expenditures for personal and commercial recreation in the nation are estimated at some $50 billion to $60 billion annually. Indiana might be considered average, or, in view of its undeveloped tourist business, somewhat below average. A rough estimate would be $270 per person in the state.

The nonprofit voluntary organizations fill a large segment of the recreation picture in Indiana. The Boy Scouts and Girl Scouts serve all sections of the state through their councils, and the 4-H Clubs are similarly widespread. The Camp Fire Girls have nine offices in the state. There are 34 Y.M.C.A.'s, 16 Y.W.C.A.'s, and 23 full-time and 18 associate Boys' Clubs. Numerous church groups and 27 centers for the aging also make their contributions to recreation in Indiana.

Some of the voluntary organizations, such as the Scouts, Camp Fire Girls, and 4-H, which function primarily through volunteer leadership, have practically no facilities except offices and camps. Other organizations, particularly the Y.M.C.A., Y.W.C.A., and Boys' Clubs, maintain their own buildings, which may range from large central buildings to small neighborhood centers.

The effectiveness of the youth programs varies greatly from community to community in accordance with financial support and leadership. Indiana has many excellent programs and compares favorably with nearby states. The increasing difficulty of finding enough volunteer leadership and enough money for salaries and facilities has hindered the development of some programs.

There are 968 private membership clubs in the state that have recreation facilities for the use of their members. These facilities include golf courses, swimming pools, bowling alleys, game rooms, club rooms, dining areas, dance floors, and fishing and hunting areas.

In Indiana, basketball is king, and each spring the fever of "Hoosier madness" infects the state as the high school elimination playoff takes place and the victor is crowned. The Indiana farmer, they say, raises corn to fatten his pigs to get the money to pay the taxes to build gymnasiums so that his son can play basketball. Certain it is that basketball is the source of many a community's pride. There is no classification of schools by size, and a Cinderella team, such as that from the little town of Milan in 1954, can capture a championship. The gymnasium of a small town sometimes has a seating capacity greater than the population of the town itself. The great amount of Indiana high school talent has provided outstanding players for college teams in many states.

For 46 years preceding 1955, Indianapolis teams failed to win a championship; but in that year and in 1956, Crispus Attucks High School brought the victory to the state capital city. Oscar Robertson went on to become one of the all-time greats of roundball competition.

The Indiana High School Athletic Association endeavors to keep a firm hand on basketball and from time to time has found it necessary to punish excesses that have occurred. Overenthusiastic community promotion, rather than the schools themselves, is generally responsible for abuses.

In college competition, Purdue has won five Big Ten crowns in basketball. Indiana, under Branch McCracken, has had four Big Ten titles and two NCAA crowns. Butler University, under Tony Hinkle, has produced a series of great teams, often upsetting one of the Big Three. Notre Dame, too, has had some outstanding teams and in the 1957 season produced the runner-up to Kentucky in the NCAA. The colleges of the state included in the Hoosier Conference and the Indiana Intercollegiate Conference have had some excellent teams. In 1965 three of the four coaches in the finals of the

NCAA tournament were Hoosiers. Evansville College has attained particular national distinction in recent years, winning the National Collegiate Athletic Association college division title in 1959, 1960, 1964, and 1965.

Football in Indiana has never commanded the attention that basketball has received. Purdue has twice tied for first place in the Big Ten, and Indiana won it in 1945 under the coaching of Bo McMillin. Notre Dame has produced some of the best teams in the nation. The immortal Knute Rockne brought fame to Notre Dame and established the tradition that brought outstanding players to that university. Year after year Notre Dame has ranked among the first ten in Associated Press polls. Frank Leahy had one of the best records in American football, winning 87, losing 11, and tying 9. Colleges of the state all play good football and probably place less emphasis on out-of-state recruiting than do the Big Three.

In track and field events, Indiana schools have done well but are not outstanding. Purdue has had a number of fine golfers, including several NCAA champions. In tennis, Indiana has had its fair share of players. In recent years, swimming has attained a place of national importance, particularly at Indiana University under Coach James Counsilman.

Professional teams in basketball, hockey, and football have had only moderate success in Indiana. Interest in high school basketball has probably stifled interest in the professional field. Baseball in Indianapolis has had good and bad years, with the management often being confronted with deficits.

In summary, with the exception of basketball, Indiana does well but is not outstanding in sports. There is a very evident need to balance the sports offerings, particularly in the high schools. Overemphasis on basketball may have hampered development of an athletic program that might permit large numbers of persons to participate.

Although Indiana is not as favorably endowed for camping as some of the Northern states, there are now over 240 organized youth camps in the state. About 66 percent of these are operated by voluntary youth-serving agencies and 22 percent by religious groups. There are very few private camps, although some of these are excellent.

The state has provided 11 camp facilities for organized groups in state parks and, through Indiana University, 5 facilities at Bradford Woods. Bradford Woods is also the headquarters of the American Camping Association, a national organization dedicated to the improvement of camp standards.

Hoosiers are inveterate family campers, and their numbers have been increasing by leaps and bounds. The state parks and forests have been unable to meet the demand for camp sites, and some private family camps are developing. About twice as many sites are needed to accommodate present users, despite efforts to increase the number of sites.

The outstanding single sporting event in Indiana is the 500-mile automobile race held annually at the Indianapolis Motor Speedway, a 2.5-mile oval track where many speed records have been shattered. An estimated 250,000 fans, said to be the largest crowd to attend a single sports event in the United States, attend the big race. The races date back to 1911, when an Indianapolis-made car, the Marmon, won the day. Today the race is the occasion for numerous social events, both before and after the race itself.

Many other special events serve recreation interests. The state fair not only displays the resources of the state but also offers horse shows, races, social events, and commercial entertainments attracting thousands of visitors. On a smaller scale are the county fairs and festivals, which combine economic, educational, and recreational features that draw spectators as well as active participants.

The Parke County Covered Bridge Festival is an example of another type of special attraction. Other festivals celebrate spring, fall, or local features. The Madison boat regatta brings a large group of participants and spectators to this Ohio River community.

The people of Indiana are entering a new day of leisure. With an increasing level of family income, city living, automation, improved roads, and shorter work hours, recreation in coming years will occupy an ever larger place in the lives of the people. Programs and facilities of public and private agencies and commercial enterprises, particularly those related to tourism, should be expanded immediately. Indiana now has the natural resources, the leadership, and the legal foundation upon which to move into an era with attractive leisure opportunities for both its citizens and its visitors.

Provision for recreation begins in the local community. Many Indiana communities have recreation programs of which to be proud, but there are others with serious deficiencies. There is reason to believe, however, that they are awakening to their needs and potentialities and will in coming years give increased attention to recreation needs. They must expand their community park and recreation facilities and employ professional leadership with an eye not only on present needs but also on the requirements of a growing population with increasing leisure.

If all schools would open their gymnasiums, auditoriums, craft rooms, and other facilities to the public—under adequate supervision, of course—when not used for school purposes, the state's acute need for indoor recreation resources could be nearly met. Closer cooperation and coordination is needed between the schools, planning authorities, and recreation agencies, public and private, to meet the total needs of the communities which they all should serve.

Indiana communities are particularly lacking in swimming facilities, especially indoor pools. More schools should construct indoor swimming pools in which to offer swimming instruction. These pools should be available to the public when not needed by students. The schools also need to encourage wide participation in a variety of sports to balance the emphasis on basketball.

The higher levels of government have the responsibility of encouraging and enabling local communities to develop their programs. State services to local communities need to be expanded. The state is currently cooperating with the federal government in the implementation of the Land and Water Conservation Fund bill, passed by the 89th Congress, which will provide Indiana a sum of nearly two million dollars yearly for the next 25 years, to be matched by local and state funds, for outdoor recreation planning, acquisition, and development. This bill has already stimulated about 20 counties to establish park and recreation departments to take advantage of the funds. It has also prodded planning for recreation services on community, county, and state levels. The increased sources of money provided by the state legislature for outdoor recreation is indicative of state interest in this aspect of leisure use.

Awareness of Indiana's needs was evidenced in the publication by the Indiana Department of Conservation in 1964 of *A Master Plan for Acquisition and Development*. Here is a blueprint for the development of state recreational lands for the next decade. It recommends the acquisition of new areas, expansion in present areas, and the development of facilities. The needs for inns, cabins, camping and picnic grounds, pools, beaches, boating facilities, fishing and hunting areas, roads for pleasure driving, hiking trails, and naturalist services are all considered. If the plans can be realized, Indiana's state parks, forests, and fish and game lands should serve not only the needs of its citizens but also the interests of visitors.

The 1964 master plan also proposes that many of the organized camps in state parks, now dilapidated, should be moved. Family camp grounds should be modernized, redesigned, and expanded. Increased swimming, picnicking, and other facilities are also recommended. The expansion of state forest holdings and recreation facilities in some of the forests is also recommended. Camping, picnicking, fishing, and hiking in these areas are increasing, and improved roads, hiking trails, camp grounds, and water resources are needed.

For the first time, the state parks are permitting private developers to erect public accommodations on state lands. This departure from past policy gives promise of the provision of needed facilities in the near future, although no private developer to date has availed himself of this privilege. The policy will necessitate very careful controls so that money-making does not take precedence over the main purposes of the parks.

Only now is the state government awakening to the economic

values of tourism and its responsibility for encouraging the tourist industry. The 1965 legislature established the Department of Tourism and provided for the first time an actual budget for the promotion of tourism. The tourists should not be encouraged, however, unless facilities and recreation attractions are ready for them. The cooperative efforts of state and local governments and private investors are necessary to the success of the tourist business. The large lakes being created by the U. S. Army Corps of Engineers and the smaller lakes constructed by the local Conservancy Districts will provide the water resources so attractive to residents and tourists alike—resources which have been especially scarce in the central and southern parts of the state.

The federal government's involvement in the state's recreation is growing. Planning has been done by the Bureau of Outdoor Recreation, the U. S. Army Corps of Engineers, the Soil Conservation Service, the Bureau of Sport Fisheries and Wildlife, and the Department of Commerce. The National Park Service is considering additions to its system and is interested in places with national significance scenically, scientifically, or historically. Among places considered are the Tippecanoe Battlefield and Vincennes, first capital of Indiana Territory, with which the names of George Rogers Clark, William Henry Harrison, and Abraham Lincoln are associated. The Dunes on Lake Michigan, the scene of a bitter conflict between economic and conservation interests, may, even with the port development, become in part a holding of the National Park Service. The U. S. Forest Service likewise is moving ahead in Indiana, though it has not secured as much land as would be desirable. Like the state forests, the national forest lands are becoming more attractive to visitors each year. Plans must be carried out as soon as possible if the demands of the public are to be met.

Throughout history, work has been our great motivating force, the reason for our existence, and the measure of our worth. For many people, work will continue to serve these ends. For many others, however, automation will render work less meaningful. Personal fulfillment will have to be found during leisure—through community service, religion, cultural activities, education, and recreation. The family, the schools, business, and public and private agencies of Indiana have an increasing responsibility for helping people develop the attitudes, interests, and skills that will bring fullness rather than emptiness in leisure, challenge rather than surfeit, and a creative rather than a decaying society.

RAYMOND T. BOSLER
JOHN G. ACKELMIRE

Human Relations

Human relations, pure and simple, is people and how they treat
each other. Few knotty problems arise when the people are of like
mind, when they share a common heritage and culture, worship
at the same altar, have the same color skin, and possess an equal
amount of the world's goods. Trouble comes when the scales do
not balance. The aim of good human relations is to put the scales
back in balance with justice, compassion, and charity.

Whatever its claim to civilized behavior, to productive, cultural,
or intellectual progress, the ultimate test of a humane society is its
treatment of minorities—racial, religious, national, economic, or the
physically or mentally handicapped. Evidence for judging a society's standing is found in constitutions and courtrooms, customs
and traditions, pulpits and newspapers, jails and orphanages. Indeed, wherever and whenever the big guy deals with the little one.

Indiana's record in this respect is better than some of her sister

Rev. Raymond T. Bosler, editor of *The Criterion,* is a member of the In-
dianapolis Human Rights Commission and of the Indiana State Advisory
Committee to the U.S. Commission on Civil Rights. He is pastor of St.
Therese's Church, Indianapolis.

With 33 years of metropolitan and international newspaper experience,
John G. Ackelmire, a native of Shelburn, Indiana, is associate editor of *The
Criterion.* He is also executive secretary of the Winona Memorial Foundation.

states, worse than others. Her position as a border state had made for anguished periods of wrestling with the slavery problem both before and during the Civil War. The state entered an era of humanitarian enlightenment during the nineteenth century that resulted in constructive concern by government and private benevolent organizations for a broad range of dependent and disabled, for orphaned or mistreated children, and for the imprisoned. Yet it was not until 1965 that the General Assembly removed another legal vestige of white supremacist sentiment, laws prohibiting interracial marriage. Indiana boasts, and properly, about "Hoosier hospitality." The gracious, kindly treatment of visitors and newcomers impresses strangers. Yet, even today, there are towns that still observe an unwritten law, the infamous "sundown ordinance," that warns Negroes to be out of town before the sun sets.

Here, as in most states, the record of human relations is a spotty one, often exhibiting ironic twists, with sentiments changing drastically to conform to time and circumstance. But it is a record that, in many areas, has shown continuous dedication to individual rights and freedoms, that has honored the intentions of early patriots and preserved their faith. Indiana is far removed from a state-wide observance of the spirit as well as the letter of the laws of equality, justice, and freedom for all. But, even without rose-colored glasses, one can see a decided trend to a more wholehearted effort to erase inequalities, to allay prejudices, to replace vaudevillian images with realistic appraisals. It is an effort that is being joined by forces that have too long remained aloof and unconcerned but now recognize the logic and wisdom of becoming involved. Later we hope to deal more fully with harbingers and promise but, for now, let's look at the record.

Merely by being part of the Old Northwest Territory, Indiana got off to a good start. The Ordinance of 1787, enacted by the Congress of the Confederation and one of history's great freedom documents, provided the articles of compact under which the territory and the several future states comprising it would live. Article 1 guaranteed complete freedom of worship and religious conviction. Article 3 enjoined good faith and fair dealing with the

Indians. Article 6, the most significant in light of the terrible events of the succeeding century, provided that there was to be neither slavery nor involuntary servitude.

In 1800 the Indians still claimed all of Indiana except a few small areas that had been given up in the Greenville Treaty of 1795. The policy of the federal government was to obtain the consent of the Indians to land cessions as rapidly as possible. It was a difficult task at best, considering the long periods of time needed for conferring and confirming between the Indians and the national government, the fever that infected land-hungry individuals and companies anxious to invade the newly opened territory, the overlapping Indian claims to many tracts, and the understandable suspicion and recalcitrance of the various tribes. So, even before Indiana became a state, there began a shameful period of exploitation of prior residents and usurpation of their rights. In treaty after treaty, federal representatives bamboozled the tribes out of many millions of acres for worthless trinkets, plus money, and worthless promises. Settlers, individually and in parties, took over without waiting for cessions. Resistance was met with arms.

Often overlooked in the scandal of Indian exploitation is the neglect accorded the majority of French settlers. This point is significant because the discriminatory actions and sentiments predicted later reaction to foreign-born immigrants. The majority of the early travelers and letter writers dealt unkindly with the foreigners. The French did not adhere to the Anglo-American Protestant ethic dominant among the pioneers. They did not place a premium on thrift and so were judged lazy, shiftless, irresponsible. Their growing poverty was viewed as a result of indolence, not the drastic decline of fur trading or the pillaging of rowdy frontier soldiers. Their dances and games proved vice and immorality were rampant. But most abhorrent of all, in American eyes, was the friendship between Frenchmen and Indians and the occasional intermarrying that resulted.

Few descendants of those early French remain in Indiana today. Their forebears, however, contributed a sense of security and tradition that has served as a balance wheel in periods of religious prejudice. Where the French raised their villages, the Catholic Church was established and religious minorities were accepted. The Jesuit missionaries and their followers who ministered to the early French engaged, as time and distance would allow, in work among the Indian tribes. And they were not alone in their concern for the spiritual and temporal welfare of the Indians.

For as American Protestants entered the Northwest Territory in numbers, they were joined in short order by circuit-riding Baptist and Methodist preachers. Far-flung congregations were established and revivals were held regularly to attract those unaffiliated with any particular denomination. The circuit riders at times carried the gospel to Indian camps as well. Their church associations sent special missionaries to the Indians and started schools for the instruction and care of Indian children. A strong obligation "to convert the heathen" pervaded the various denominations.

One religious group that displayed a special interest in the welfare of the tribes was the Society of Friends. Chiefs of the Miami and Potawatomi tribes had met Quakers during trips East to visit President John Adams and invited their aid in introducing agriculture and in banning the sale of whiskey. Three Quakers from Baltimore created a model farm near the present city of Huntington that flourished only briefly.

Whatever the success or failure of this initial endeavor of the Quakers, it should be noted that the Friends, more than any other religious group, has consistently, through persuasion, entreaty, action, and reaction, served as the conscience-keepers of Hoosiers. Public records attest to their presence in almost every endeavor which forwarded the rights and welfare of minorities. Whoever the underdog was—Indian, Negro, orphan, exploited prison laborer, ill or infirm—Quakers gave a hand. Much of the more enlightened state and local humanitarian legislation was promoted, if not conceived, by Quakers.

Throughout the state's history there has run a strong feeling among the majority that it possesses an inherent right and duty to legislate, propagandize, and intimidate its neighbors into "acceptable" conduct. In pioneer days a community was at times set right by the handiest means available—a sumptuary law, a vigilance committee, a public whipping, or a shotgun. One of the prime requisites was "to care for your own." In those rawboned, risky, hard days few had the wherewithal to do for others. But as civilization and comparative comforts came to the frontier there evolved a sense of social responsibility.

"As soon as circumstances will permit," the 1816 Constitution called for a penal code based on reformation and not vindictive justice and "one or more farms, to be an asylum for those persons who . . . have a claim upon the aid and beneficence of society." The 1851 Constitution repeated these fundamentals and acknowledged the need for education for the deaf and blind, treatment of the insane, and the reformation of juvenile offenders.

In the pioneer era the county poor farm was the only public welfare institution. Not until 1845 did the General Assembly provide for the purchase of "a state lunatic asylum," although the next year the name was changed to the Indiana Hospital for the Insane, and the first patients were admitted in 1848. The State School for the Deaf began in 1844 and the School for the Blind in 1851.

The history of treatment of criminals in Indiana, as elsewhere, may be divided into three periods: outright vengeance by the injured party, official punishment, and penalty plus reform. In 1821 a state prison was opened at Jeffersonville and in the 1860's a second prison was built at Michigan City. Until 1846 convict labor was hired out to the highest bidder and the prison was operated by superintendents who had bid for the job. That year the warden system was installed. Largely through the efforts of the Society of Friends abuses in the prisons were corrected. A separate prison for women opened in Indianapolis in 1873 and later an institution was added for younger male prisoners at Plainfield.

In 1852 the state authorized county commissioners to contract with doctors for the care of paupers on county farms and prisoners in county jails. Later, township trustees provided medical care for the poor. Aside from the Civil War military hospitals, the only early example of a public-supported hospital was Indianapolis City Hospital, authorized in the late 1850's.

Dependent children, under laws in 1852, were bound out as apprentices or cared for in county poor farms. The apprentice provision followed the custom of territorial days and was in reality a form of indenture which resulted in young, cheap labor for farms and homes. A number of private orphanages were established in the next three decades, mostly by religious groups.

Gradually, public officials and the populace at large began to realize the need for special care for special groups. The sins of omission and neglect that stain the state's record were not peculiar to Indiana. Indifference throughout all the other states is easily documented.

Despite those famous words of the Ordinance of 1787 prohibiting slavery, nearly all of the limited Negro population of the territorial period was held in slavery or under long-term indentures tantamount to slavery. As interpreted generally, Article 6 was not retroactive. Before statehood, proslavery advocates unsuccessfully petitioned Congress for a ten-year suspension of the ban but did succeed in passing territorial indenture laws. Such action did not remain unchallenged or unchecked. The chief proslavery sentiment was centered around Vincennes and in the Kaskaskia and Cahokia areas in what is now Illinois, while the antislavery element was mainly located in eastern Indiana. The division of the Indiana and Illinois territories in 1809 significantly reduced the ranks of proponents, and the indenture laws were repealed in 1810.

At the time of the framing of the first state constitution in 1816, opponents of slavery were in the majority. But the antislavery sentiment did not signal any great humanitarian interest in the Negro. There was a decided feeling that the state should be preserved for whites only, a feeling enunciated in repeated proposals to prevent Negroes from settling in the state. The Constitution of 1851 proposed, and offered some financial support to, a Liberian colony for Negroes already resident in the state.

At no time before the Civil War did Indiana's Negro population exceed one percent of the state's total population. (In 1860 there were 11,428 Negroes and 1,338,710 whites.) Yet the Negro in Indiana—as in many other states—is a definitive benchmark in the history of human relations. The status of this minority has been and still is a perennial political issue and one which has consistently engaged popular thinking and debate. In no other area of human and inhuman relations do tempers flare so readily, grievances rankle, and consciences shame. The belief in the inherent inferiority of the Negro was espoused without question through much of the state's history. In line with this doctrine, a spate of legal and social barriers separated the races.

By 1850 most of Indiana's citizens were characterized by a devotion to the Union and a desire to avoid disruptive controversy. They supported compromise regarding slavery in the territories. Some citizens, however, were involved in the Underground Railroad movement that transported Southern slaves to Canada and many opposed the federal Fugitive Slave Law of 1850.

Prior to and during the Civil War some Hoosier white supremacists rallied round the hate banners of a secret society known as the Knights of the Golden Circle, which was followed by the Sons of Liberty, whose Supreme Commander was one Clement Vallandigham of Ohio. Agents of Governor Oliver P. Morton infiltrated the latter organization and reported treasonous plans. The alleged menace became involved in partisan politics and the governor used the information—although there had been no overt action—to the best political advantage. Several persons were convicted of treason on what seems to have been flimsy evidence.

The years immediately after the Civil War were marked by legal and political gains for Negroes. Despite "on the books" progress, discrimination continued unabated, however. A double standard of justice was generally accepted. An ugly tradition of mob violence persisted and lynchings of Negroes became increasingly frequent as the century ended. All lynch victims were not Negroes, however. Vigilante committees and night riders lynched far more whites than Negroes, although the number cannot be determined with complete accuracy. As recently as 1930 two young Negroes accused of murder and rape were taken from the county jail at Marion and publicly lynched.

As they had the French earlier, some of the Indiana settlers of the early nineteenth century regarded with suspicion, often intolerance and hatred, the European immigrants among them, yet the Constitution of 1851 gave suffrage to aliens even before they became citizens. Most of the influx of territorial days was of native stock, but here and there a colony of foreign-born was established. The Swiss settled at Vevay and later at Tell City, and German peasants at Harmonie, making a unique chapter in the state's social and economic history. Other Germans settled in Dubois County and along the Ohio River and then over the rest of Indiana. The Irish began to come into the state in the 1840's and 1850's to build the canals and the railroads. By 1880 there were 144,178 foreign-born, and Indiana ranked ninth in the United States in the number of German-born, fifteenth in the number of Irish-born, and thirteenth in the number of all other nationalities. Economic exploitation and social rejection were common. Popular dissatisfaction with the disproportionate influence of the alien electorate is seen through the records of the Constitutional Convention of 1850-51 and subsequent political campaigns. The "lop-eared Dutch" and "red-neck Irish" were favorite targets of the Whig and Know-Nothing parties.

Arriving late in the nineteenth and early in the twentieth century, the Slavs and related groups who worked in Gary's steel mills faced similar discrimination, often more acute because of their lesser numbers. There were instances of lumping the darker-skinned "dagos" with "blacks and mulattoes."

During the first decade and a half of the twentieth century the state was too busy becoming the miracle of growth which characterized the whole Midwest to concern itself actively with racial and religious prejudice. But biased attitudes, inherited and acquired, seem only to have lain dormant. The Ku Klux Klan brought them to hysterical activity once more. The shameful story of the Klan in the 1920's is well known. Catholics, Jews, and "Mongolians" were pilloried with gusto. In many towns, when the fever ran high, families found themselves ostracized. Men lost jobs or found their businesses ruined by Klan zealots. For religious minorities that period was one of varying degrees of hardship.

The Klan era, moreover, was catastrophic for the Negro. Up to that time generations of Negro children in many Indiana communities had been schooled on fairly equal and largely friendly terms with white children. Because of Klan insistence, Crispus Attucks High School in Indianapolis was built, and Negro students throughout the city were required to attend it. There was also a great increase in segregation in the elementary schools. In 1926 the Klan-owned Indianapolis City Council passed a racial zoning ordinance, later declared unconstitutional, which solidified traditional resistance to school and social mixing and disrupted what little progress toward desegregation had been made in the decades since the Civil War.

Though Indiana's Jews have had to suffer religious prejudice, deliberate and concerted persecution did not become an issue until Klan days. In the political arena their influence was noted on a few occasions. One of the more interesting occurred during the Civil War when a petition was presented to the General Assembly asking that the constitution be amended to acknowledge God as the source of authority and "Jesus Christ as the ruler among nations." The petition had the blessing of an impressive army of churchmen. But Jewish citizens protested strenuously against its adoption and the legislature rejected it.

The minority groups have not been without their own prejudices. Many Catholic immigrants, tending to withdraw as much as possible into parochial enclaves, nourished prejudices against Protestants and Jews. Though Catholic schools were desegregated before the public schools, there were many instances of white parental protest. In 1944 the admission of two Negro children to Holy Name grade school in Beech Grove caused a furor that abated only when Archbishop Joseph Ritter threatened to close the school and place the parish under interdict.

During the Klan's heyday Gary's white high school students, many of them the children of immigrant Slavs, staged a strike over the admission of a few Negroes. Construction of an all-Negro school was the result of that protest. And when Alabama's Governor Wallace invaded Indiana during the 1964 primary, Lake

County's first- and second-generation Americans voted heavily in favor of the Southern racist doctrine that Wallace represented.

Today in Indiana there are varying degrees of anti-Catholicism, but Catholics, by and large, enjoy social and economic status equal to their peers. Jews, under the leadership of such hardy organizations as the Anti-Defamation League, have virtually overcome discrimination in the years since World War II. The relatively few Asians in Indiana no longer feel the sting of oppression or ostracism.

The Negro has been making notable progress in the state since World War II. When the Fifteenth Amendment to the U. S. Constitution was ratified in 1869, there were no restrictions on Negro voting rights, and no effort was made to deprive them of their franchise. Their votes now have made them a political force in the state. By 1960 there were 274,000 Negroes in Indiana and the projected figure for 1970 is 475,000. Today about 22 percent of the population of Indianapolis and 40 percent of Gary is Negro.

In 1945 the state legislature passed a noncompulsory fair employment practices law. The craft labor unions began easing up on exclusionist policies, although too many of them still exist. In many cities discrimination in places of public accommodation began to be relaxed, although it too is far from eliminated, despite a prohibition by state law.

The legislature banned all school segregation in 1949, although de facto segregation, resulting from residential housing practices, remains in Indianapolis, Gary, and some other communities. This law also banned discrimination in the hiring and tenure of teachers, and some progress has been made in this area. But even today there are only two Negro high school principals in the state, both at all-Negro schools, and in 1960 Negroes were teaching in only 15 of the state's 775 school corporations.

Negroes have been making some progress in education. Twenty-five years ago less than 2 percent had college educations. In 1960 the figure was 3.1 percent compared to 6.5 percent for whites. Also in that year 16.5 percent of Negroes had finished high school as against 29 percent of whites. The Negro dropout rate remains alarmingly high, however.

Statistics show a slight increase in Negro employment in white-collar and professional jobs between 1950 and 1960, but 85 percent of the Negro breadwinners remain concentrated in the blue-collar jobs that are steadily being eliminated by automation. Only in government service has the Negro made appreciable gains, despite the equal employment campaign and such legislation as the 1961 Indiana Civil Rights Act.

To this day housing is the most sensitive, volatile area of discrimination. Despite federal and state laws and the work done by the Indiana Civil Rights Commission, city commissions on human relations, and a variety of religious and private human relations groups throughout the state—and despite noncompulsory legislation against discrimination—open occupancy remains the exception rather than the rule. But the past decade is not a totally dismal one. Neighborhood associations have made inroads on the panic-selling trend that usually follows the introduction of a Negro family into a formerly all-white neighborhood. The state Civil Rights Commission has succeeded in forming a Housing Advisory Committee composed of representatives of real estate, human relations, banking, and other interested groups to set guidelines for a gradual, peaceable, and equitable solution.

Because of the concentration of Negroes in urban areas, Indiana's cities have the most at stake in open occupancy as in almost every other area of social progress. Whatever one's politics, there is little dispute that the liberalization of the state legislature by reapportionment and the consequent gain of voice and vote by the cities can only result in added stress on social, economic, and cultural disparities. In years past rurally dominated legislatures paid little heed to festering slums and ghettoes and the ills they breed. Slums produce giant problems that can be tackled effectively only with federal assistance, too long a bugaboo of the conservative, rural assemblies. Housing, education, unemployment, and urban blight call for massive aid and broad cooperation.

It is in the realm of cooperation and common recognition of social ills that the greatest promise lies. Churches have committed themselves, irrevocably it seems, to vigorous action in behalf of the poor and handicapped of all types. This is in the face of stern resistance from "Bible-belt" groups with their cries of socialism. A burgeoning spirit of ecumenicism is fostering inter-faith cooperation that has the twofold effect of mitigating religious prejudice and providing effective social and civic action.

Those who bemoaned increasing welfare costs but refused to recognize the basic causes of generation-after-generation poverty are becoming aware of the need to break the vicious circle of ignorance and unemployment, poor nutrition and lack of medical care, squalid housing and cultural deprivation. The Indiana Chamber of Commerce and industrial leaders, as well as labor union officials and educators, have awakened to the particular problems of the chronically unemployed and unskilled.

A retooling of the middle-class-oriented public school system, coupled with federal and state special aid programs, recognizes for the first time that multiple approaches are necessary to rescue underprivileged children from a lifetime sentence to slums.

Time, sophistication, and travel have greatly reduced intolerance for aliens. In many cases, the foreigner, resident or visitor, is feted with a passion. Society pages feature the customs and cuisine of the foreign-born. Over 800 Cuban refugees have been absorbed in communities around the state in a friendly, sympathetic fashion.

Indiana's attempts at rehabilitating the criminal have been sporadic and listless. Hope in this area, however, has been justifiably revived lately by increasing attention to psychiatric counseling, job training, and official acceptance of a more enlightened philosophy of correction. Religious groups have established "half-way" houses to aid parolees.

Recent approval of plans for mental health treatment centers in Indianapolis and mental retardation centers in Richmond and Lafayette—supported by state and federal funds—marks progress in the mental health field. Even the best of the state's mental health institutions have been perennially overcrowded and understaffed.

Local centers can be of inestimable help to those not in need of full-time institutional care and instruction.

There are many bright spots, it is true, emerging in the state-wide human relations and social welfare picture. But it would be disastrous to ignore those dark regions of despair, exploitation, and deprivation that remain to be lighted by compassion and justice. We have written about human relations from the viewpoint of who gets pushed around the most and by whom. Evils must be recognized and defined before they can be eliminated.

Indiana, presently and historically, is a friendly, hospitable place. Response to the need for change is accelerating at almost every civic and social level. It is doubtful that such un-American hate-mongering groups as the Ku Klux Klan can ever again gain a significant foothold. The task of individual Hoosiers is one of broader knowledge of and relationship with others of diverse races, religions, colors and economic, cultural, and social standing. Only person-to-person experience demonstrates so clearly that all people are essentially the same whatever their creed, skin tone, national origin, or bank account.